IMAGES
of America

NORFOLK'S CHURCH STREET

BETWEEN MEMORY AND REALITY

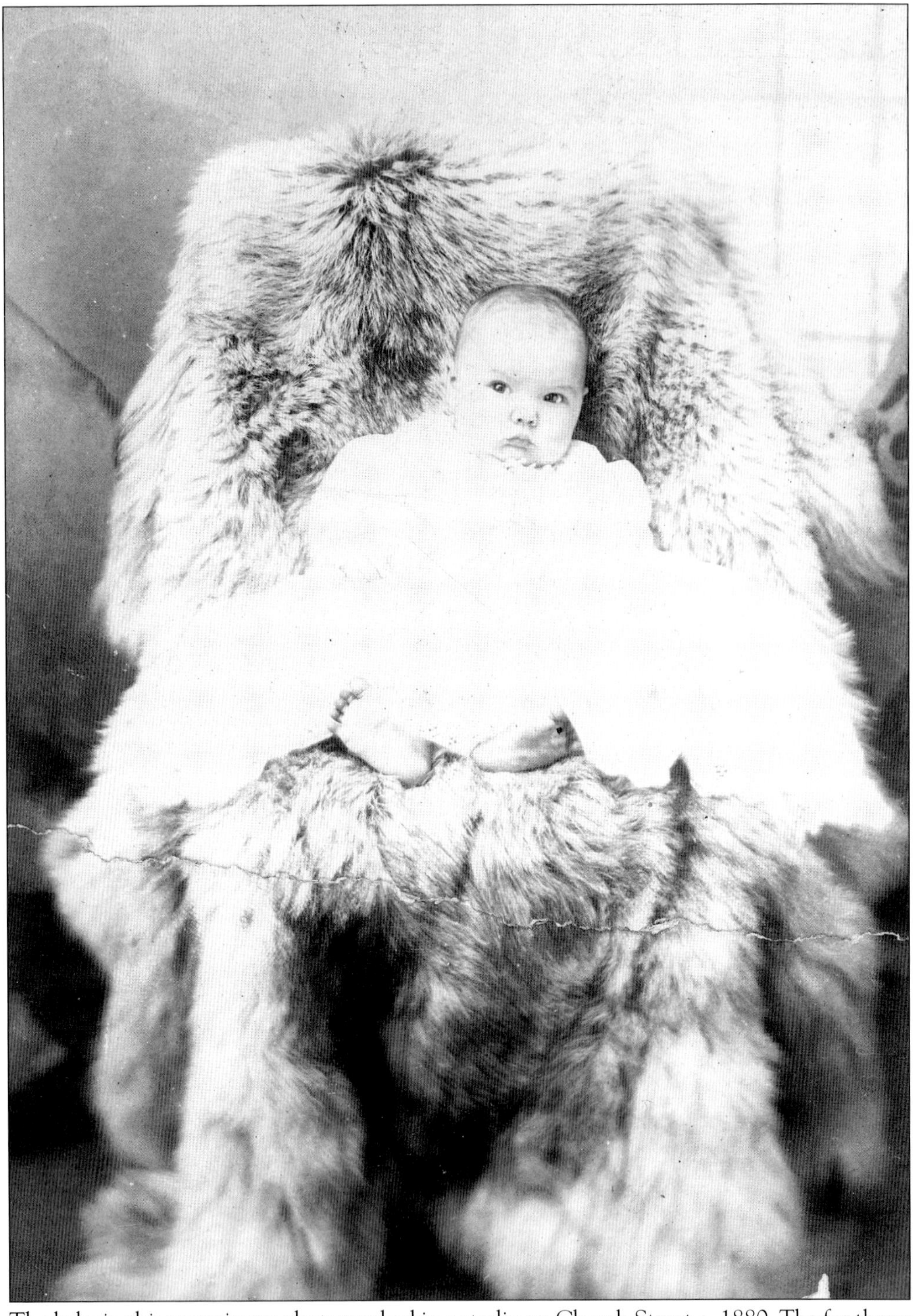

The baby in this portrait was photographed in a studio on Church Street *c.* 1880. The fur throw makes an interesting and cozy backdrop for the infant, whose identity is unknown.

IMAGES
of America

NORFOLK'S CHURCH STREET
BETWEEN MEMORY AND REALITY

Amy Waters Yarsinske

ARCADIA
PUBLISHING

ISBN 978-0-7385-0103-1

Published by Arcadia Publishing
Charleston, South Carolina

Printed in the United States of America

Library of Congress Catalog Card Number: 99-60277

For all general information contact Arcadia Publishing at:
Telephone 843-853-2070
Fax 843-853-0044
E-Mail sales@arcadiapublishing.com
For customer service and orders:
Toll-Free 1-888-313-2665

Visit us on the Internet at www.arcadiapublishing.com

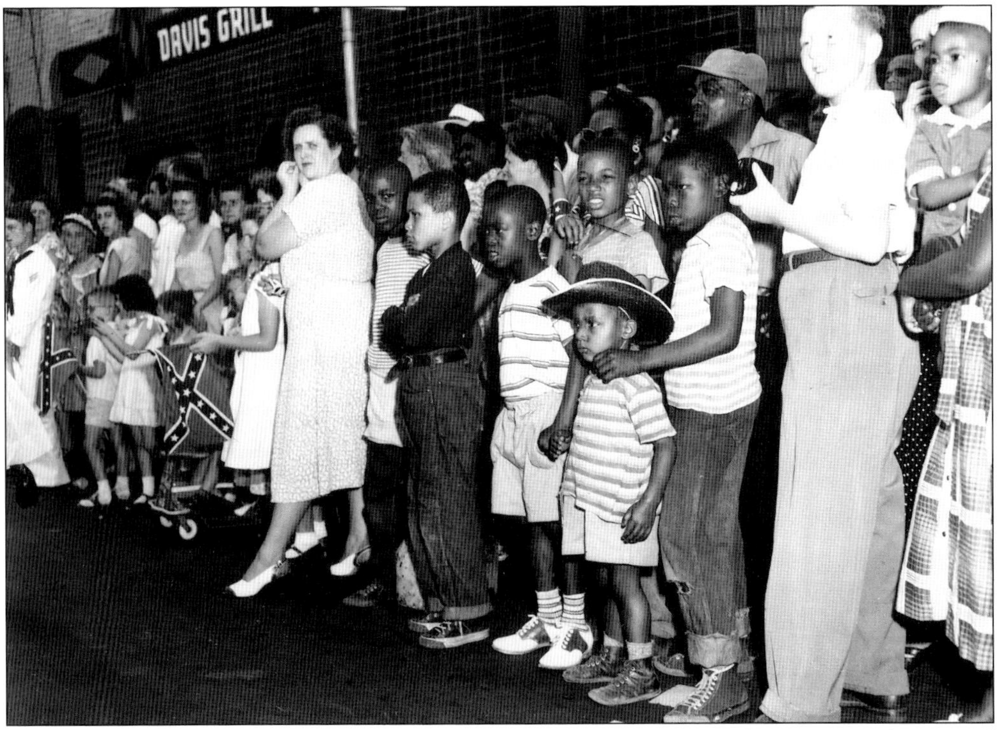

Children watch a parade on June 2, 1951. The occasion was the final reunion of the United Confederate Veterans. The celebration in Norfolk lasted from Memorial Day, May 30, through June 3, which in times past, had been celebrated as Confederate Memorial Day in certain southern states, and as Jefferson Davis's birthday in Virginia. Confederate veterans attending were William J. Bush, 104, of Fitzgerald, Georgia, and William D. Townsend, 105, of Olla, Louisiana. John Salling, 105, of Slant, Virginia, was in such poor health, he was unable to attend the reunion in Norfolk. (Charles S. Borjes, photographer. Courtesy of Kirn Library.)

Contents

ACKNOWLEDGMENTS

Polish novelist and Nobel Prize winner Henry Sienkiewicz (1846–1916) once wrote of America that "other lands grant only asylum; this land recognizes the immigrant as a son and grants him rights." Sienkiewicz came to the United States in 1876 to publish his letters in a newspaper, *Gazeta Polska*, so that his views on freedom might be heard in a free land. When they were "sickened at last of poverty, bigotry and kings," wrote another immigrant, "there was always America!"

Church Street became a search for Norfolk's diversity, a perspective of the city's and region's ethnic multeity that has rarely, if ever, been addressed properly in historical narratives and public discussions. This book is a tribute to all who ever lived on, worked on, or remember Church Street, a testament to the human spirit that draws our anamnesis always to that fine line between memory and reality. In its character and contribution, Church Street is that place where Henry Sienkiewicz might have found immigrants living free of persecution while others struggled long and hard for rights that eventually would be within their grasp. This is a story of one road's tale of diversity and prosperity, decline and renaissance. The motto of the United States, *E pluribus unum*, "out of many, one" speaks to what Church Street was and what it was to become. As early as 1790, the first census of the new nation revealed that in Virginia, perhaps the most "English" of the states, three out of every ten individuals were of German origin. It is not surprising that this notion of an ethnic melting pot was the foundation of Church Street.

If Church Street and its surrounding community belonged to anyone in its long and rich history, it was Norfolk's immigrants. From the English, Irish, Scottish, German, French, Dutch, Italian, Hungarian, Czechoslovakian, and Russian, to Japanese, Chinese, and African people who all struggled to become American, this street was their home and their history. To acknowledge their invaluable contribution is imperative as we move to rebuild the Church Street community, making room for all that this street has done to define diversity in Norfolk. I like to remember the words of American poet Robert Penn Warren (1905–1989), who wrote in his poem *History* (1935): "In the new land/Our seed shall prosper, and/ In those unsifted times/Our sons shall cultivate/Peculiar crimes,/Having not love, nor hate,/ Nor memory." We should strive not to forget that we prosper because we are all different, but one in the same. Our collective memories define us, and from the pervasive spirituality of our history, communities grow.

Though I generally have a number of people to acknowledge in the front-matter of my books, I found that researching and writing *Norfolk's Church Street: Between Memory and Reality*, was a journey I had to make alone. Diverse communities such as those which once lived and worked along Church Street scatter over time, and those who had possession of important historical pieces of the puzzle were possessive at best. In the end, the effort required travel and the purchase of invaluable historical documents and photographs. Without them, an accurate picture of "The Road That Leadeth Out of Town" would have been impossible. As always, I cherish the support of my husband, Raymond, and his prescience that I will be given the time and latitude to successfully complete a book. Our children, Ashley, Allyson, and Raymond III, have been, as they always are, patient with their mother, and continue to make me proud.

INTRODUCTION

Established as a town by the Virginia Assembly's Act for Cohabitation and Encouragement of Trade and Manufacture in 1680, Norfolk was on a 50-acre site in Lower Norfolk County on Nicholas Wise's land, abutting the Eastern Branch of the Elizabeth River at the entrance to the branch. Directed to survey the town, John Ferebee completed his initial survey of the town's boundaries on October 19, 1680. "The Road That Leadeth Into the Woods," subsequently called "The Road That Leadeth Out of Town," was established as one of the town of Norfolk's first thoroughfares when, on October 19, 1681, surveyor John Ferebee received payment as "Clerke of the Militia" for the purpose of "laying out the Streets of the Towne." Clearly, the town of Norfolk was established by law in 1680, was surveyed almost immediately thereafter, and was ready for occupation by settlers before the end of 1681. It is contrary to historical facts that the city of Norfolk displays the date of 1682 on its city seal. The streets Ferebee mapped were Main Street; "The Street That Leadeth Down to the Waterside," later called Market Square, the Parade, and Commercial Place; "The Street That Leadeth to the Publique Spring," later determined to be Metcalf Lane; a small street north of Main Street's eastern terminus, which later became known as East Street and Bermuda Street; and, of course, "The Road That Leadeth Into the Woods," later Church Street. As part of Norfolk's original 50-acre townsite, "The Road That Leadeth Into the Woods" may have been nothing more than a short-walk's distance, but its parameters would soon change as the town expanded to a borough in 1736 and a city in 1845. Over the same period of time, the changes which would take place to Church Street would also expand the width of the street and its cross-streets. The narrowness of streets as the town was first mapped was due to the prevailing ideas of ancient times when cities had walls around them, and since it cost a great deal of money to build and maintain a wall around a town, the width of streets was narrow, nothing as expansive as would be constructed in the late 19th and 20th centuries. Early European settlers in Virginia continued the practice of building towns with streets of relatively narrow width.

The first residential expansion of Norfolk beyond the first 50 acres occurred when Colonel Samuel Boush started subdividing his land along the northwest side of the main thoroughfare, Church Street, and went northeasterly from the churchyard of the Borough Church to a point just beyond the Town Bridge, near the corner of present-day Charlotte Street. Those who purchased the lots from April 13, 1728, through August 17, 1732, included Walter Clothier; Captain John Phillips, a mariner; shoemaker John Scott; John Guy; Philip Dison, recorded as a shipwright; John Munds, weaver; Edward Portlock; George Tucker; James Moore, another mariner; William Ives, joiner; Edward Pugh; John Munds; Henry Gristock; John Roberts; Margaret Novcutt; and Edmund Jenkins. The area around Town Bridge was called by that name into the 19th century. Market Street was later cut through the lots belonging to John Munds and Tucker; Freemason Street between Phillips's and Guy's land; and Charlotte Street cut through Scott's and Ives's land almost exactly where the bridge was located.

This important street, home to the city's first church and common school, was called Church Street, which appeared on a deed dated 1737, preceding the construction of the present Saint Paul's Episcopal Church by only two years. Traveling over the ruts of this unpaved route jolted the carts of farmers going to town to sell and buy in the thriving village on the Elizabeth River. When inland settlers sought a route to sea by land, they were compelled to make a sweeping detour into Norfolk from Suffolk by way of Kemp's Landing and the same Church

Street. The street was Norfolk's first highway connection to the west. Then came, of course, the Revolutionary War and Lord Dunmore. Sympathizers to the minutemen's cause retreated Norfolk via Church Street, some with carts of household belongings, to seek refuge in the forests and homes of friends in the county. Lord Dunmore sent an expedition into the county, which marched triumphantly back into Norfolk over Church Street. At the close of the struggle for independence, one of the first acts of the town council in 1782 was an order for alterations to Church Street. At the intersection with Main Street, two Tory buildings protruded into the thoroughfare. The town council decided in 1786 to establish an academy for the education of the town's children, choosing a building site on the school land "across from Saint Paul's on Church Street." The land for construction of a school had been set aside in 1728, but no building had been built on it until the council's aforementioned order. The building erected on the site was a two-story frame schoolhouse that remained the home of Norfolk Academy until construction many years later of the Grecian building on Bank Street, which also later housed the Norfolk Juvenile and Domestic Relations Court and, presently, the Norfolk office of the Hampton Roads Chamber of Commerce.

By 1806, the Norfolk City Directory listed Church Street as "still the only avenue by which the town may be entered by vehicles." It was described as a "noisy, busy thoroughfare," built up with stores and tenements. At the southern end of the street, there were dry goods stores, shoe shops, and grocery stores; but from No. 50 northward were the homes of the middle-class tailors, cabinet-makers, sea captains, blacksmiths, plasterers, and butchers. Saint Paul's Episcopal Church stood gracefully at the corner of Cove Street, and across the street stood the Norfolk Academy and the new Episcopal church. The street was still unpaved, muddy in winter, dusty in summer, always crowded with "horses, carriages, phaetons, chairs, carts, and drays."

When resentment over the federal government's embargo reached its zenith and the War of 1812 loomed near, citizens of the borough hastily threw up fortifications around the village, and erected one of the breastworks on Church Street at its intersection with Princess Anne Road—Fort Tar. Though it is difficult to pinpoint precisely when Church Street was first paved, a visitor to the borough in 1818 stated that all the principal streets of the borough were paved at that time. The *Norfolk Herald* of 1835 stated: "Church Street, formerly a bog in winter and dusty in summer, is now a handsomely paved street from the lower termination near the courthouse to the town bridge." The *American Beacon* noted: "It is the most delightful promenade in Norfolk." By April 2, 1819, the cornerstone of the customhouse, built at the corner of Widewater (Water) and Church Streets, was laid. President James Monroe, John C. Calhoun, and Commodore Stephen Decatur were among the distinguished guests at this event. Unfortunately, the building burned down in May 1861 as the Confederates retreated the city.

Church Street 150 years ago was vastly different from the one we know today. In 1850, Church Street was described as running north from the Elizabeth River, and extending through the city to the northern boundary. The northernmost limit of the city was near the head of Smith's Creek, on a line with what was then upper Union Street. The easternmost boundary was above the head of Newton's Creek, where the boundary line crossed Princess Anne Road. The southernmost boundary of the city was at Higgins' Wharf, the westernmost at the west end of York Street. Holt Street extended farther to the east than any street south of it, or than the two above Holt to the north. Church Street had five curves, and Main Street just two, but Church Street was more of a straight line between the curves than Main. Aside from Main and Widewater Streets, Church Street was the only street in Norfolk's early history that ran through the entire city. In 1851, Widewater Street was about 4,600 feet long, or 680 feet less than a mile; Main Street was roughly 4,300 feet long, or 980 feet less than a mile; and Church Street was 6,400 feet long, or 1,120 feet more than a mile. Today, Main and Church Streets are the oldest in the city, and Church Street is the oldest street of its original description—"The Road That Leadeth Into the Woods" and "The Road That Leadeth Out of Town"—in the United States.

By the middle of the 19th century, there were 84 streets in the city, and nearly 50 lanes. Most of the city's streets ran on a grid of north and south, east and west, with very few streets running at off-angles from the grid streets. Many streets had not been opened at this time. There were plans to open a street from the eastern terminus of Liberty Street to the western terminus of Moseley at Church, thus forming another direct thoroughfare through the city from west to east. Plans were also in the works for a street, east from Church, near Nicholson. The names of some of the streets around Church Street had also changed in the period between 1811 and 1851. Wood Street had been known as George Street. Some of the thoroughfares in the Church Street section of Norfolk had been named before the Revolution and bore the names of English nobles, princes, princesses, and so forth, in honor of whom they were named. There were three cemeteries close to Church Street: Catholic Cemetery, on the southeast corner of Chapel and Holt Streets; Saint Paul's Cemetery, on Church and Cove Streets, east of Cumberland; and Potter's Field, north of Cedar Grove Cemetery at the head of Smith's Creek. There were significant public buildings and offices also located within the physical bounds of Church Street. The City Gas Works could be found at the southwest corner of Mariner and Third Cross Streets at Briggs' Point. The customhouse was found at the southwest corner of Widewater and Church Streets. Collector and Depository William Garnett oversaw the customhouse operation. The Female Orphan Asylum, located at the corner of Holt and Third Cross Streets was not to be confused with the Norfolk Female Institute, fronting Holt, at the corner of Second Cross. Norfolk's educational system began with what became known today as Norfolk Academy, and the Lancastrian School (1815–1856), located on the southwest corner of Fenchurch and Holt. The Lancastrian School had one teacher in 1851, Mr. W.B. Micks. The president of the school's trustees was Tazewell Taylor. The Masonic Hall once stood on the east side of South Church Street between Cove and Bermuda Streets, but moved to a larger building fronting on Church.

The churches and synagogues, which would eventually proliferate Church Street, were diverse, speaking well to the cultural diversity that would eventually identify the street as unique in the city of Norfolk. The Hebrew Synagogue at 137 South Church Street, with an entrance on Widewater Street, was led by Rabbi Reuben Oppenheimer from 1850 to 1852. The members of the Congregation House of Jacob moved into this location for one year, in 1851, and it was about this time that talk began of building a new synagogue structure on land purchased from Jacob and Fanny Umstadter. This did not occur until March 3, 1859. The Umstadter property was located on the east side of Cumberland Street. Jacob Umstadter ran a dry goods store at 70 South Church Street and a clothing store at 4 West Widewater (later Water) Street, both of which he established in 1844 (see advertisement below). Saint Paul's Episcopal Church, ministered by William Jackson, was erected on the west side of South Church Street near Cove in 1739, and a short distance away was Saint Patrick's Roman Catholic Church, located on the south side of Holt near Chapel. Father A.L. Hitselberger was pastor of Saint Patrick's at that

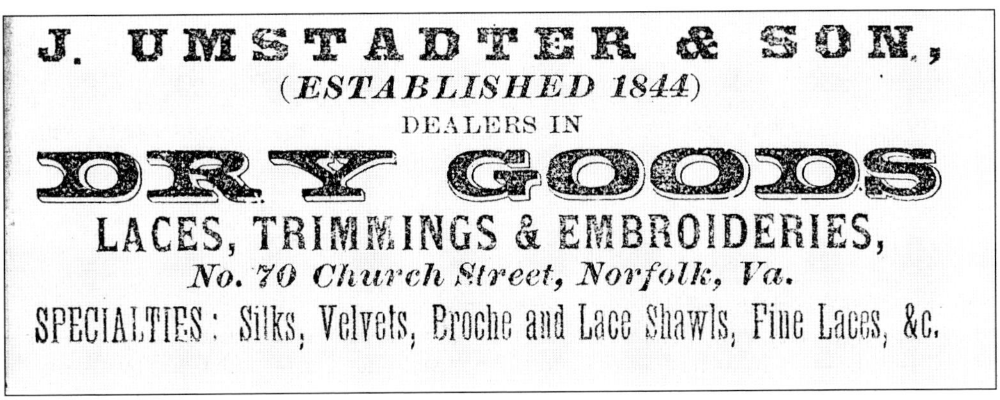

time. The African-American church was the Methodist Episcopal Church, South, on the south side of Bute, opposite Union, near Church, and its pastor was Reverend F.J. Mitchell.

There were other amenities to living on Church Street in the middle of the 19th century. The National Hotel was conveniently located on the corner of Main and Church Streets, and the City Hotel on the north side of Main, west of Church Street. There were also two fire companies nearby: Union, on the west side of Fenchurch, near Bermuda; and Relief, found on the south side of Holt, near Church Street. The Union Fire Company was led by Captain Edward E. Delany, and Relief by First Captain H.M. Marcus.

The boundaries of Church Street in 1866 encompassed Church Street north from East Freemason Street north and northeast; Church Street south from East Freemason southwest to East Widewater Street; and Soutter's Wharf, east of Church Street, then west above the city ferry. The street's limits were basic. By 1874, it is safe to assume that the boundaries were stretching well beyond the original acreage plotted by Ferebee. Church Street was described as beginning at the Elizabeth River and running north to the city boundary, Fenchurch and Cumberland, on the southern extremity, and Chapel and Smith on the northern boundary.

In the 1880s, Church Street was a city unto itself. It was described as having "a blend of everything in the shape of habitations upon its long and crooked length from churches, synagogues, hospitals, graveyards, dry goods, boot and shoe, furniture, and grocery stores, meat markets, stables, liquor houses, bars, undertaking establishments, human hair stores, junk stores, to alligator-tooth jewelry establishments." On Church Street, one could encounter Odd Fellows Hall, Saint Paul's Episcopal Church, the Central Presbyterian Church, St. Vincent DePaul Hospital, and finally, Lesner's Garden. For years after the Civil War, the town's principal theater was the old Church Street Opera House, which shared a building with the Odd Fellows.

The area encompassing Church Street was originally settled by successive waves of immigrants from Europe, beginning with those from England, Ireland, Scotland, France, Germany, and Italy. The last significant, and large, group of inhabitants that settled along the Church Street corridor was primarily made up of East European Jewish immigrants who migrated from New York City, New York, between 1890 and 1914. They established small businesses and prospered. By the late 1920s the East Europeans had moved to the outlying suburbs of Norfolk, but maintained ownership of the land and continued their businesses on Church Street. Although African Americans were one of the first groups to settle in this area, with this residential population shift, the black population increased dramatically, and Church Street became the center of African-American family life, religion, entertainment, business opportunities, education, and political power for the better part of the 20th century.

Since its zenith in the 1920s, the Church Street of yesteryear has gradually disappeared, reflecting both the economic and social trends of the times. The area continued to thrive until the post-World War II era, when dramatic changes to Church Street and the Huntersville neighborhood can be traced up until the present. Between the 1950s and 1960s the decline of the Church Street area was principally due to two major factors. The first was the increased mobility of the African-American population through opportunities created by the Civil Rights Movement. Coupled with this was growing affluence of African Americans and their greater acceptance of living in suburban areas. The second factor was the severing of the lower end of Church Street with the construction of the Downtown Plaza shopping center, truncating Church Street and becoming the southern terminus of the once-famous street. A third and often overlooked factor in the decades since desegregation is the loss of a sense of community within the Church Street area. As middle- and upper-income African Americans moved away from Church Street, lower income individuals and families were left struggling without the benefit of financial stability created by middle- and upper-income blacks reinvesting their money and time in the community, ensuring that there would be capital improvements and safe conditions in which to live and work. Gone in large measure were the community leaders and success stories, the people who could keep the best and brightest of the Church Street's young people from slipping into obscurity and the world of drugs, crime, and mischief on the streets by setting powerful examples of their own opportunities and good fortune. There would also be a laundry list of projects, which, in their planning, were not necessarily intended to end the vibrant and important contributions of Church Street to Norfolk. The completion of the Norfolk-Portsmouth Bridge-Tunnel and the new Berkley Bridge permitted downtown commuters to bypass Church Street's commercial corridor. Urban renewal projects in the 1950s, which cleared 200 acres of downtown Norfolk, eliminated the connection between the city's center and Church Street. Changes, particularly in traffic patterns with the closing of East Main Street and the construction of Saint Paul's Boulevard, which parallels Church Street, forever altered the complexion of "The Road That Leadeth Out of Town."

In the end, Church Street is a testament to the human spirit that draws our anamnesis to that fine line between memory and reality, where the smells of bakeries and distilleries permeate our nostrels, and the sweet, cool sounds of blues and jazz music penetrate our ears and bring a smile to passersby. Children and their parents, businessmen, and laborers thronged the street, as well as youngsters running loops around lamp posts and street signs, their laughter peeling down the street. The street life was electric, and the entertainment and accommodations along the Church Street of yesteryear were legendary. There are few places tucked in our collective conscience that refresh our memory and stir our hearts like those of Church Street, known by generations of immigrants and African Americans as the "Harlem of the South."

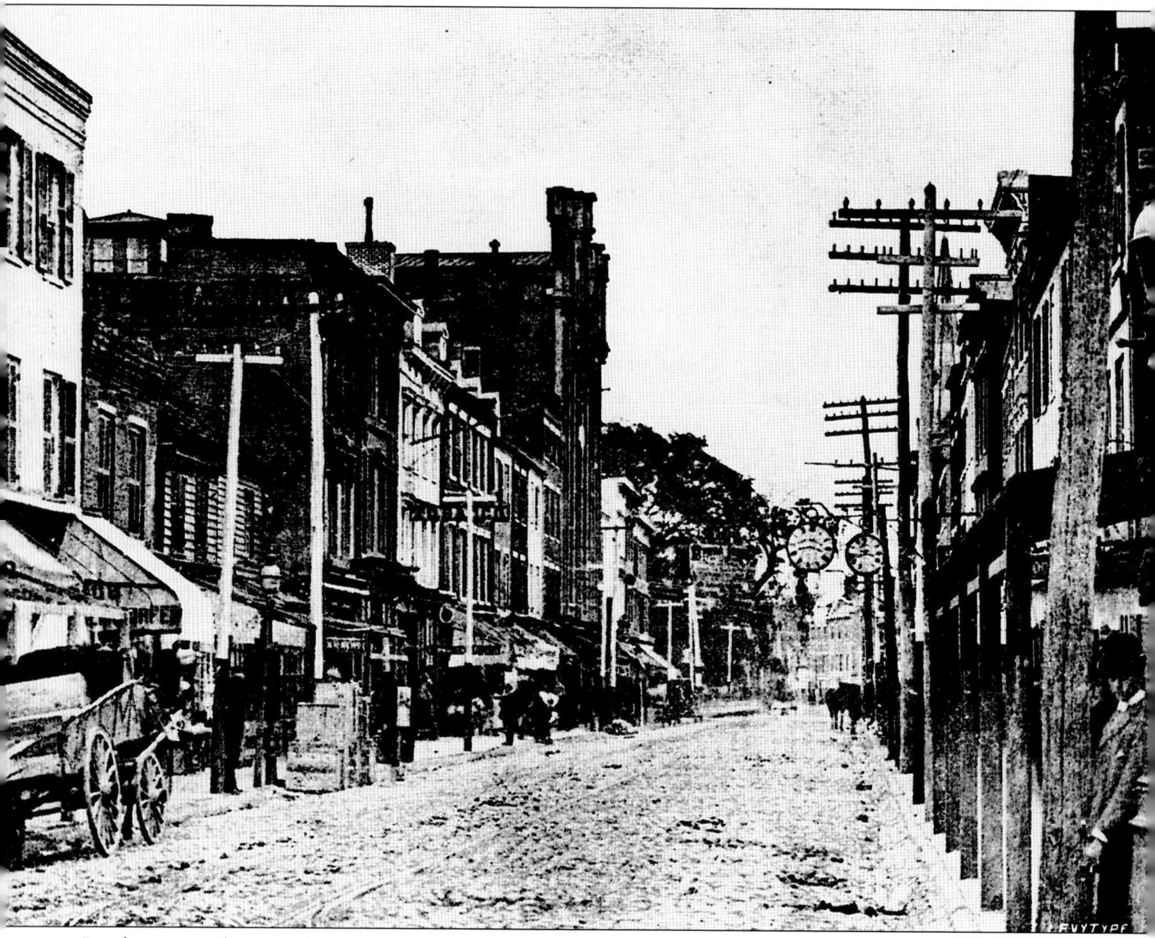

Looking north on Church Street in 1885, a photographer from the Levytype Company of Philadelphia took this picture, probably standing on the corner of East Main and Church Streets at the foot of Purcell House, a local hostelry. The street was paved with cobblestones, and the tracks visible in the foreground were used by supply cars drawn by horses down the middle of the street. Many business establishments lined the street on both sides: Frank Dreisell's Jewelry Company, Compere & Sons (dye works), and, of course, Jane Gillerlain's millinery, famous for its fine hat wear. The Odd Fellows Hall (previously called the Church Street Opera House), sharing quarters as the Norfolk Opera House, is the tall building on the left. The trees in the center of the photograph mark the location of St. Paul's Episcopal Church, then situated at the corner of Church and Cove Streets, now St. Paul's Boulevard and City Hall Avenue, respectively. All the buildings in this picture, with the exception of the church, are now gone, and Church Street has been widened and renamed St. Paul's Boulevard. It is of interest to note that the picture was taken at approximately 8:20 a.m., and the street is bustling with activity.

One

Religion and Revolution

"What means the Old Dominion? Hath she forgot the day
When o'er her conquered valleys swept the Briton's steel array?
How side by side, with sons of hers, the Massachusetts men
Encountered Tarleton's charge of fire, and stout Cornwallis, then?"

—From *Massachusetts to Virginia*, 1843*
John Greenleaf Whittier, American poet (1807–1892)

* This poem was composed by Whittier on reading an account of the proceedings of the citizens of Norfolk, Virginia, in reference to George Latimer, the alleged fugitive slave, who was seized in Boston without warrant at the request of James B. Grey, of Norfolk, claiming to be his master. This was a contentious case in the North and South, Latimer finally being given free papers for the sum of $400.

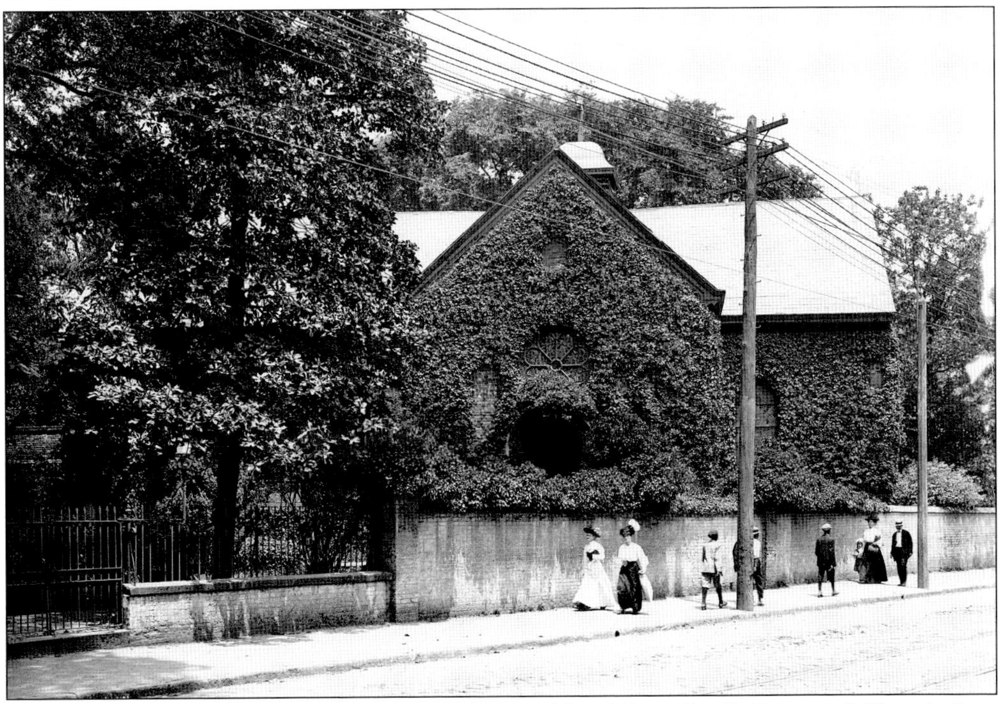

Harry C. Mann took this image of the southern gable of Saint Paul's Episcopal Church from Church Street on a hot summer's day in 1908. The cannonball, purportedly fired into the church by Lord Dunmore during his attack on January 1, 1776, is visible in the church wall to the far right, to the left of the second utility pole.

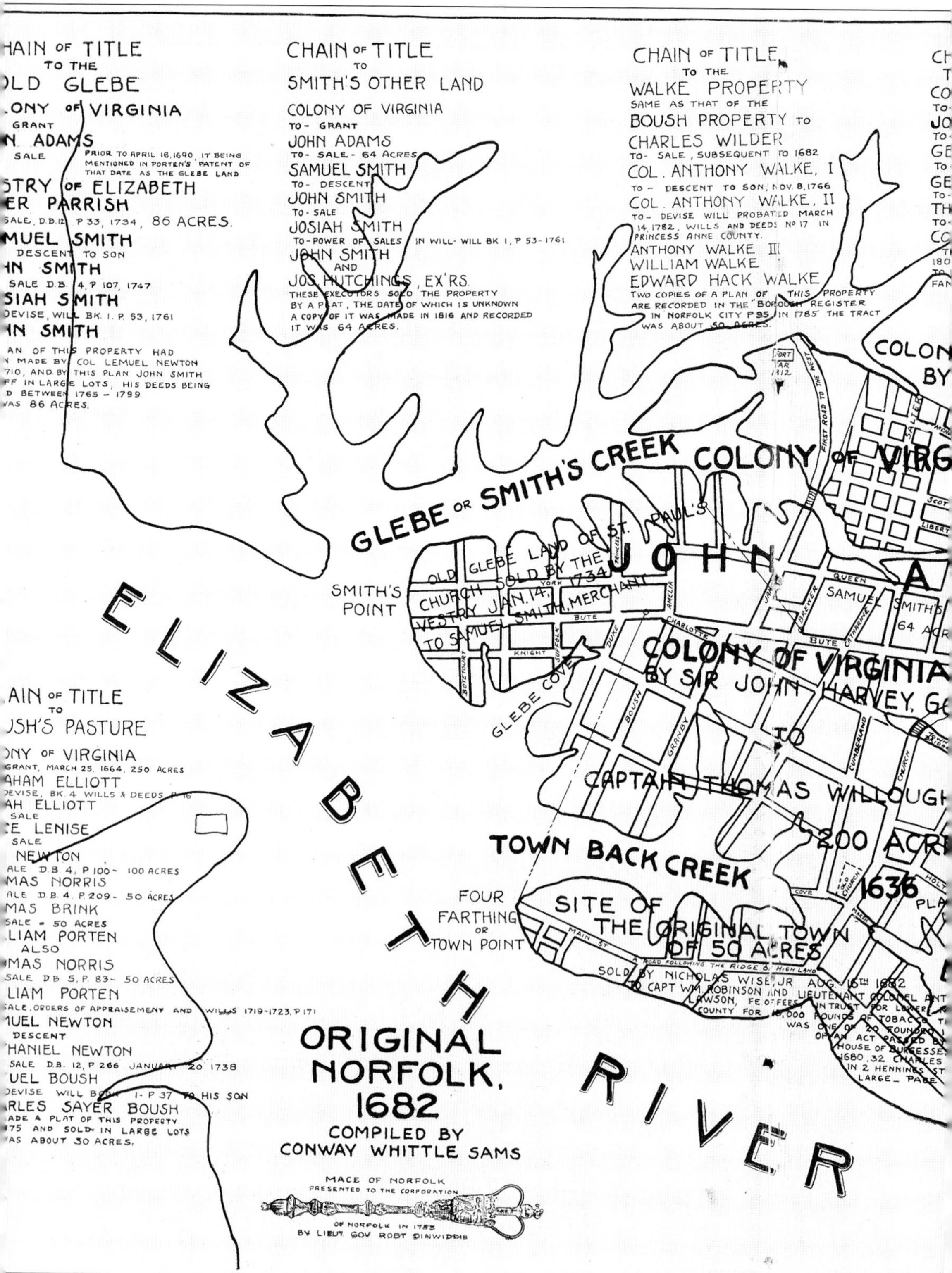
CHAIN OF TITLE TO SMITH'S OTHER LAND
COLONY OF VIRGINIA
TO- GRANT
JOHN ADAMS
TO- SALE - 64 ACRES
SAMUEL SMITH
TO- DESCENT
JOHN SMITH
TO- SALE
JOSIAH SMITH
TO-POWER OF SALES IN WILL- WILL BK 1, P 53-1761
JOHN SMITH AND JOS. HUTCHINGS, EX'RS.
THESE EXECUTORS SOLD THE PROPERTY BY A PLAT, THE DATE OF WHICH IS UNKNOWN A COPY OF IT WAS MADE IN 1816 AND RECORDED IT WAS 64 ACRES.
CHAIN OF TITLE TO THE WALKE PROPERTY
SAME AS THAT OF THE BOUSH PROPERTY TO CHARLES WILDER
TO- SALE, SUBSEQUENT TO 1682
COL. ANTHONY WALKE, I
TO - DESCENT TO SON, NOV. 8, 1766
COL. ANTHONY WALKE, II
TO- DEVISE WILL PROBATED MARCH 14, 1782, WILLS AND DEEDS No 17 IN PRINCESS ANNE COUNTY.
ANTHONY WALKE III
WILLIAM WALKE
EDWARD HACK WALKE
TWO COPIES OF A PLAN OF THIS PROPERTY ARE RECORDED IN THE "BOROUGH REGISTER" IN NORFOLK CITY P 95 IN 1785 THE TRACT WAS ABOUT 50 ACRES.
PRIOR TO APRIL 16, 1690, IT BEING MENTIONED IN PORTEN'S PATENT OF THAT DATE AS THE GLEBE LAND
GLEBE OR SMITH'S CREEK
OLD GLEBE LAND OF ST. PAUL'S CHURCH SOLD BY THE VESTRY JAN. 14, 1734 TO SAMUEL SMITH, MERCHANT
SMITH'S POINT
GLEBE COVE
ELIZABETH RIVER
TOWN BACK CREEK
FOUR FARTHING OR TOWN POINT
SITE OF THE ORIGINAL TOWN OF 50 ACRES
CAPTAIN THOMAS WILLOUGH
200 ACR
1636
ORIGINAL NORFOLK, 1682
COMPILED BY CONWAY WHITTLE SAMS
MACE OF NORFOLK PRESENTED TO THE CORPORATION OF NORFOLK IN 1753 BY LIEUT. GOV. ROBT DINWIDDIE

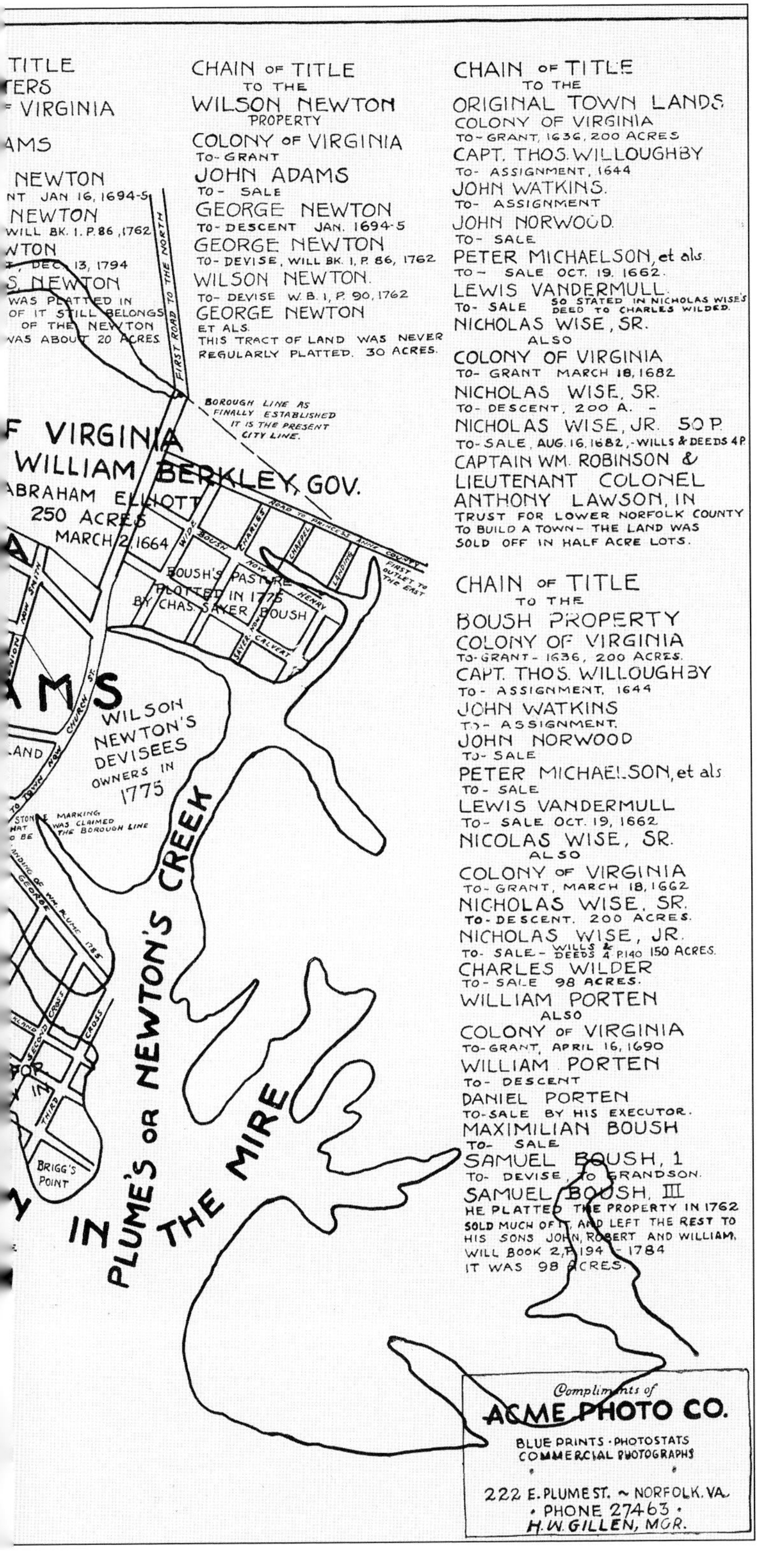

"The Road That Leadeth Into the Woods," later known as "The Road That Leadeth Out of Town," initially traversed a natural causeway connecting the land on which the town of Norfolk was first mapped by John Ferebee and the country to the north of Town Back Creek and Dun-in-the-Mire Creek. The street was later named Church Street for the old Norfolk Borough Church, known today as Saint Paul's Episcopal Church, sitting on its west side. The map shown here, compiled by Conway Whittle Sams, shows Norfolk as it appeared in 1682.

Ye Chappell of Ease

Sometime before 1634, Norfolk County was part of Elizabeth City County, encompassing the southern shore of Lower Tidewater as well as the Peninsula. Between 1634 and 1637, Lower Norfolk County was established, taking in the area that eventually became Norfolk and Princess Anne Counties. In 1691, Princess Anne County was established, named for Anne, Princess of Denmark and the daughter of James II, who ascended the English throne in 1702. James II was dedicated to bringing the teachings of the Church of England to the American colonies. As early as 1637, wealthy colonists with estates and plantations established on the southside of Lower Tidewater were visited by clergy, the first of whom was the Reverend John Wilson. Though there had been a small chapel located on "Mr. Seawell's Pointe" in this time frame, completed by March 15, 1640–41, members of the Elizabeth River Parish needed a place of worship closer to the town where the majority of the population resided. The house of Robert Glascock was chosen for this purpose while a church was built. Ye Chappell of Ease was completed in October of 1641, down the Elizabeth River between Lambert's Point and the area known today as Town Point. The chapel on Henry Sewell's property was eventually abandoned, but to its credit, all of the Episcopalian churches in Norfolk are descended from this little chapel on Henry Seawell's (Sewell's) property. Chapels of ease were so named for a chapel or dependent church built to accommodate an expanding parish.

As Norfolk was surveyed in 1680 and its streets mapped in 1681, the area later known as the Borough Church churchyard was put aside as a church site and graveyard for the town. There was not a church constructed on the site until after July 15, 1698. A second Ye Chappell of Ease, located on the site of the church known today as Saint Paul's Episcopal Church, was likely completed by 1700. The first Samuel Boush presented a London-manufactured silver chalice "to the Parish Church of Norfolk Towne March 1700." The second chapel of ease was a brick and timber structure, which stood at Cove Street in the corner of the yard between Cove and Market Streets on a 100-acre tract of land presented to the parish as glebe in a land grant dated October 30, 1686. This church is referenced in the Norfolk County Deed Book "F," pages 23 and 63, dated May 17, 1722. Under the term of Reverend Moses Robertson (1734), 84 acres of the glebe had already passed out of the church's possession, lands which might today carry a value of millions of dollars. The deed of Colonel Samuel Boush to Captain Simon Hancock in November 1737, and the deed of Peter Malbone to Captain Nathaniel Tatem in November 1738 indicate that the first church was standing next to and north of Malbone's land and gave its name to Church Street.

The name "Church Street" was not bestowed on "The Road That Leadeth Out of Town" until the town limits were extended under the Charter of 1736 to Town Bridge. The road took the name Church Street from the first church, which was razed after the erection of Saint Paul's Episcopal Church. Built in 1739, Saint Paul's Episcopal Church remains standing today.

The town of Norfolk was established by the Town Act of 1680, but in September 1736, the Norfolk Borough was established by Royal Charter because the town had proven itself to King George II as amenable to trade and navigation. Samuel Boush was appointed mayor but died before qualifying for office, and in November, George Newton was chosen as mayor of the borough. Two years later, in 1738, the old Ye Chappell of Ease had become inadequate to serve the religious needs of the borough's growing population. In 1739, the Borough Church was completed as indicated by the date on the southern gable. The new church stood in the yard near the old building. The Borough Church was built in the form of a Roman cross of red and bluish semiglazed brick. Colonel Samuel Boush gave the bricks for this church, and it may be that he had his father's initials, S.B., placed on the southern gable in memorial, or that the vestry placed the good colonel's initials there in recognition of his generous contribution to the church's construction. The bricks and timbers of Ye Chappell of Ease, the first church structure in Norfolk, were sold in 1750 by the vestry.

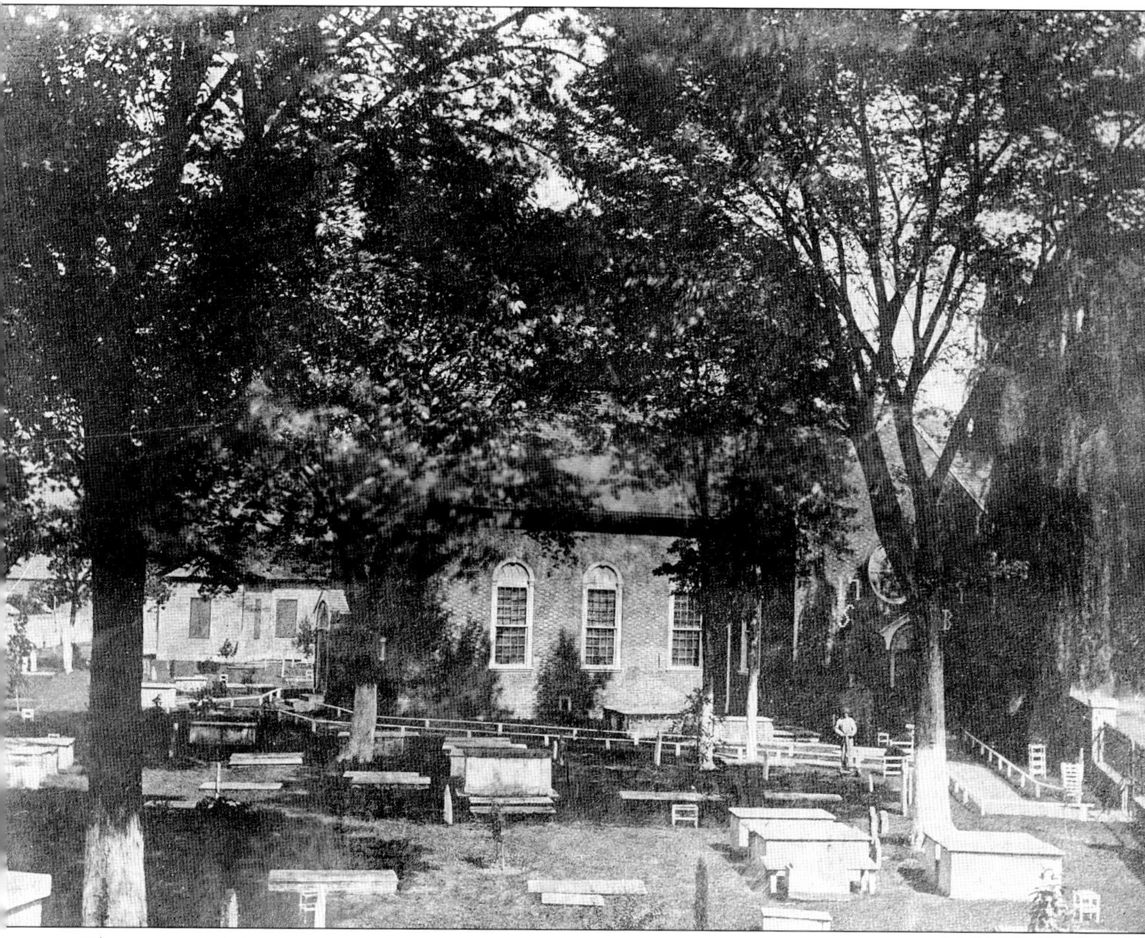

This image of the Saint Paul's Episcopal Church and its cemetery was taken about 1880 by an unknown photographer.

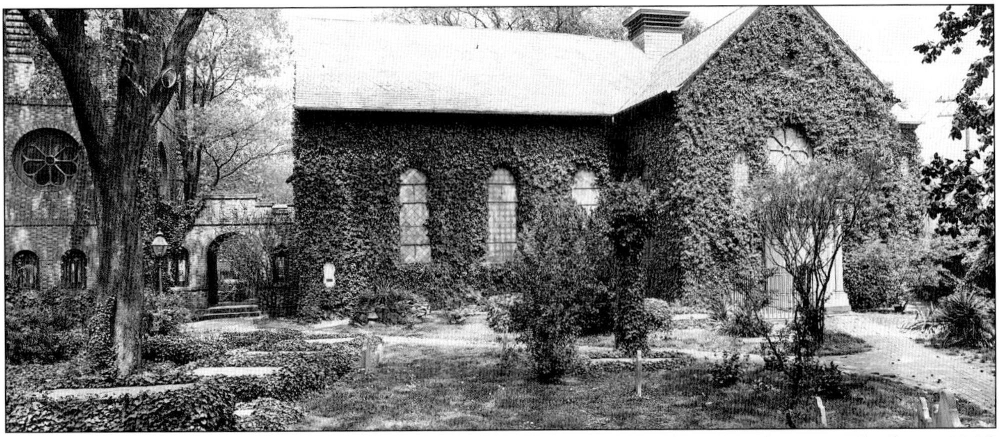

Saint Paul's Episcopal Church and its surrounding graveyard were photographed in 1908 by Harry C. Mann. There were 265 tombstones in the churchyard in 1902 when they were inventoried, but so many had already disappeared. The oldest tombstone in the yard was found on the south side of the church and was documented in the 1902 survey. The stone was inscribed: "Here lies the body of Dorothy Farrell who deceased the 18th of January 1673." The presence of 17th-century tombstones in the churchyard, predating the construction of the second Ye Chapell of Ease and the Borough Church, were brought from other places to be reinterred on the site.

Sacred Sites

A general law was passed in the Virginia colony in 1667 vesting the right in county courts that when expedient, it was a county court's responsibility "to set aside and appropriate not more than two acres of land for Church and Burial purposes." As there are 1 3/4 acres of land encompassing Saint Paul's cemetery within the walls, it was obviously given to this use by the law of 1667. Many of what would have been the oldest grave markers in the yard were made of soft sandstone and have crumbled with age, or were carried away by unscrupulous British troops during the Revolutionary War. Some of the earliest headstones were also constructed of wood plank because tombstones in the 1600s and 1700s had to be imported from Europe and were quite costly. It was also customary in the 17th and 18th (and even early 19th) centuries to have family vaults for burials adjoining the residences of wealthier citizens. These vaults have been found throughout Hampton Roads over the years, especially in Norfolk, and also gave rise to stories of houses haunted by unrequited spirits. These tales did little more than bend the imaginations of the superstitious. In the earliest years of the town's and borough's history, generations of the same family occupied a residence, those being the days of primogeniture and entails. Substantial residences once stood throughout the city of Norfolk, surrounded by convenient outhouses and enclosed by brick walls, early storm-proofing against high winds. When loved ones died, family members buried them in the vault in the garden, in the shadow of their roof-tree and away from public displays of mourning.

There are graves underneath the floor of Saint Paul's Episcopal Church, following a European religious custom of burying the dead in churches. Henry Sewell and his wife were buried beneath the chancel of the first Ye Chappell of Ease. The floor of the original church rested on the ground and was made of stone to facilitate this purpose. The same is true of the 1739 structure. By 1835, the cemetery was closed to interments with seven exceptions, four of whom were Mrs. Collins (no marker); Mary Chandler, 91 years and 5 months, a daughter of Colonel Anthony Lawson, who died in 1859; Reverend Nicholas Albertson Okeson, in 1882; and Reverend Henry Harris Covington, rector of the church from 1913 until his death on February 12, 1933.

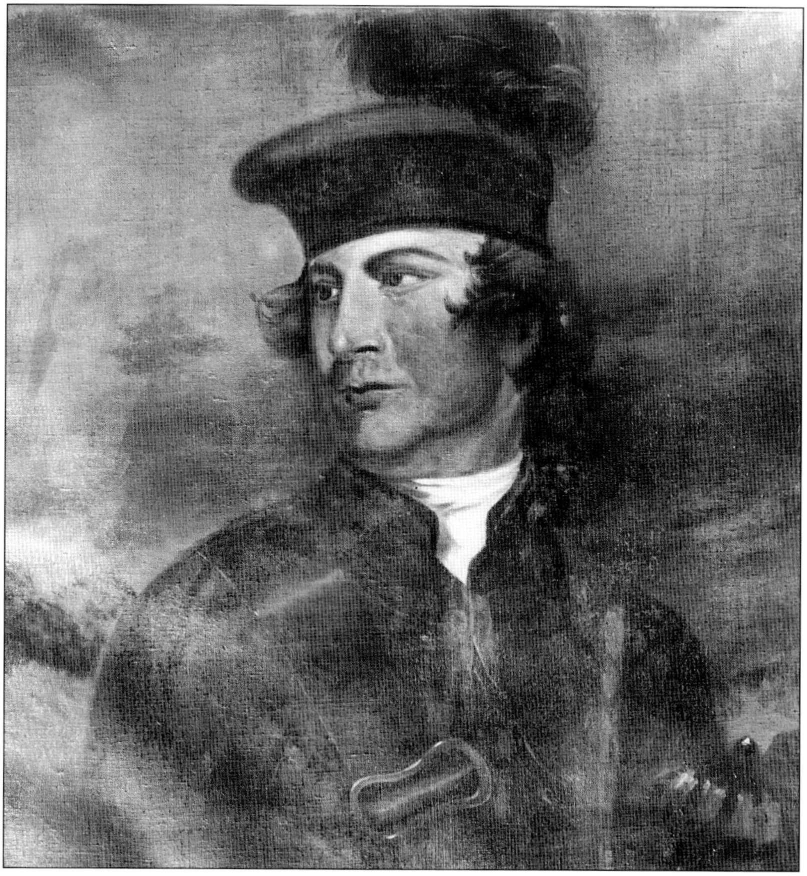

This photograph of a painting of Lord Dunmore, the fourth earl of Dunmore and last royal governor of Virginia (1771–1775), was taken in 1906 by the Jamestown Official Photograph Corporation. The Earl of Dunmore, John Murray, has never been depicted in a wholly positive light in the annals of Norfolk history. After the royal government of Virginia was dissolved in April of 1775, an independent governing body was formed by convention in Richmond, and the colony of Virginia was divided into four districts. The borough of Norfolk along with Nansemond, Norfolk, Isle of Wight, and Princess Anne Counties formed one of these districts, the intent of which was to organize opposition to the British, including recruitment of minutemen. We find in the records of December 1, 1775, an ordinance was passed as a direct result of Dunmore's proclamation of November 1775, pertaining to the royal governor's release of slaves and indentured servants to bear arms on the side of the British. The preamble to the Virginia Convention's ordinance read: "Whereas Lord Dunmore, by his many hostile attacks upon the good people of the colony, and attempts to infringe their rights and liberties by his proclamation declaring freedom to our servants and slaves, and arming them against us, by seizing our persons and properties and declaring those who opposed his arbitrary measures to be in a state of rebellion, made it necessary that an additional number of forces be raised, for our protection and defense." In response to Dunmore's action, the *Virginia Gazette* of November 5, 1775, carried a letter from a citizen who declared Dunmore's action "a cruel declaration to the Negroes."

As an aside, Dunmore was so unpopular with Virginians by this time, Dunmore County, formed from Frederick County in May 1772 and named for him, had its named changed by the General Assembly to Shanando (today known as Shenandoah) County, effective February 1, 1778. Located in the Valley of Virginia, Shenandoah County's largest town is Woodstock.

Norfolk Under Fire and the Legend of the Cannonball

The Revolutionary War wrought a great deal of damage on the Norfolk Borough and its venerable Borough Church, so much so that only the walls of the church stood at the conclusion of hostilities. The onus for most of the church's destruction falls on the shoulders of Lord Dunmore. Dunmore and seven of his best ships covered Norfolk with their guns from what is now the Berkley Bridge to the western end of Main Street. The *Liverpool* stayed off Church Street flanked by the HMS *Otter*, HMS *Kingfisher*, HMS *Eilbeck*, HMS *Dunmore*, HMS *Mercury*, and HMS *William*. What was left of Norfolk's population was preparing for Christmas when Dunmore's forces initiated their first assault on the town. The fleet sent up a barrage of bar shot, chain shot, and grape that tore through the trees and buildings located near the waterfront. Norfolk's defenders were sure British troops would next attempt a landing ashore. Colonel Edward Stephens and two hundred Culpeper Minutemen charged Dunmore's landing parties, forcing them back to their ships. The minutemen's success was short-lived. On January 1, 1776, Dunmore bombarded the city, and buildings caught fire. Women and children fled to the Borough Church, protecting themselves from the hail of shells under its eaves. Though history assigns complete blame on Dunmore for Norfolk's destruction, it is actually not known whether he alone is responsible or whether American patriots under the command of Colonel Richard Howe fired the city to prevent the quartering of British troops in the town. There are no remaining records to indicate what really happened.

One of Dunmore's cannon shots did leave the Borough Church with an indentation in its corner wall. Not until many years later was the cannonball permanently affixed in the indentation. Accounts in the *American Beacon* dated May 13, 1848, tell of the "cannonball that made the well-known indentation upon the corner of the wall of [Saint Paul's Church]. It was discovered by one of the vestrymen [Captain Seabury] of that church (whom a laudable curiosity prompted to dig for it) about 2 1/2 feet below the surface of the ground, immediately under the indentation. Tradition says it was fired from a British man-o-war during the bombardment of Norfolk by order of Lord Dunmore." The frigate HMS *Liverpool* fired the shot on the Monday afternoon of the January 1, 1776 attack. In response to the *American Beacon* article, one reader recounted the following in the May 17 edition:

"I remember conversing as late as the year 1836 with Robert Farmer, Esq., who recently died at the advanced age of 86, respecting the ball found the other day in the yard of St. Paul's, when he observed that the ball was still in the building where it first struck; but upon my telling him that I have never seen the ball there from my childhood he added: 'I did not know that it had fallen down.' So, it appears that the ball remained embedded in the wall of the church a long time after it was discharged from the cannon."

The reader went on to recommend returning the cannonball to its original resting place as a memorial to the city's bravely fought revolutionary contest. Of course, this was done. The Borough Church was ordered re-roofed by the Virginia Assembly in 1785, but sat without a parish. The first Christ Church was constructed across Church Street from the Borough Church in 1800. In the interim, the former Borough Church building was used as a racially mixed Baptist church until 1832, when the Reverend Henry William Ducachet of Christ Church restored the former Borough Church and renamed it Saint Paul's Protestant Episcopal Church. The word "Protestant" has since been dropped from the name.

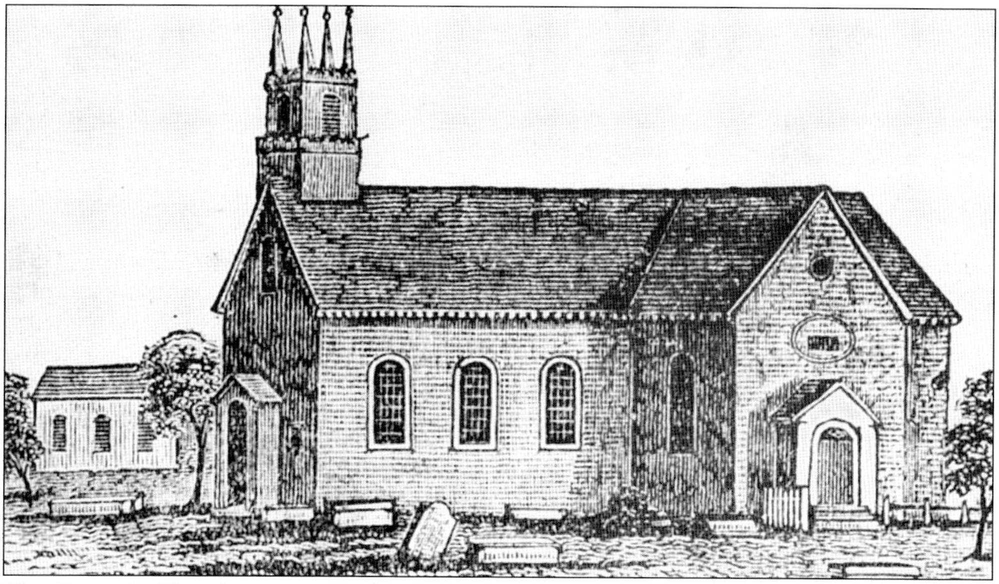

The Borough Church was repaired in 1785, but it was not until 1832 that the Saint Paul's parish was organized. This illustration was rendered of the venerable church about 1800 and shows the sanctuary still unoccupied.

The marble font in Saint Paul's Episcopal Church is a copy of one given by Robert "King" Carter to Christ Church in Lancaster County, Virginia, in 1734. The bowl is upheld by three cherubs, one of which is visible in this Harry C. Mann photograph taken about 1909 of the church's interior. The font was carved by a Danish artist in New York, and was presented to the church by Sarah Francis (Leigh) Pegram, who died on August 14, 1905. The church has five memorial windows. The two in the rear of the chancel are visible here. These windows are inscribed to the memory of Reverend William Myers Jackson, who was born on October 19, 1809, and who died on October 3, 1855, and Nicholas Albertson Okeson, who was born November 5, 1819, and died September 16, 1882. On Jackson's window is a representation of Saint John on Patmos receiving the revelation from an angel, and on Okeson's window, a representation of Saint Paul on Mars Hill. Aside from the memorial windows, the church also contains several Norman windows of cathedral glass, and two beautiful rose windows, the glass of which is richly accentuated with color.

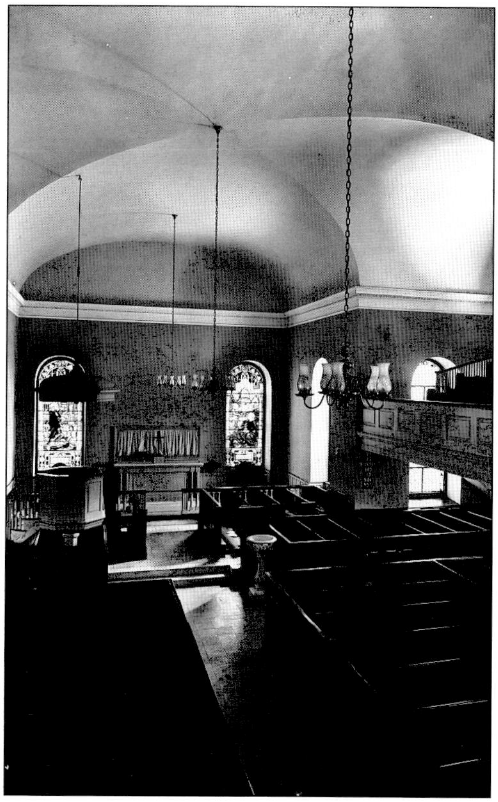

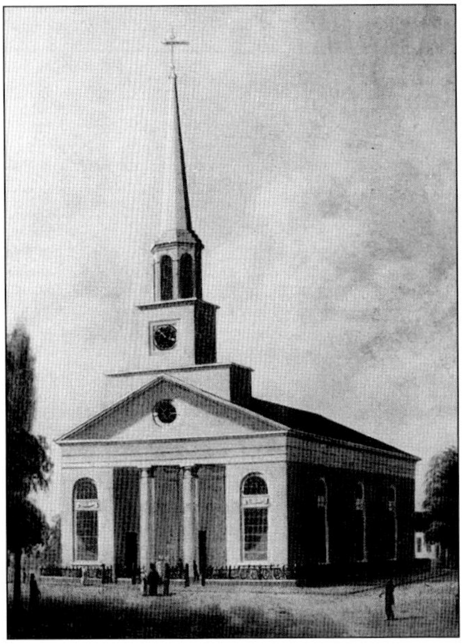

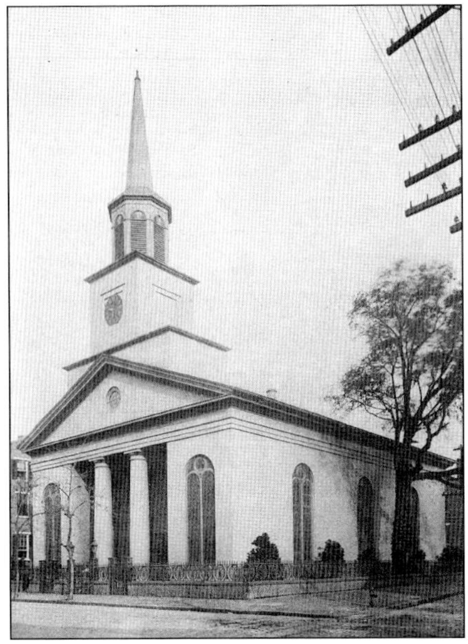

Left: Christ Church (Episcopal) was consecrated on November 9, 1828, and replaced the first Christ Church on Church Street, built in 1800 and burned in 1827. Thomas Williamson (1776–1846), an amateur architect and a cashier at the Virginia Bank in Norfolk, designed the new edifice, shown here as it appeared *c.* 1830. The church was located at the corner of Freemason and Cumberland Streets, but was demolished in 1973. *Right:* Pictured here is Christ Church, *c.* 1902.

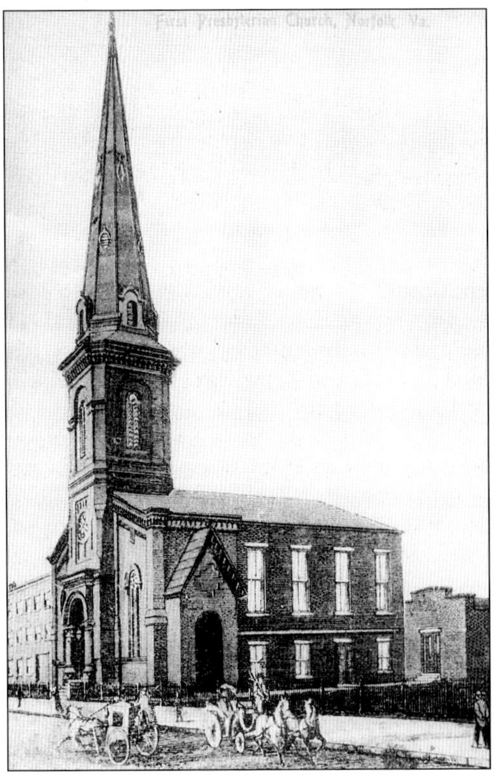

By 1836, the majority of the Bell Church's faithful had withdrawn to form a new church, built on the foundation of the first Christ Church on Church Street. Parishioners attended a dedication ceremony conducted by the Reverend William S. Plummer on November 20, 1836, and it was this edifice (shown as it appeared *c.* 1840) that became the First Presbyterian Church. First Presbyterian was led by Reverend Dr. George W. Armstrong from 1851 to 1891. On March 17, 1912, the congregations of First and Ghent Presbyterian Churches agreed to merge into one church. First Presbyterian Church ceased to exist, abandoning the Church Street edifice in 1912 and joining members of Ghent Presbyterian on Colonial Avenue. The Reverend Stuart Nye Hutchison of the Ghent church became pastor. (Courtesy of Kirn Library.)

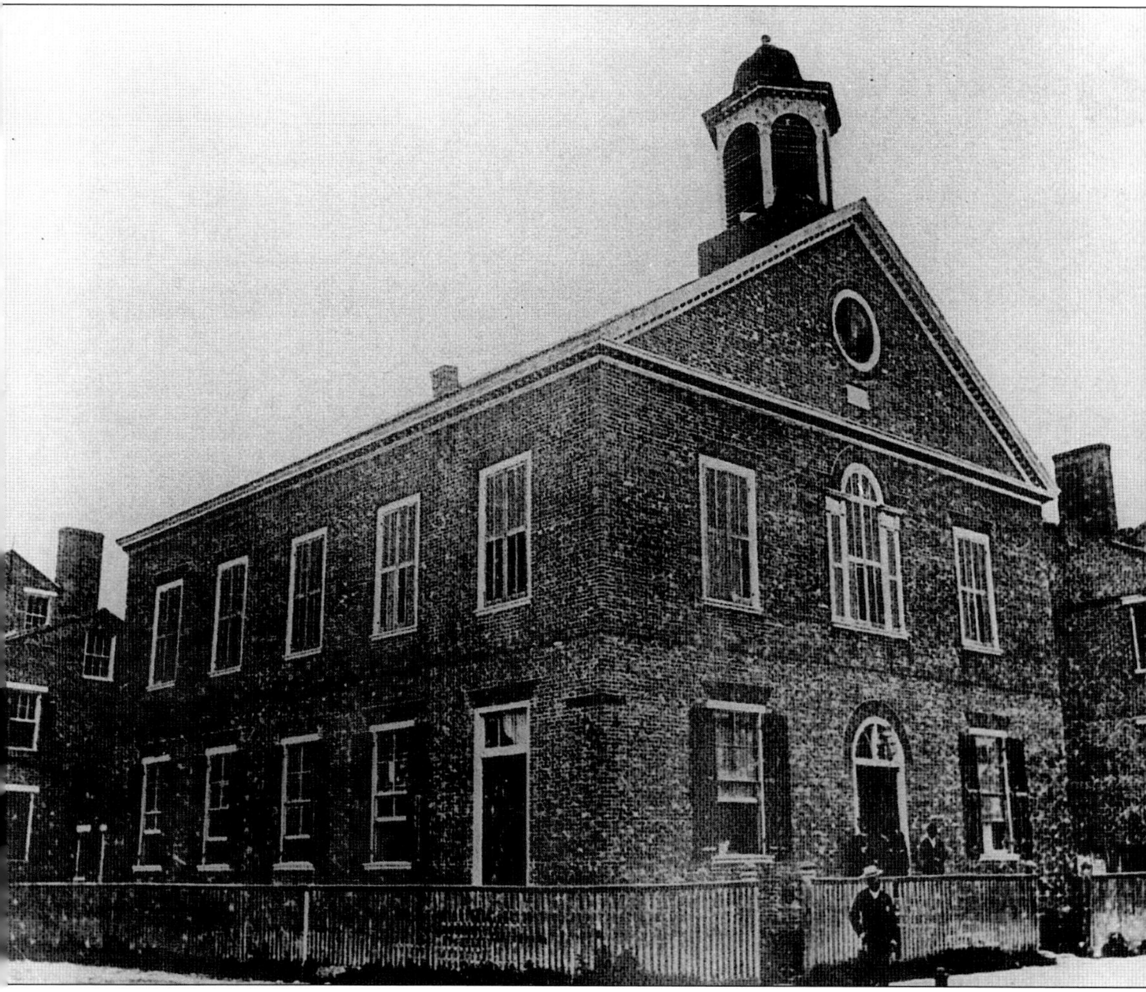

There was no record of a Presbyterian church in Norfolk from 1680 to 1710. Religious intolerance and persecution were still too pervasive in the town to allow other denominations to practice their faith openly. Norfolk County Court licensed Reverend Josias Mackie in 1692 to minister at three locations: Thomas Ivy's house, located on the Eastern Branch of the Elizabeth River; Richard Phillpot's house on Tanner's Creek; and the house of John Roberts, built on the Western Branch of the Elizabeth River. Mackie died in 1716, and in papers of the Philadelphia Presbytery documenting his passing, Mackie's faithful were called the "the congregation on the Elizabeth River." In 1801 the Virginia General Assembly appointed Reverend Benjamin Grigsby to itinerate in the lower parts of Virginia. Grigsby succeeded between 1802 and 1803 in having a building erected for his congregation at the corner of Bank and Charlotte Streets (the Bell Church, pictured above as it appeared before the turn of the century). Unfortunately, Grigsby died of yellow fever in 1810, and his congregation began to split along progressive and traditional lines.

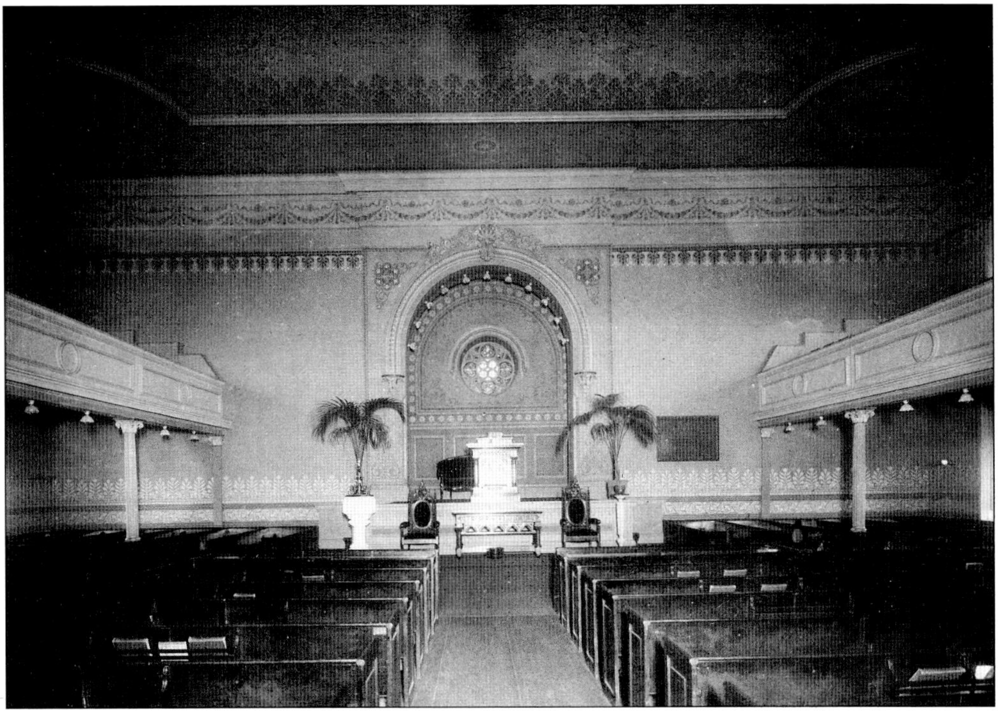

This image of the interior of First Presbyterian Church was taken by an unknown photographer in 1895.

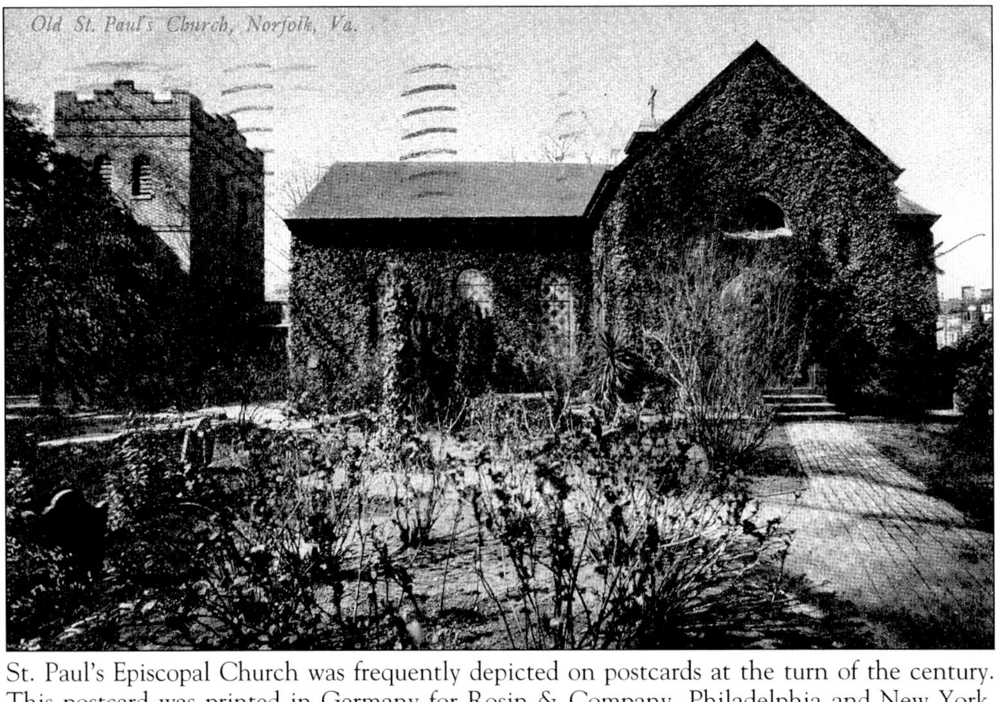

St. Paul's Episcopal Church was frequently depicted on postcards at the turn of the century. This postcard was printed in Germany for Rosin & Company, Philadelphia and New York, about 1908. The card was hand colored and shows the southeast side of the churchyard. Church Street is visible over the ivy-covered wall on the right.

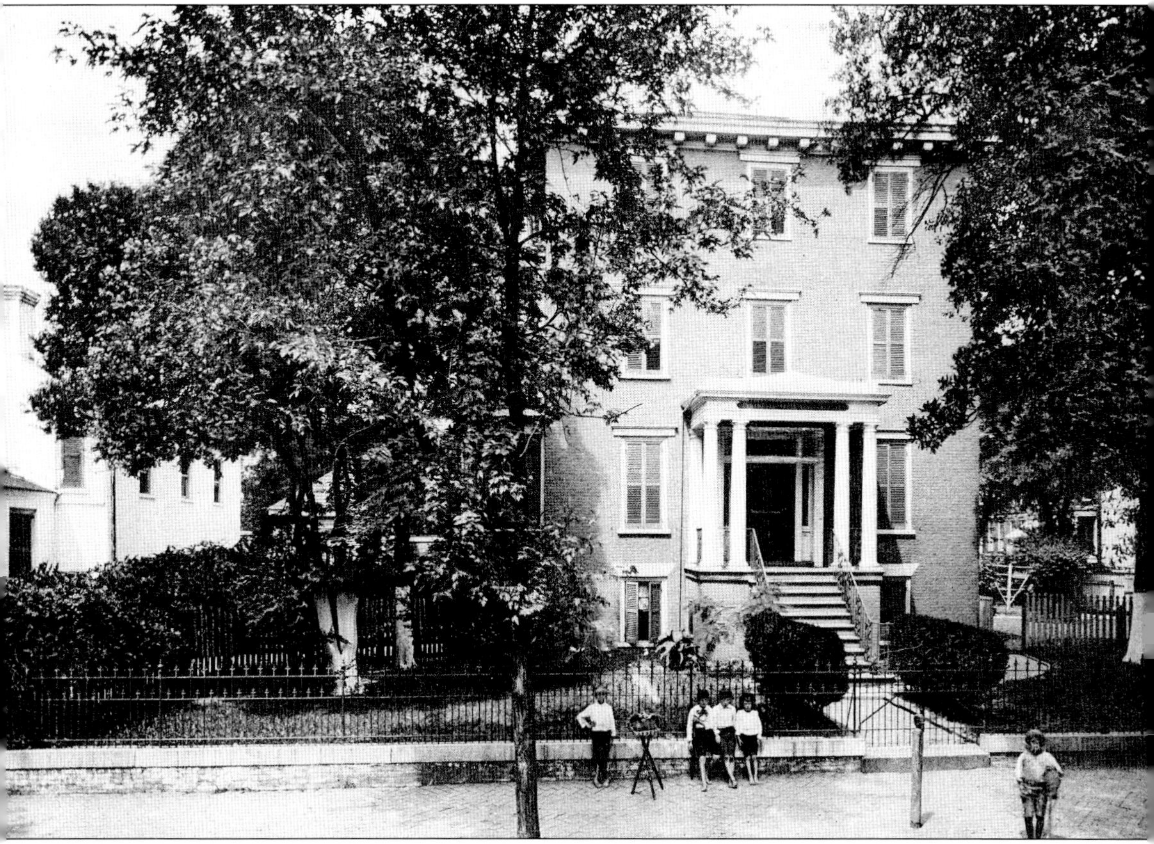

The Norfolk Female Orphan Asylum, located at 93 Holt Street near the corner of Walke Street (née Third Cross Street), was photographed by an unknown photographer in 1892. Pattie S. Hart became matron of the asylum the year the picture was taken, succeeding Mary R. Andrews. It was founded by Bishop Francis Asbury of the Methodist ministry on March 24, 1804. Asbury was born in Hamstead, England, part of the British Black Country, on August 21, 1745. He came to the American colonies in 1771 at a time when there were perhaps only a dozen Methodist ministers. Asbury was never to return to his homeland. By 1784 he was ordained a Methodist Bishop of America. He died on March 31, 1816, at the age of 71. In 1924, President of the United States Calvin Coolidge unveiled a statue of Asbury in Washington, D.C. The orphan home was undenominational and dependent on an annual contribution made by all the area's churches, supplemented by a small stipend from the city of Norfolk. The facility was incorporated as the Norfolk Female Orphan Asylum by an Act of Assembly in January 1816. When the yellow fever epidemic of 1855 left countless orphans, both boys and girls, a group of businessmen known as the Howard Association set about to rent a house and provide for the children properly. Contributions toward the children's care came from people all over the United States. By the time the Civil War came, the orphanage owned its building and the little girls and young women residing in the house could continue to be provided a place to stay by the Howard Association. A board of managers consisting of members of the Methodist, Presbyterian, and Baptist churches administered the asylum. Children anywhere from three to 12 years of age were accepted by the orphanage, and the girls were provided for until they were 18 unless adopted or employed.

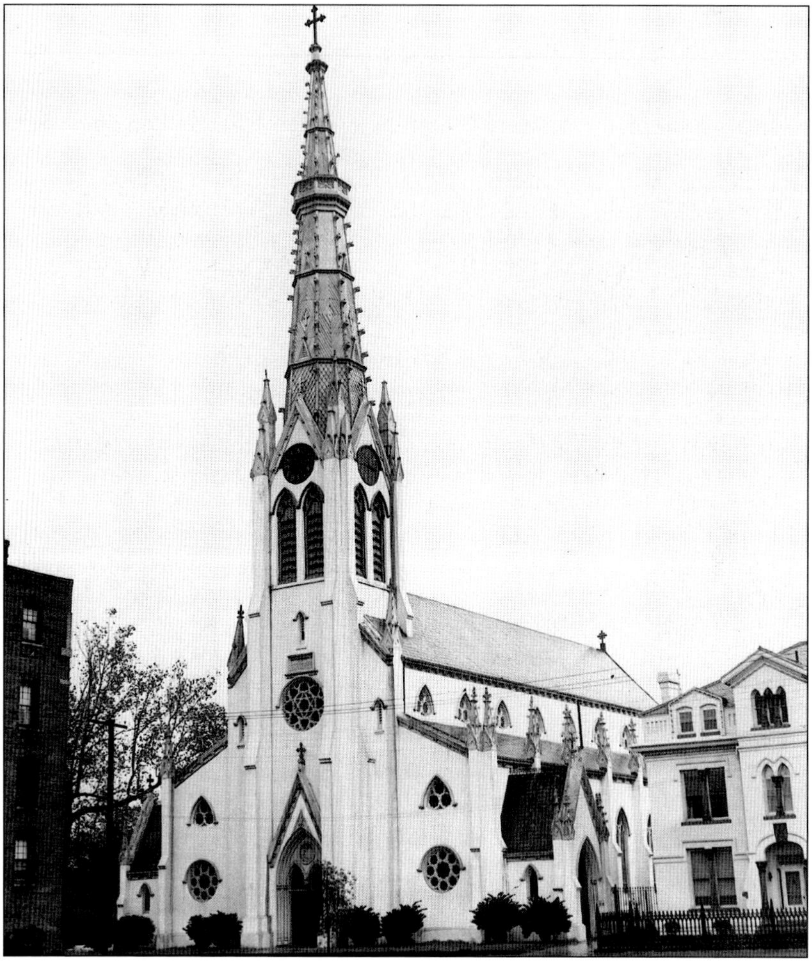

This photograph of St. Mary's of the Immaculate Conception Catholic Church, located at 232 Chapel Street, was taken in 1953. The most significant history associated with the magnificent structure shown here began 100 years before this picture was taken. Father Matthew O'Keefe became pastor of St. Mary's predecessor, St. Patrick's, in 1853 and remained in that role until 1887. On December 8, 1856, St. Patrick's was razed by fire, and though it cannot be known for sure, the fire may have been set because O'Keefe refused to conduct segregated services. O'Keefe was wrought with grief over the church's destruction, particularly coming on the heels of the 1855 yellow fever epidemic in the city. Raising money to rebuild the church using donations from Norfolk patrons was hard, so O'Keefe turned elsewhere—New York—for the bulk of contributions toward rebuilding a suitable house of worship. The result was St. Mary's Catholic Church, built in 1858. The church's imposing French Gothic influence has led many to believe that it was the creation of architect James Renwick, one of a handful of American architects of his day to infuse his designs with such strong overtones of Gallic-Gothic precedent. St. Patrick's Cathedral in New York City was perhaps Renwick's crowning architectural achievement. The church's stained-glass windows, visible here, were crafted by Franz Mayer of Mayer and Company, Munich, Germany. St. Mary's was consecrated on October 3, 1858, by Bishop John McGill of the Diocese of Richmond. St. Mary's did not add "Immaculate Conception" to its name until December 19, 1900, when it was designated a church of the Immaculate Conception by the Reverend Augustine Van DeVyver, the sixth bishop of Richmond. (H.D. Vollmer, photographer. Courtesy of Kirn Library.)

Catholicism in Norfolk

St. Mary's of the Immaculate Conception (now St. Mary's Basilica) is the direct descendant of the first Roman Catholic church established in Virginia, dating to early efforts to establish a Catholic church in Norfolk in September of 1687. At that time, a Father Edmonds was arrested for marrying a couple, and on November 16, 1687, Father Raymond was also arrested for saying Mass and, consequently, marrying another couple. The religious persecution of Catholics in the town had so deteriorated that by 1785, there were none left in Norfolk. Catholicism did not return to Norfolk until 1791 when Father Jean DuBois and some of his priests and congregation fled France seeking religious freedom and the right to practice their faith guaranteed under federal law and the Virginia Statute of Religious Freedom authored by Thomas Jefferson. Those were the days in Norfolk when most of the known Catholics were French or of French extraction. Many had come to America to escape religious persecution prevalent during and after the French Revolution. The first church under DuBois's tutelage was located on Bermuda Street. It was here that DuBois said the first Mass in Virginia after the signing of the Declaration of Independence with the exception, of course, Masses being said during the fall and winter of 1781 in French encampments and ships engaged in the Revolutionary War. Even in this formative period, Norfolk was still the center of Catholicism in Virginia. The church remained on Bermuda Street until 1794 when land was acquired by the Roman Catholic Society of the Norfolk Borough on the same site the present-day St. Mary's was later constructed in 1858.

Though much history would pass between the construction of St. Mary's Catholic Church in the waning years of the republic prior to the outbreak of the War Between the States, some of the most compelling pieces of St. Mary's and Catholicism's history in Norfolk would begin amidst the Great Depression of the 20th century. Father Edward A. Brosnan arrived at St. Mary's in 1925, coming to the parish at a time when the mother church of Hampton Roads' Catholic community had spun off outlying parishes and the African-American Catholic population of his new church was burgeoning. From the arrival of the first Josephites in 1889 to tend to black parishioners' needs at St. Mary's, to the marriage of the first black couple on February 18, 1890, by Father William G. Payne, to the consolidations and departures of large portions of St. Mary's congregation in the 1940s and 1950s, Catholicism in the city could be said to be in a perpetual state of motion.

Changes to the face of downtown Norfolk left a mark on the future of St. Mary's of the Immaculate Conception Catholic Church, and St. Mary's was hardly alone in the church's experience with what was to occur in the late 1940s and 1950s during the peak of Norfolk's urban renewal movement. Public housing projects started to replace older, dilapidated Norfolk neighborhoods, streets were widened and major interstate arteries connecting the city to the suburbs were created, and improved transportation services led to an exodus of St. Mary's parishioners to the outlying areas of Virginia Beach, South Norfolk, Lower Norfolk County, and to the northern reaches of the existing city of Norfolk. While the move by predominantly white parishioners to outlying areas was happening at a feverish pace, cultural geography was bringing African Americans closer to the Catholic church, particularly St. Mary's, which already had a strong contingent of black parishioners. By June 16, 1961, St. Joseph's Catholic Church, an all-black congregation, had moved permanently to St. Mary's from their building at the southwest corner of Cumberland and Freemason Streets. This was not an altogether smooth transition to St. Mary's because, in their enthusiasm to become a contributing faction of St. Mary's congregation, former St. Joseph's parishioners forgot that it might take a period of adjustment to blend divergent traditions. Devout Josephites, who had come to Norfolk in 1889, remained until 1974. Their presence during the pivotal 1960s and early 1970s helped unify the church. By 1987, Reverend Walter C. Barrett had become the first African-American pastor in the church's history. Under his pastorate, St. Mary's was designated a minor basilica by an emissary of Pope John Paul II, Archbishop Agostino Cacciavillan, the Pope's prelate, in

December 1991. In so doing, Pope John Paul II recognized St. Mary's for its antiquity, dignity, and historical importance as a center of worship. It is also the only black-majority church in the United States to be given the basilica designation.

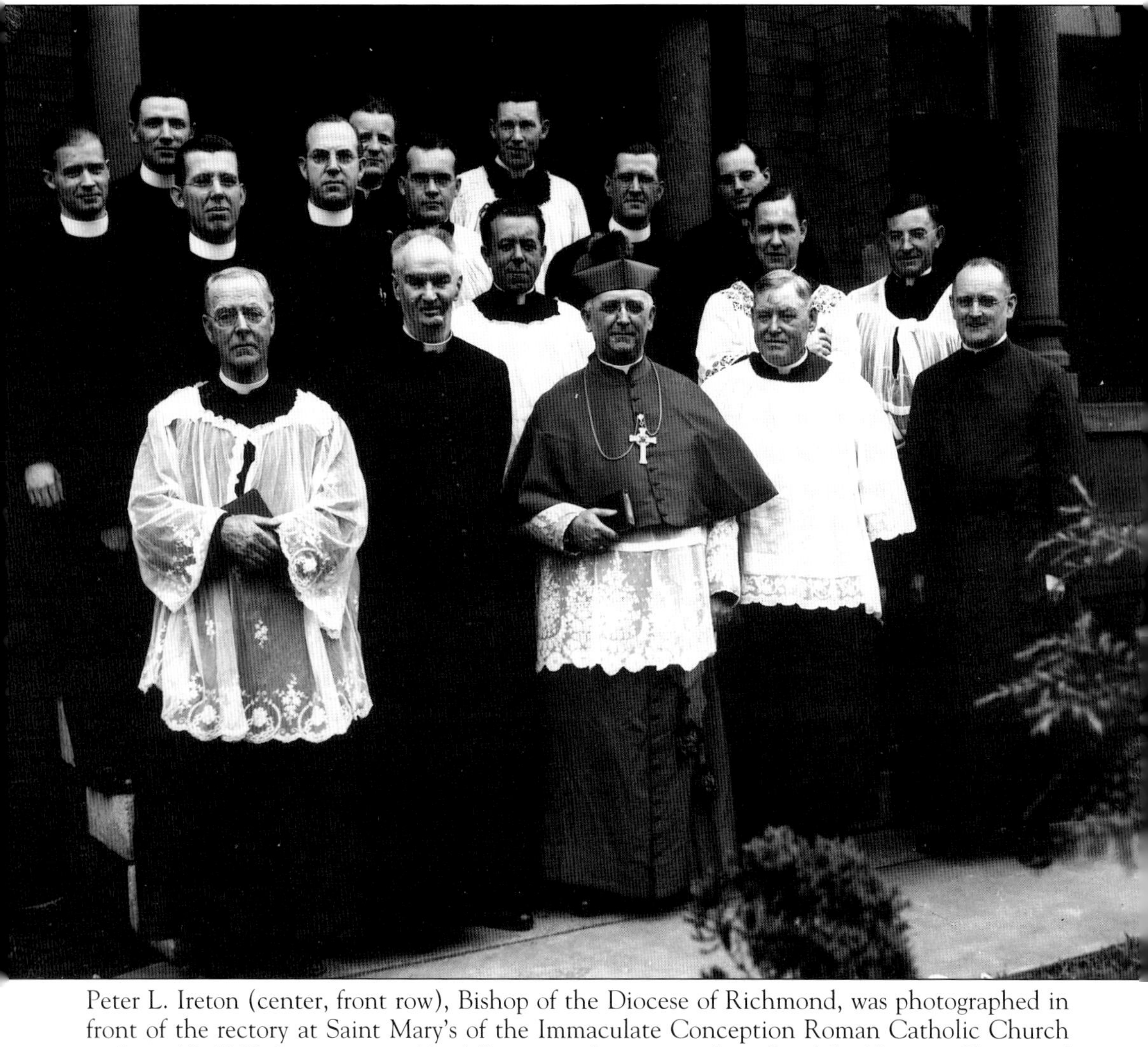

Peter L. Ireton (center, front row), Bishop of the Diocese of Richmond, was photographed in front of the rectory at Saint Mary's of the Immaculate Conception Roman Catholic Church on June 13, 1938. Ireton was in Norfolk to give the opening homily of the Virginia Chapter of the Catholic Student Mission Crusade, held at Sacred Heart Catholic Church, situated in the city's Ghent section. Bishop Ireton was joined at the altar by Father Edward A. Brosnan, pastor of Saint Mary's, and Father E.P. Kilgalen, pastor of Sacred Heart. The convention convened at Sacred Heart School, and Marie Downey, of Alexandria, was elected president of the Virginia chapter; Mary Piedmont, of Norfolk, scribe; Margaret Lescure, of Roanoke, minstrel; and Frank Lawrence, of Norfolk's Ocean View, past leader. (Charles S. Borjes, photographer. Courtesy of Kirn Library.)

Two

REBELLION AND RECONSTRUCTION

"A march in the ranks hard-prest, and the road unknown,
A route through a heavy wood with muffled steps in the darkness,
Our army foil'd with loss severe, and the sullen remnant retreating,
Till after midnight glimmer upon us the lights of a dim-lighted building,
We came to an open space in the woods, and halt by the dim-lighted building,
'Tis a large old church at the crossing roads . . ."

—From *A March in the Ranks Hard-Prest, and the Road Unknown*, 1865, 1867
Walt Whitman, American poet (1819–1892)

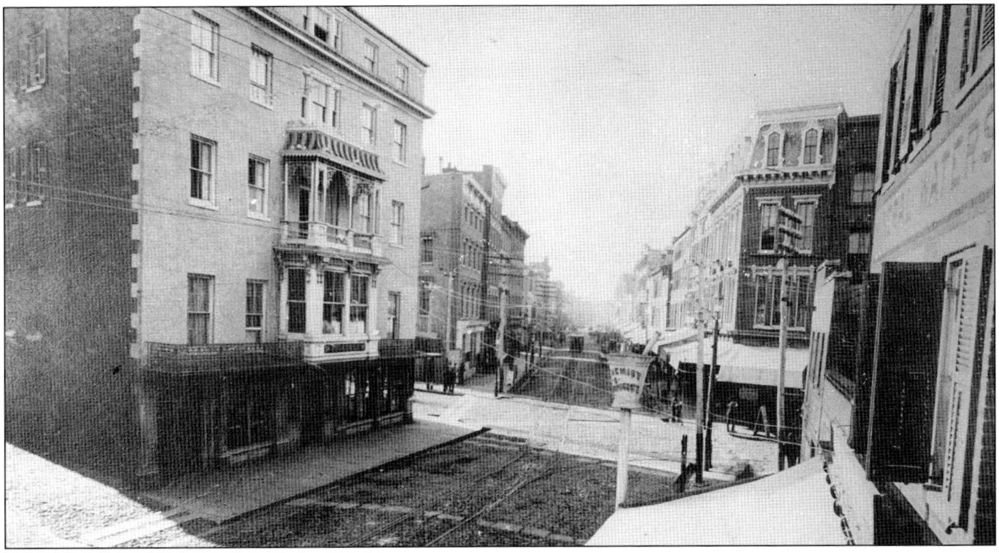

French's Hotel (on the left, looking west from Church and Main Streets) was opened in the spring of 1837 and had as its first guest Prince Charles Louis Napoleon Bonaparte of France, in exile but soon to become Emperor Louis Napoleon of France (1852–1870). Prince Louis Napoleon was the nephew of Emperor Napoleon Bonaparte I. He and his retinue arrived in Norfolk on April 19 to much fanfare. By 1846 the establishment had changed its name to the National Hotel, and on August 25, 1860, Stephen A. Douglass made a speech from the balcony of the hotel (shown here). The hotel manager, D.F. Keeling, Esq., was said to have conducted business with a flair for "gentility and good living." Sometime after the Civil War the National Hotel became the Purcell House. By 1901 the structure had become the home of Willis Furniture, Inc., wholesale and retail furniture emporium. The building was eventually razed by Norfolk Redevelopment and Housing Authority c. 1961, but its halls had once echoed with the voices of Bonaparte, Mark Twain, General Winfield Scott, President John Tyler, and President Grover Cleveland, a frequent visitor to Norfolk for duck hunting trips to Back Bay.

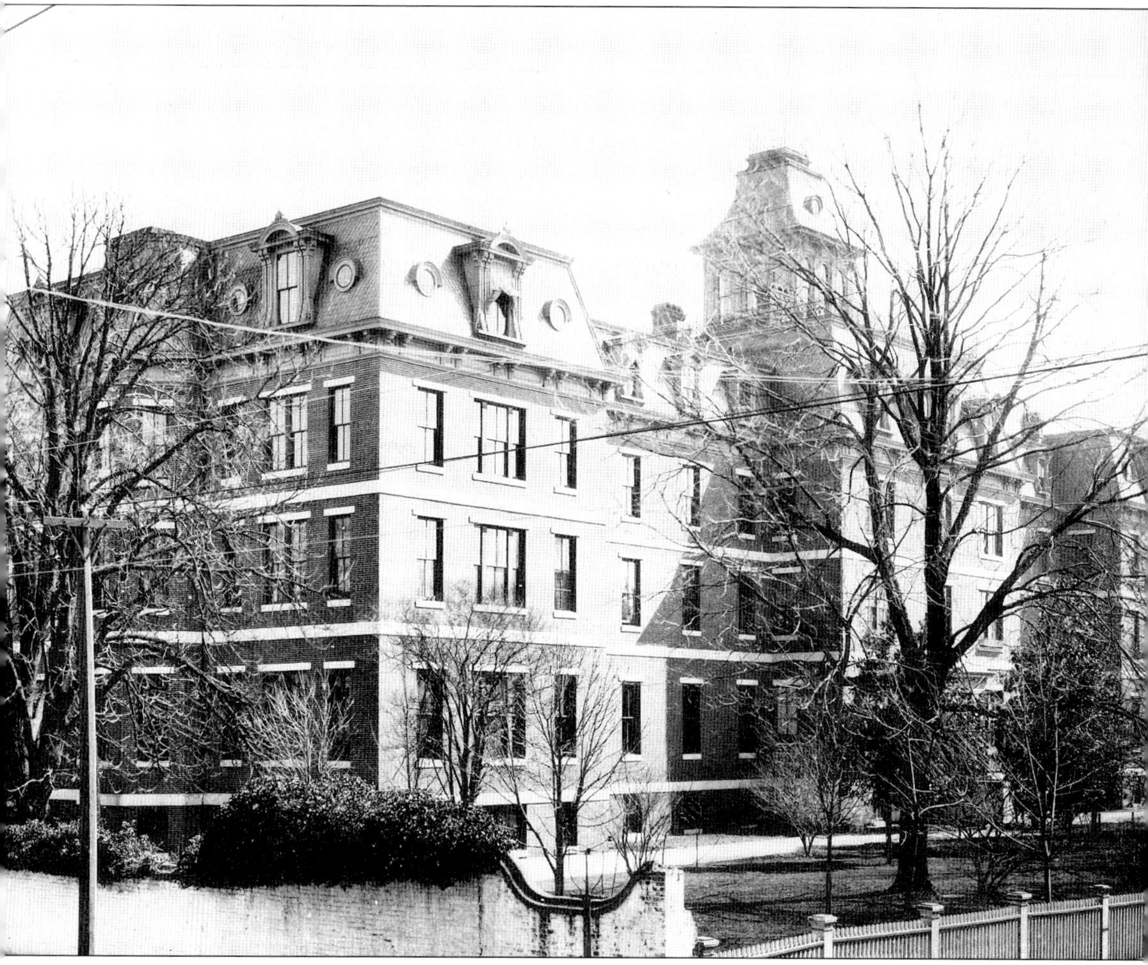

Located at the corner of Wood and Church Streets on 6 acres of land filled with an abundance of shade trees, St. Vincent DePaul Hospital was established on March 3, 1856. At the center of the building shown here, photographed in 1895, was a private residence: the 1785 mansion of William Plume, known as Plumesville. Upon Plume's death, his property was inherited by his nephew, Walter Herron, a wealthy Norfolk merchant. When Herron passed away, he willed the property to Ann P. Behan Herron, his adopted daughter. Together with her brother, Dr. James H. Behan, Ann owned the land and mansion. During the yellow fever epidemic in 1855, many residents of the city, particularly the poor and disenfranchised, were without shelter and proper care, so Ann opened the doors of her home to the sick. While helping care for them, she fell victim to the fever herself. Her dying decree was that the property be dedicated for use as a hospital. This was carried out by her brother, Dr. Behan, and the mansion was gradually converted, and additions made, to a hospital capable of caring for hundreds of patients per year.

At its peak, before being destroyed by fire on September 21, 1899, St. Vincent DePaul Hospital saw 1,473 patients in one year. Soon after the fire, workers rebuilt the hospital, doubling its capacity to house patients by providing beds for 350 patients. The Sisters (Daughters) of Charity administered the hospital.

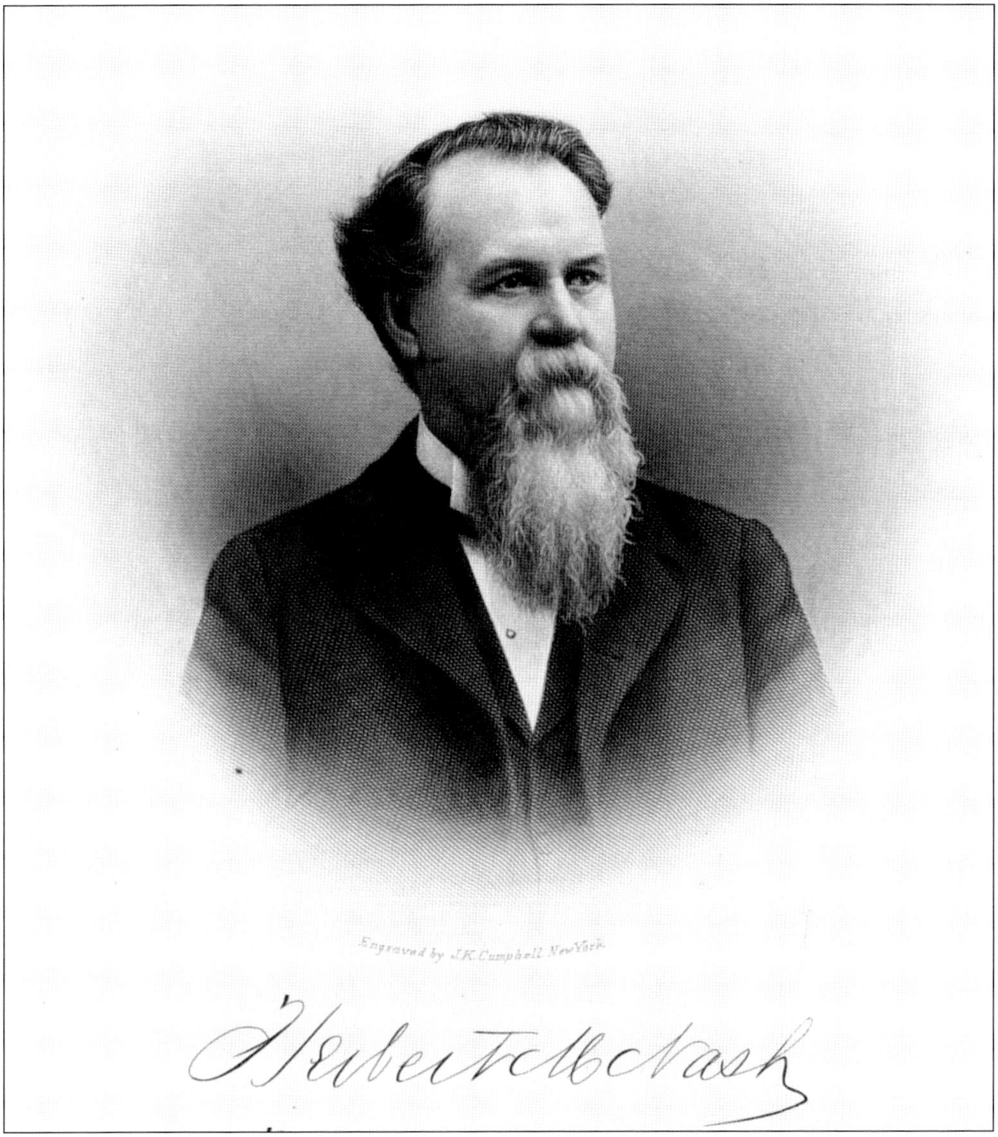

Herbert M. Nash, M.D., born in Norfolk in 1831 and whose family owned one of the first houses erected on the original plat of Norfolk in 1680, is shown here as he appeared on a turn-of-the-century engraving by J.K. Campbell of New York. The engraving is signed by Nash. At the age of 21, Nash received his medical degree from the University of Virginia, after which he came to Norfolk to begin his practice in the fall of 1853. Less than two years later, he faced the appalling loss of life from the yellow fever. The good doctor was the only survivor of the medical men who were on duty in the city after the 1855 yellow fever epidemic. He and Dr. Frank Anthony Walke were also the last surviving surgeons of the Confederate Army residing in Norfolk at that time. After the Civil War, Nash resumed his medical practice in Norfolk, where he served as president of the Board of Quarantine Commissioners for the District of Elizabeth River, an appointment by the governor of Virginia in recognition of his expertise with infectious disease. This was but one of his numerous offices and distinctions in the practice of medicine upon returning to Norfolk. Nash was a distinguished physician and surgeon with a long association as a visiting doctor to St. Vincent DePaul Hospital.

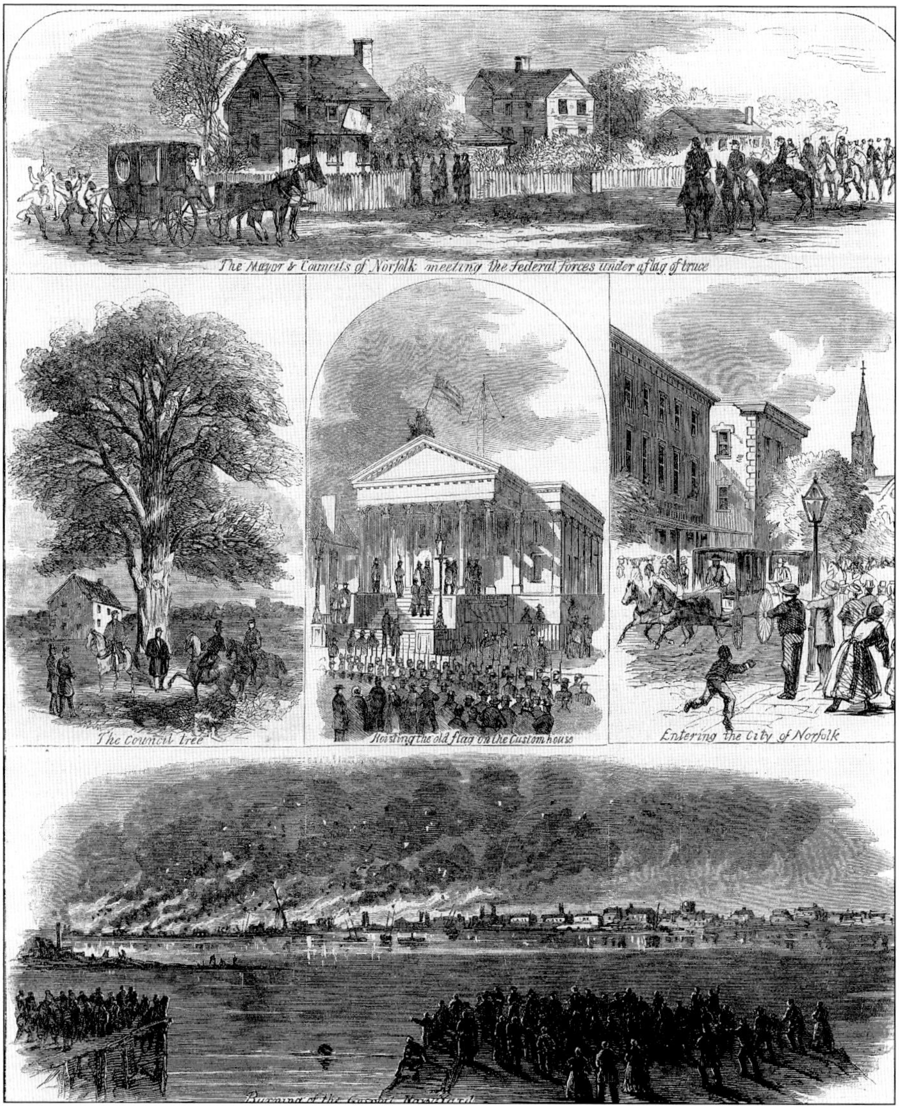

On the morning of May 10, 1862, Federal forces bent on occupying the city, took the road to Norfolk, which would have led them from the vicinity of Willoughby Spit and Ocean View toward Indian Pole Bridge, later the Granby Street Bridge over Tanner's Creek. Federal troops were led by General John E. Wool and accompanied by Abraham Lincoln's cabinet officers, Secretaries Edwin M. Stanton and Salmon P. Chase. At the bridge, Confederate troops fired on Federal troops and burned the bridge. The Federal army detoured and reached the limits of Norfolk by Princess Anne Road. Mayor William Wilson Lamb and members of the city council were waiting at the corner of Church Street and Princess Anne Road (shown here in a *Harper's Weekly* from May 24, 1862) at the home of Elias E. Guy to explain to General Wool that Confederate forces had retired. Lamb's entourage wished to surrender the city, asking that the people and their property be protected. General Wool replied courteously, and proceeded to ride in Lamb's carriage to the city's courthouse with General Egbert Ludovickus Viele, destined to be the military governor of Norfolk from May 1862 through November 1863, and Secretary Chase. Each of these events is depicted in the *Harper's*. (Courtesy of the Clerk's Office, City of Norfolk.)

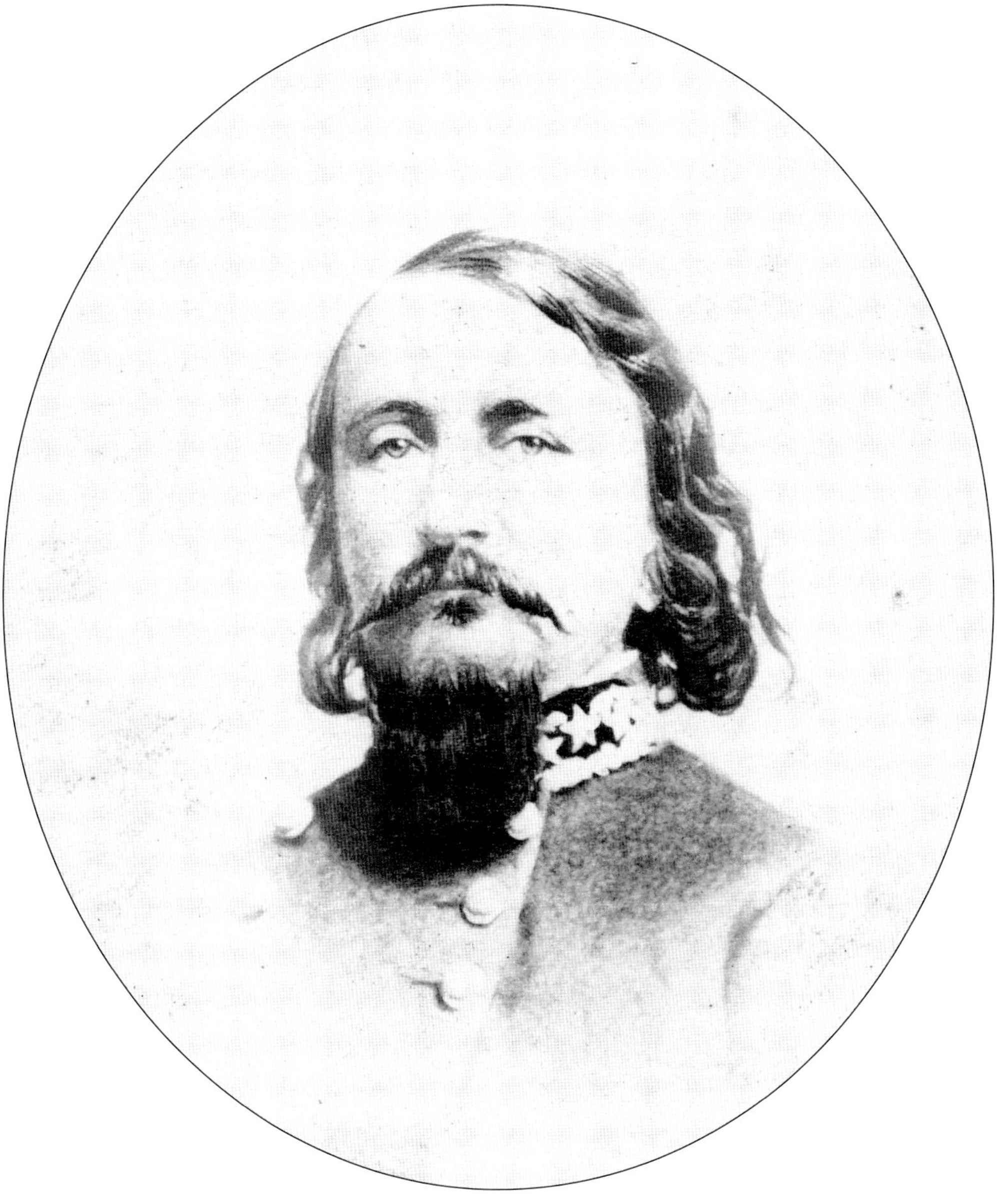

Major General George Edward Pickett, Confederate States Army, pictured here, died in St. Vincent DePaul Hospital on July 30, 1875. The general was made famous as the leader of Pickett's Charge against the center of the Union line on Cemetary Ridge, July 3, 1863, at the Battle of Gettysburg. After the war, he refused a brigadier general's commission in the Egyptian Army, choosing instead to go into the insurance business. Up until the time of his death at the age of 50, Pickett earned a sparse living as an insurance agent. Pickett was briefly interred in Norfolk's Elmwood Cemetery before being moved to Hollywood Cemetery in Richmond, Virginia, his birthplace. It is ironic that a young George Pickett was appointed to West Point by a Whig congressman from Illinois—Abraham Lincoln. This image of Pickett, a *carte-de-visite*, was published by E.& H.T. Anthony of 501 Broadway, New York, *c.* 1864. Popular souvenirs in the North and South, *carte-de-visites* are particularly collectable today if signed by the individual pictured.

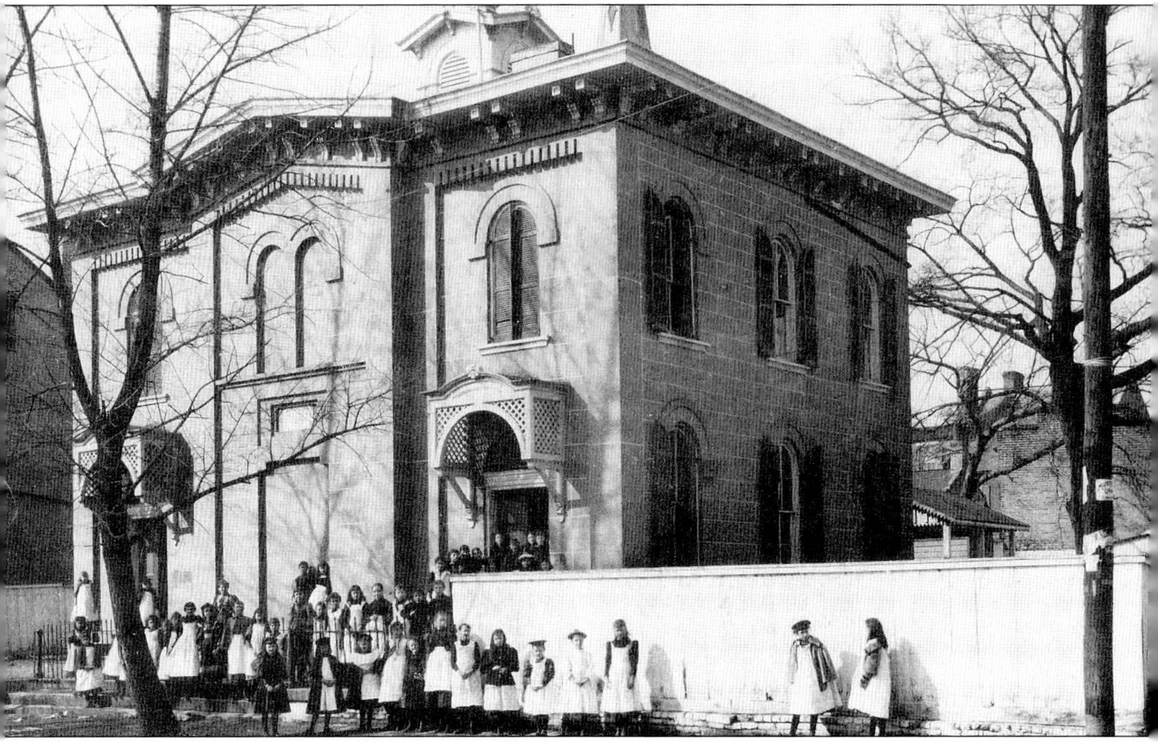

The Fenchurch Street School, also called Public School No. 3, was one of the four original free schools—one in each district of the city—built in 1858 in Norfolk. Located in the second ward district on Fenchurch near Holt Street, any white child ages six to 21, and a resident of the district, could attend the school. Norfolk was the first city in Virginia to establish a system of public schools. The system was begun in 1857 under the direction of Thomas C. Tabb, father of Norfolk Public Schools and its first superintendent. Tabb remained in his post until 1865. When it opened in 1858, the Fenchurch Street School registered 92 students. Hard times came with the Civil War. Children were not in school on March 9, 1862, a Sunday, and it is believed many of them witnessed the famous engagement between the USS *Monitor* and CSS *Virginia* off Sewell's Point. With the closure of schools to whites during Federal occupation of the city by Brigadier General Benjamin F. Butler from 1863 until the end of the war, formerly all white schools were turned over to African Americans for instruction. Butler noted that if Norfolkians wanted their schools back, they would have to be free schools, in this case meaning integrated schools. In 1867, Superintendent William Wilson Lamb (1867–1874) advocated public schools for black children. The *Norfolk Journal* on March 29, 1867, noted: "This is a wise measure, and we hope it will be successful. By educating the Negro, we not only improve his condition, but we make him a better member of society. Ignorant persons are often led into misdemeanors educated men avoid." The first African-American superintendent was H.C. Percy. By the time this picture was taken in 1895, this school taught only little girls and had three teachers supported by Alice B. Wharton as rector. Three years later, 1898, the Fenchurch Street School was sold for $90. The buyer agreed to remove the old school building within 30 days of purchase. While their new building was being constructed, Fenchurch Street students attended classes in the Sunday school rooms of First Baptist Church on Holt Street.

Norfolk's first opera house, later the site of L. Snyder's Department Store, at 151-153 Church Street, was the scene of many merry pre- and post-Civil War affairs. Opened in 1856 by Henry C. Jarrett, the Church Street Opera House reached its zenith in January 1877 with the visit of Russian Grand Dukes Alexander Aleksandrovich and Konstantin (the younger) and their party, who visited Norfolk at that time. The building was constructed in medieval English style, rejoicing in a grand display of great windows and pinnacles. After the erection of the Academy of Music on Main Street in 1880, use of the old opera house declined. In 1904, the Odd Fellows rebuilt the structure for lodge quarters with three stores on the ground floor, one of which had been occupied by L. Snyder since 1894. L. Snyder took over the entire building in 1929, later remodeling the edifice. Snyder's remained in business at 151-153 Church Street until 1969.

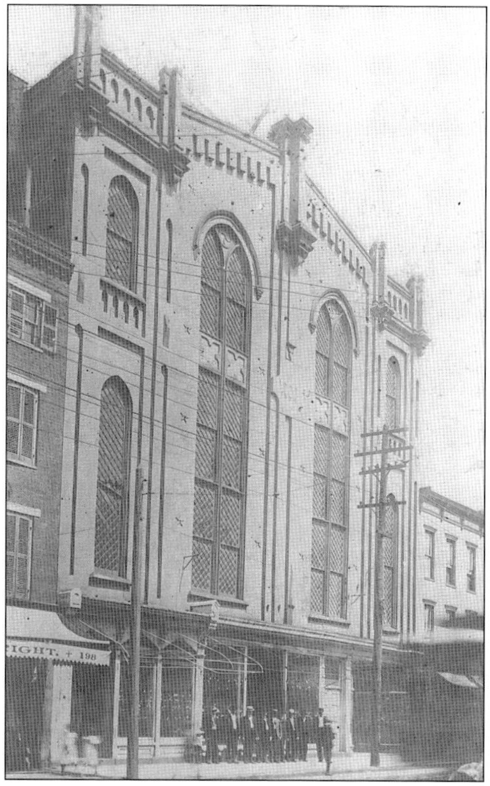

Command Performances

Prior to the American Revolution, theatrical performances were held in a wooden building formerly used as a pottery on the south side of Main Street, near the Elizabeth River. A regular theater building was in operation in 1793 in a large wooden warehouse on Calvert's Lane. A brick playhouse was constructed in 1795 on the east side of Fenchurch Street, one block off Church Street. It was in the Fenchurch Street theater that Junius Brutus Booth performed after he arrived in Norfolk from Madeira, June 30, 1821. This theater was Norfolk's only theater until 1823, when the Fenchurch Street theater was sold to the Methodist Protestant congregation. It was not until October 16, 1839, that Norfolk had another theater, the Avon Theatre on Avon Street, to entertain the population. From the time the Avon Theatre burned in February 1850 until the completion of the Church Street Opera House or Norfolk Varieties, the people of Norfolk held performances in the old Mechanics Hall on Main Street. The cornerstone of the Church Street Opera House was laid on July 4, 1854, and opened to the public in 1856. The opera house stood on the west side of the second block of Church Street on the site in more recent memory occupied by L. Snyder Department Store. The Church Street Opera House was built with façades reflecting medieval English style, which was most evident in its great windows and pinnacles. The ground floor was occupied by storefronts and the upper floor used by the Odd Fellows as a meeting hall. The seating capacity of the opera house was 937, with stage boxes that could accommodate yet another 22 people. The Church Street Opera House stage was graced by the finest performers of their day. Most notable among the theater's many fine performances was the gala performance of Shakespeare's *Romeo and Juliet*, performed for the benefit of Russian Grand Duke Alexander Aleksandrovich, son of Emperor Alexander II of Russia, and Grand Duke Konstantin (the younger) and their entourage during the Russian's famous visit to Norfolk in 1877. The photograph here was also taken in 1877.

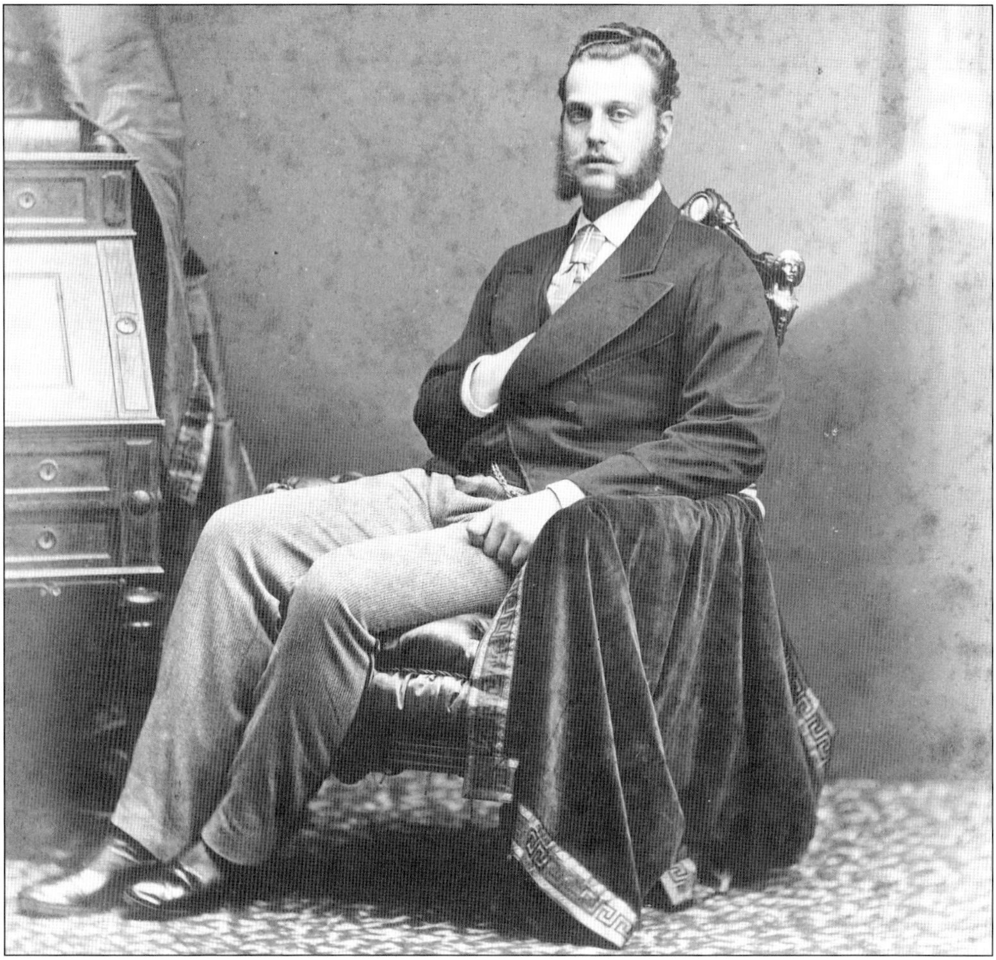

This imperial *carte-de-visite* by Mathew B. Brady's National Portrait Galleries was taken of Grand Duke Alexander Aleksandrovich of Russia, second son of Russian Tsar Alexander II, in 1871, ten years before he was to become Tsar Alexander III, Emperor of Russia. Grand Duke Alexander Aleksandrovich and Grand Duke Konstantin (the younger) came to Norfolk six years later aboard the Imperial Russian Navy battleship, *Swetlana*, arriving on Saturday, January 13, 1877, and preparations were immediately set afoot to entertain the royal visitors at the Church Street Opera House. Max Strakosch, the renowned opera manager of New York, brought Lillian Adelaide Neilson, a vivacious and talented actress, to Norfolk to treat the Russian cortége and their city hosts to Neilson's portrayal of Juliet in Shakespeare's *Romeo and Juliet*. The first performance was held January 22, before a packed house. The grand dukes were seated in handsomely decorated private boxes to the right of the stage. Private boxes to stage left were occupied by Imperial Russian Navy officers and Russian Prince Stcherbaton. The boxes were decorated with large American and Russian flags. The future Russian tsar, born in 1845, married Princess Dagmar, daughter of King Christian IX and Queen Louisa of Denmark, his deceased elder brother Nikolai's fiancée, in October 1866. Princess Dagmar took the name Maria Feodorovna when she converted to Orthodoxy. Upon becoming Emperor Alexander III after his father's assassination on March 13, 1881, he and Empress Maria Feodorovna gained a reputation as a devoted couple. He and the Empress Maria's first son, Nikolai Aleksandrovich, took the throne of Russia upon his father's death on March 1, 1894, thus becoming Tsar Nicholas II, the last Romanov ruler of his country.

The Norfolk Varieties, then managed by C.T. Tooker, advertised its distinction as "The Only Permanent Place of Amusement in the City" at 75 & 78 Church Street (the street numbering at that time) in 1870.

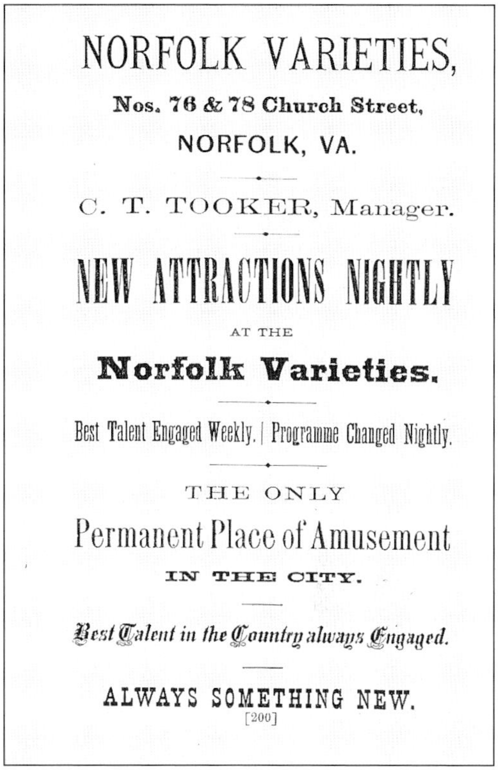

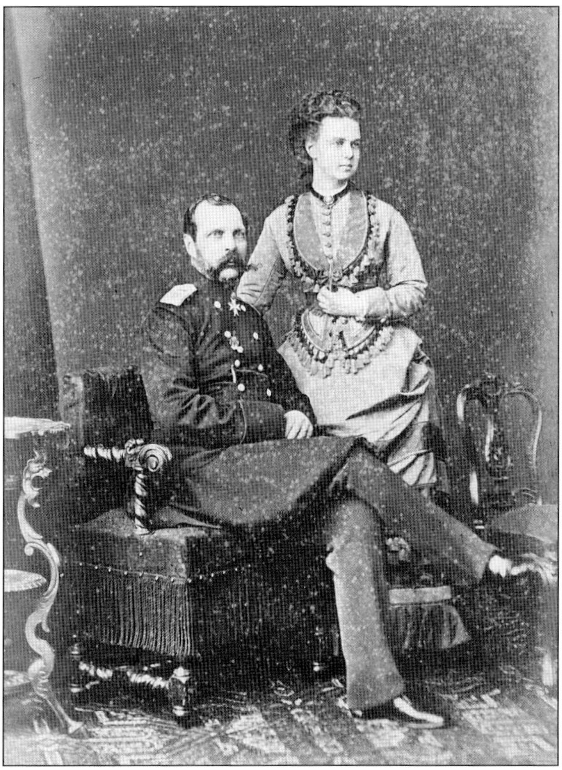

In the photograph shown here, another *carte-de-visite*, Grand Duke Alexander Aleksandrovich's father, Alexander II, poses with his eldest daughter, Grand Duchess Maria Aleksandrovna, also about 1871. Maria married Alfred, Duke of Edinburgh, and became the Duchess of Edinburgh. The portrait was taken by William Notman of Montreal, Toronto & Halifax, Canada, who advertised himself as photographer to Her Majesty Queen Victoria.

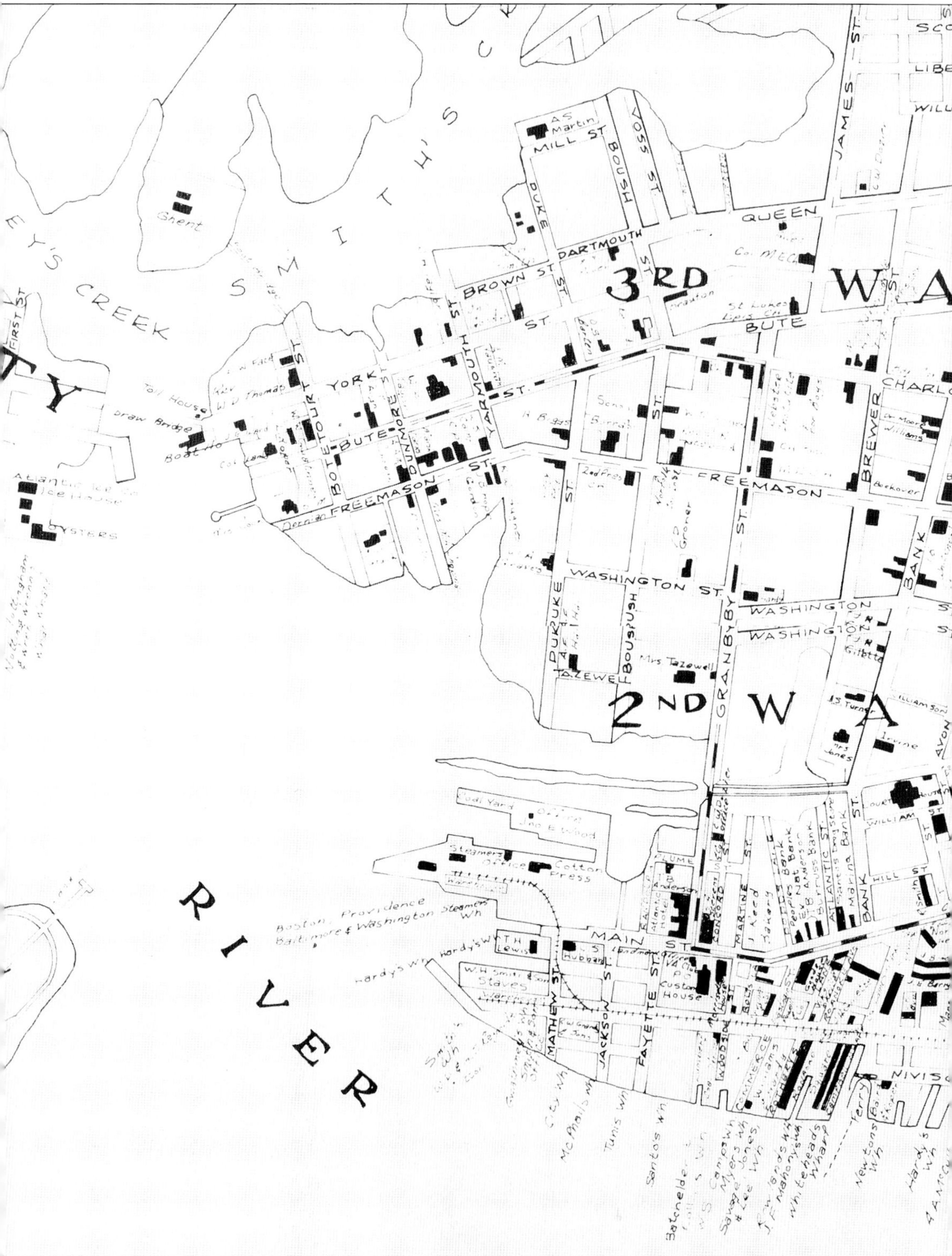

This map, drawn from special surveys, was produced by Grays in 1877.

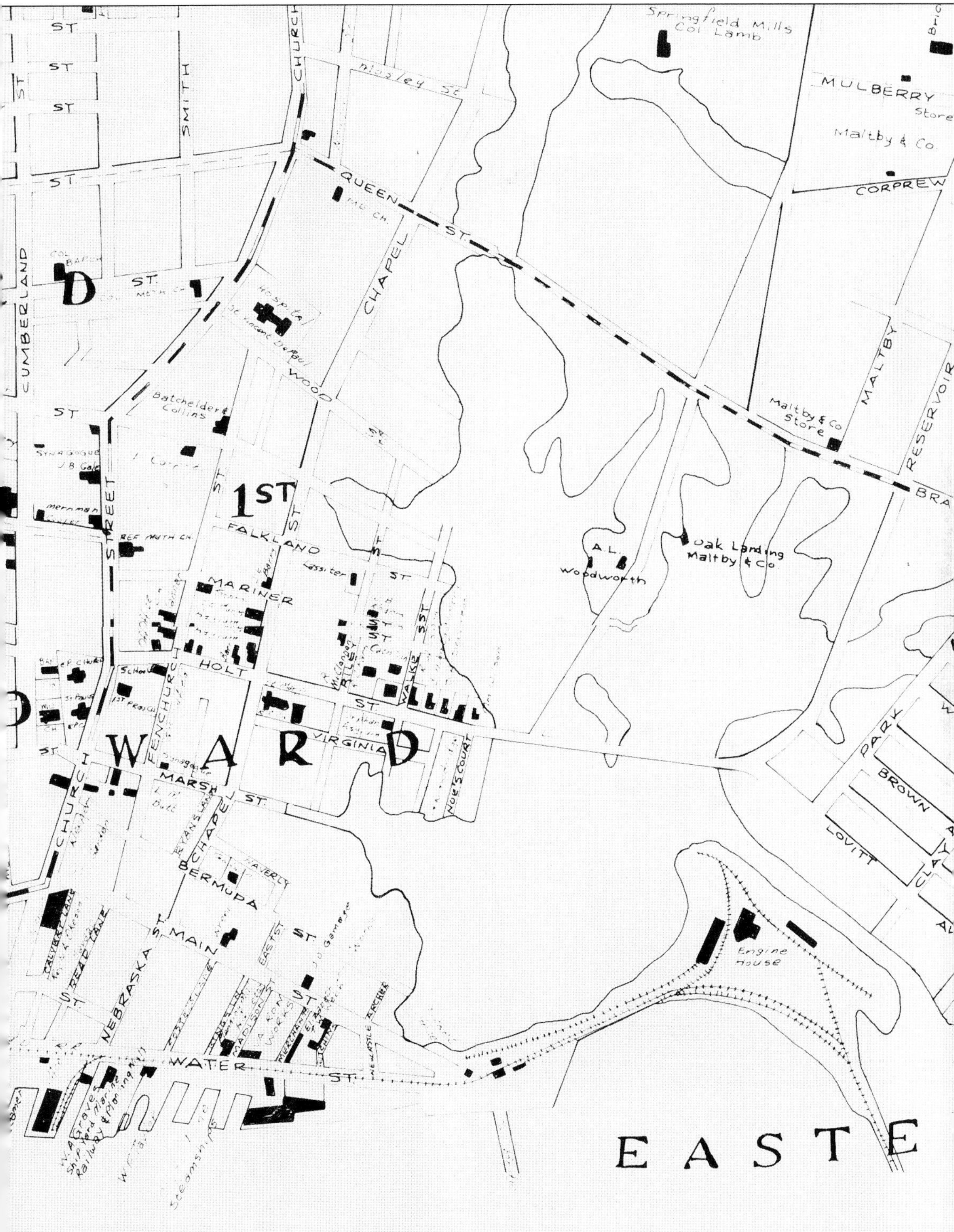
Springfield Mills
Col Lamb
MULBERRY
Store
Maltby & Co.
CORPREW
QUEEN ST
CHURCH
SMITH
CUMBERLAND
CHAPEL
Hospital
WOOD
Batchelder & Collins
SYNAGOGUE
MALTBY
RESERVOIR
Maltby & Co Store
D
1ST
FALKLAND
MARINER
HOLT
VIRGINIA
STREET
REF METH CH
Oak Landing
Maltby & Co
A.L. Woodworth
SCHOOL
FENCHURCH
W A R D
MARSH ST
NOE'S COURT
PARK
BROWN
LOVITT
BERMUDA
WAVERLY
MAIN
NEBRASKA
EAST ST
Engine House
WATER ST
MADISON
MERCHANT
NEWCASTLE
ARCHER
W.A. Graves Ship Yard Marine Railway & Planing Mill
Steamships
E A S T E

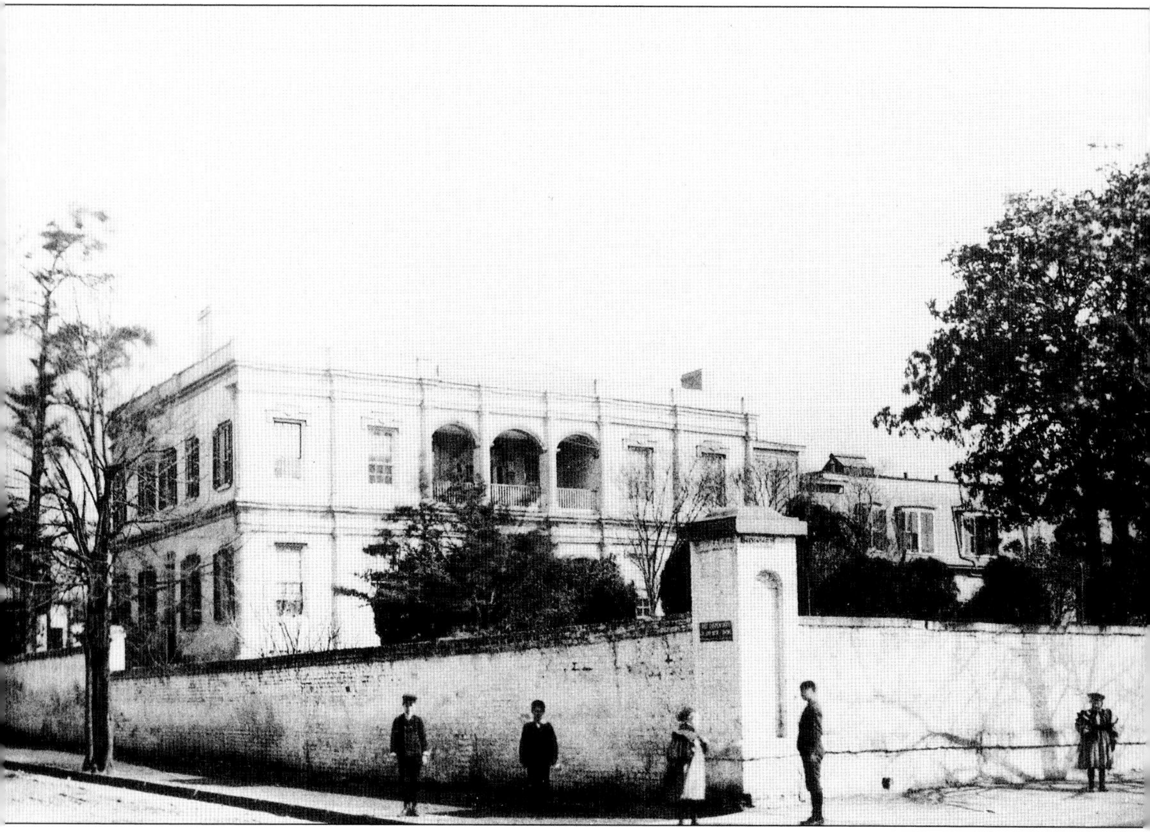

The Retreat for the Sick at the corner of Holt and Reilly Streets was opened in 1888 in a building noted for its early Spanish-style architecture. The hospital consisted of 25 beds. The hospital's creation was the brainchild of ladies associated with the Women's Christian Association in conjunction with many of the city's leading citizens and physicians, most of whom contributed to the purchase price of the land and existing house: $8,574.99. Captain John L. Roper was named first president of the hospital, and Bessie Williams Reid, its first superintendent. At the time of its establishment, there were fewer than 200 hospitals in the entire United States. Norfolk had The Retreat for the Sick as well as St. Vincent DePaul Hospital serving the people of the city at that time. As Norfolk continued to expand, the need to enlarge the hospital became readily apparent. Captain Roper and his board of directors opted to move the hospital to the Colley residence, an imposing old home in Ghent overlooking The Hague. The Holt Street property was sold, and, in 1896, The Retreat for the Sick moved to the Colley property, expanding to a 100-bed facility. This earliest precursor of Sentara Norfolk General Hospital would experience many growing pains over the next 100 years. The image shown here was taken in 1893.

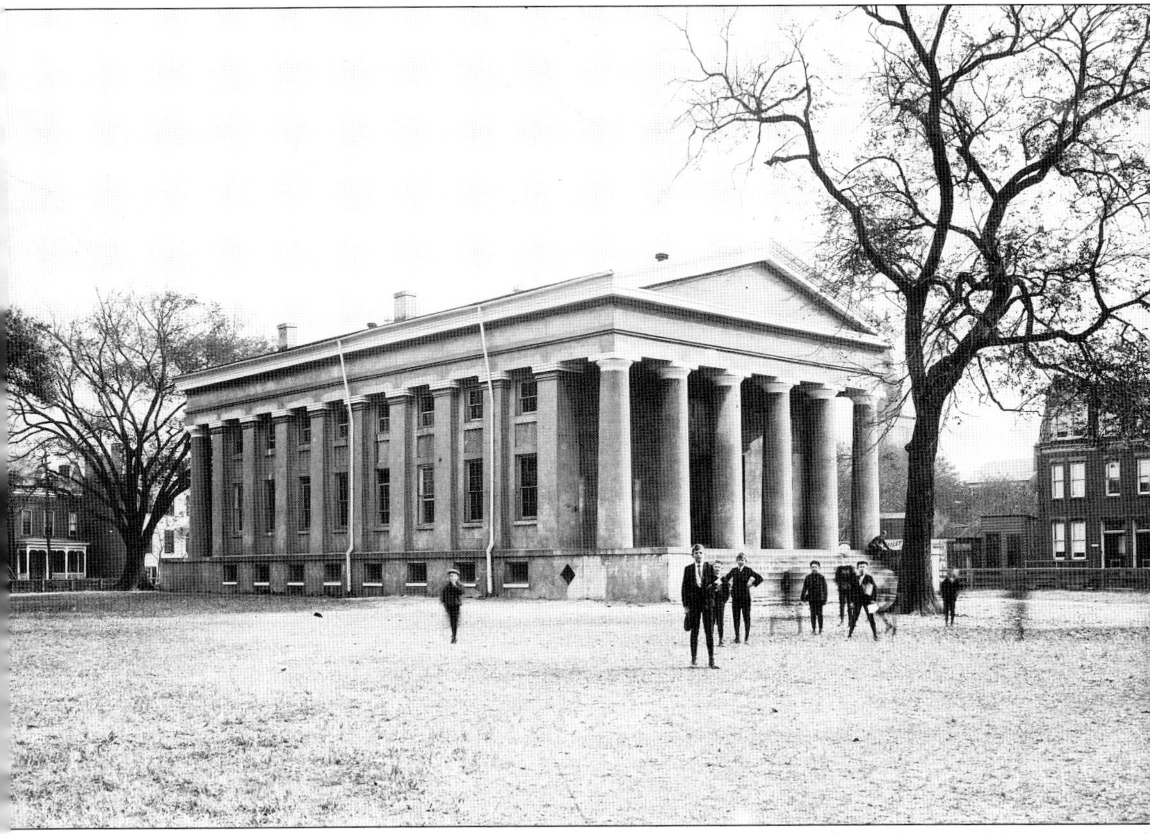

The cornerstone of the Norfolk Academy building at 420 Bank Street, shown here *c.* 1892, was laid on May 25, 1840.

Norfolk Academy

The first building occupied by the town school, Norfolk Academy's earliest precursor, was a two-story frame school across Church Street. In October 1786 the Reverend Walker Maury, the new minister of Saint Paul's, became the school's master. After Maury's death in October 1788, Reverend Alexander Whitehead took his place, but on November 23, 1792, Alexander resigned and appointed the Reverend James Whitehead. The school was then located at 103 Church Street, and free education in Norfolk seemed to be going well until January 19, 1804, when Norfolk Academy was incorporated by an Act of the General Assembly. At this time, a board of trustees was appointed and Norfolk Academy ceased to be a "free" or public school as it had been since 1728. The Act of Assembly gave the board of trustees the right to appoint teachers and staff, and within the year of 1804, Reverend James Whitehead ceased to be master of the academy. Two years later, Norfolk Academy's trustees bought from the Overseers of the Poor the former parish glebe, bounded by Catherine (Bank), Charlotte, and Cumberland Streets, and former Grigsby Place, though no building was erected on the site for another 36 years.

After 1830, Norfolk Academy declined in popularity, and by 1836, the old site and building on Church Street were ordered to be sold so a new building could be built. The construction of a larger and much more impressive building appeared to peak public interest in Norfolk Academy. The cornerstone of the 1840 building contained a silver plate with the names of its trustees and the building's architect, Thomas Ustick Walter, of Philadelphia, engraved on it.

Walter was already famous in the architectural world as the designer of the wings and dome of the National Capitol in Washington, D.C., and as the chief advisor during the construction of Norfolk's City Hall in 1850. Norfolk Academy was modeled after the Temple of Theseus in Athens, Greece. John P. Scott (1840–1843) was the first headmaster of the new school (shown here), known at that time as the Norfolk Military Academy.

Between 1845 and 1861, the school's history was not closely documented. Educational institutions operating within the city lacked organization. Ordered public education did not come to the city of Norfolk until the middle of the 19th century when an Act of the General Assembly authorized free schools in 1845. A definitive decree was issued in 1855, and within one year Norfolk was divided into four districts, and schools were built in each one of them on Boush Street, Charlotte Street, Holt Street, and Queen Street (Brambleton), respectively.

Just as public education was gaining a foothold and Norfolk Academy began to flourish, the War Between the States broke out. Norfolk Academy was turned into a hospital in 1862 by occupying Federal troops. The school building was returned to the board of trustees in September 1865 and reopened in October with the Reverend Robert Gatewood as headmaster. It is interesting to note that in 1877 the city of Norfolk tried to take over Norfolk Academy as its high school on the premise the school was originally intended as a public educational institution, but this initiative failed. In 1894, the city bought another private school, the Hemenway School, in Brambleton, as its first high school. During the First World War, Norfolk Academy closed and the building was used as a Red Cross headquarters. Opening once again after the war, Norfolk Academy's trustees opted to buy a site west of Granby Street near Ward's Corner in 1924. The old building was sold to the city and converted to the Norfolk Juvenile and Domestic Relations Court. Norfolk Academy moved to the site near Ward's Corner, closing only once more, during WW II. After a merger with the exclusive Country Day School for Girls of Virginia Beach in 1966, Norfolk Academy moved to its present location off Wesleyan Drive, becoming officially coeducational at that time.

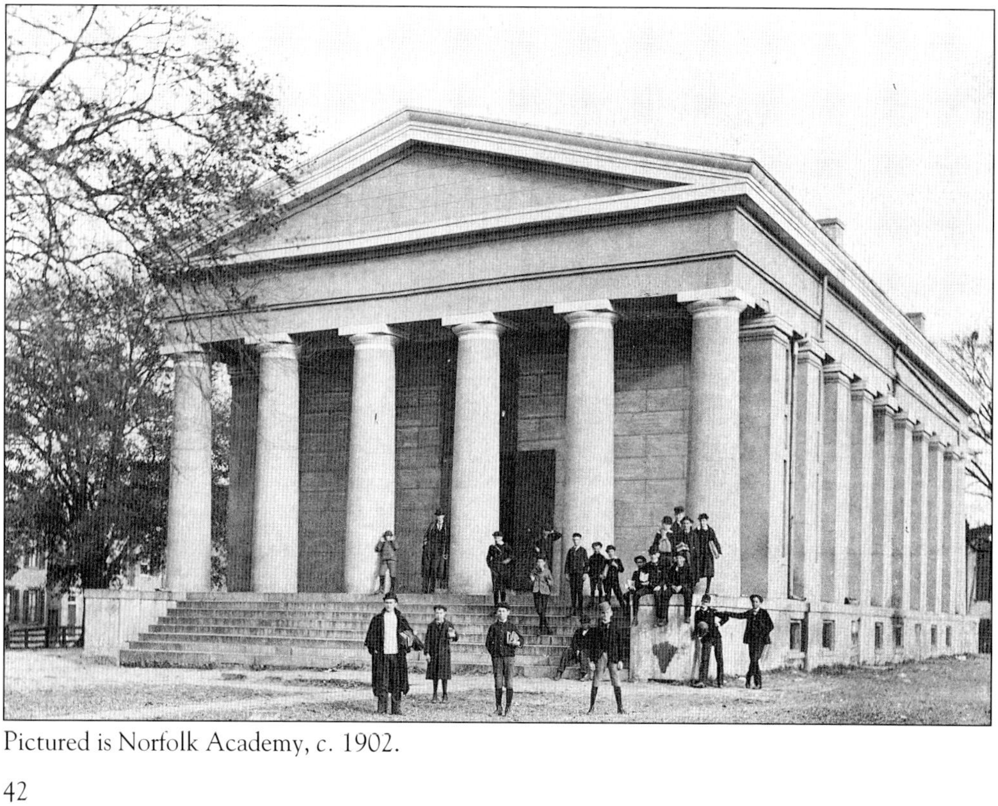

Pictured is Norfolk Academy, c. 1902.

Three

East European Jewish Immigration

"How strange it seems! These Hebrews in their graves,
Close by the street of this fair seaport town,
Silent beside the never-silent waves,
At rest in all this moving up and down! . . .

Pride and humiliation hand in hand
Walked with them from town to town, from street to street;
At every gate the accursed Mordecai
Was mocked and jeered, and spurned by Christian feet.

For the background figure, vague and vast
Of patriarchs and of prophets rose sublime,
And all the great traditions of the Past
They saw reflected in the coming time.

—From *The Jewish Cemetery at Newport,* 1854
Henry Wadsworth Longfellow, American poet (1807–1882)

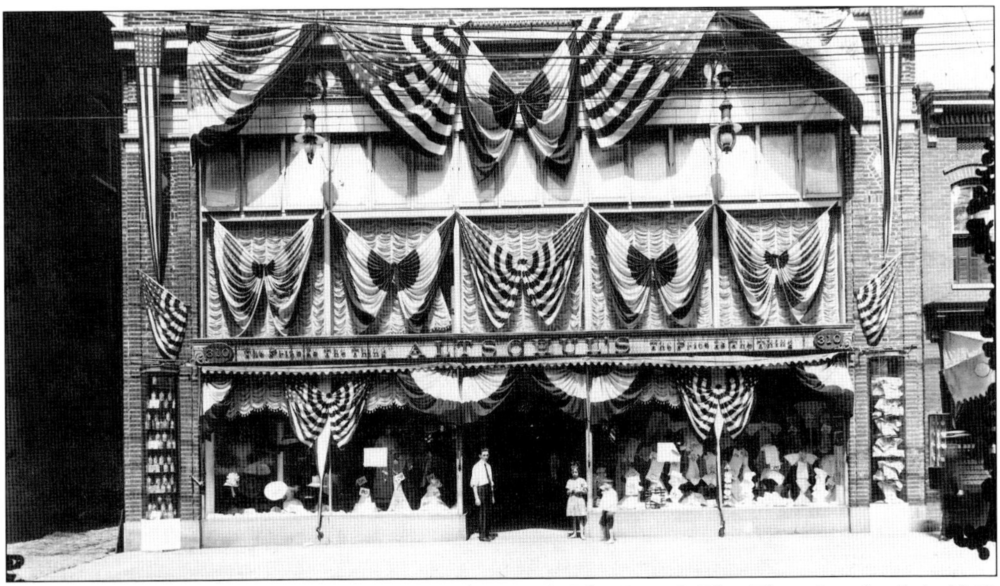

The Altschul's store at 310 Church Street advertised "The Price Is The Thing" in this July 1912 sales week photograph taken by Harry C. Mann. All the stores along Church Street participated in sales week decoration of their shops and restaurants. (Courtesy of the Library of Virginia.)

A Culture In Conflict

Novelist Leon Uris tells the story of a fictitious Jewish gentleman from Prodno, Russia, Abraham Cadyzynski, in his book *QB VII* (Doubleday, 1970). Cadyzynski left his homeland for Palestine but ended up owning a small bakery on Church Street in the ghetto in Norfolk, Virginia. The city's famous "black belt," as it was called by whites, was home to Cady, who had Americanized his name, and his two daughters. Since the daughters' husbands were not interested in the bakery business, Cady left the bakery to his brother Morris. "The Jewish community was tiny and close knit, hanging together unable to shake off all the ghetto mentality. Morris met Molly Segal, also an immigrant in the Zionist movement, and they were married in the year of 1909." Uris is careful to note that out of deference to her father, the couple was married in a synagogue, though neither was particularly religious, but, nonetheless, unable to break away from most of the customs of their faith and country. The fictitious couple had three children, Ben, Abe, and Sophie, though they could have been as real as any of the Jewish children who lived in and around Church Street at the turn of the century. Morris's bakery became enormously popular, particularly during the First World War as the bakery's output "tripled and quadrupled" but lost much of its Jewish identity because of mandatory conformance with government specifications for their product. After the war, Morris was able to return to the traditions of a nearly all-Kosher kitchen. The bakery was so popular, Morris shipped to grocery stores, even those in gentile neighborhoods. When Morris and Molly found a place to live on their own in Norfolk, they moved into a small row house with a white porch on Holt Street, where their children were born. "The Jewish section started in the one hundred block of Church Street at St. Mary's Church and ran for seven blocks to where the Booker T. Pharmacy started the Negro ghetto. The streets were lined with little shops out of the old country and the children were to remember the smells and sounds of it all their lives. Heated discussion in Yiddish where the two newspapers, the *Freiheit* and the New York *Vorwärts* vied for opinion. There was the marvelous odor of leather from Cousin Herschel's shoe repair shop and the pungent aroma of the cellar of the 'pickle' man, where you could have a choice of sixty different kinds of pickles and pickled onions from briny old vats. They cost a penny each, two cents for an extra."

Uris would go on to explain that despite Morris and Molly Cady's simplicity, "their affluence caught up with them and after a year of discussion they bought a big shingled ten room house on an acre of land at Gosnold and New Hampshire Streets with a view to the estuary. A few Jewish families, upper-middle class merchants and doctors, had penetrated Colonial Place but further down the line around Colley Avenue and Thirty-first." The fictitious baker and his family had moved into an all-gentile community, and it was not as easy a move as it may have sounded. "Not that the Cadys were black, but they weren't exactly white in the eyes of their neighbors." Their boys were "'Jew boys. The Hebes, Yids, Sheenies, Kikes. Much of this was changed at the big circle at Pennsylvania and Delaware," Uris writes, "where they played ball near the pumping station." Both of Morris's boys, characters Ben and Abe, established "an understanding to live by with the neighborhood kids" with their fists, but fist fights gradually gave way to friendships and an honored place in the community. As Uris concludes, "After a time the neighbors pointed with certain curious pride to the Jewish family. They were good Jews. They knew their place. But the strangeness of entering a gentile home never exactly wore off." The affluence of Jews in Norfolk, especially those who invested in Church Street and saved their money, provided Norfolk with great economic stability during the Depression years. Few of them had invested in the stock market and while a small percentage of their Jewish friends and gentile contemporaries faced financial difficulties, they were able to purchase properties and businesses and build a very stable and affluent future.

Later, as Uris describes the death of Ben, the family's rebellious son, brother Abe reminisces, "I guess what I remember most about my brother Ben were those quiet days we just horsed around. Maybe we'd go to the marsh behind J.E.B. Stuart School and catch a couple of frogs." He continued, "Best of all were the times around the creek. We'd get up early in the morning and take our bicycles down to the docks and buy us a watermelon for a nickel. They sold them to the kids cheap because they had split in shipment. Then we'd bike to the creek. I had my dog in the front basket and Ben carried the watermelon in his. We'd sit on the bank and put the watermelon in to cool it and while it was cooling we'd walk to a small pier and fish for soft shell crabs." Ben would die defending innocent Spaniards against the evils of Francisco Franco and his Nazi friends.

Persecution experienced by these East European, particularly Russian, Jews made them incredibly sympathetic to the plight of African Americans in the American South. But as Uris describes in painful detail, the allegiance only went so far. The dialogue between Morris and son Ben, set in the late 1930s, becomes wrought with tension as they argue about Ben's communist tendencies and his son's fraternizing with people the elder Cady refers to as schwartzes, a derogatory term for blacks. Morris tells Ben, "All right, son, it's fashionable for young people to go into the colored section and dance with schwartzes. First you dance with them, then you bring them home to your mother." Not willing to let his son get in a word in what can only be described as contentious discussion, Morris continues, "Ben, I don't have a prejudiced bone in my body. I'm a Jew from the old country. Don't you know I know how these black people suffer. Who, after all, are the most liberal thinkers and the most decent to the colored people? The Jews are. And if something goes wrong, if the blacks explode . . . who do you think they'll turn on . . . us." Nothing quite as grim as Morris describes ever occurred, but the friction was certainly present as the widely understood parameters of race and social class were the divining rod of Church Street.

Uris's depiction of life on Church Street is borne on the shoulders of characters who are as alive and compelling as any of the real people who once brought life and prosperity to Norfolk's oldest thoroughfare. Uris said recently that "One of the things that sets us apart from all other species is the desire to perpetuate ourselves and leave behind a record," but he continued, "A writer has to unlock a series of doors." The doors Uris opened with his descriptions of Norfolk's Church Street in *QB VII* are not wholly pleasant, but they provide a realistic impression of how happy, and some might say content, life could have been for the multitude of Jews and African Americans who once cohabitated Church Street.

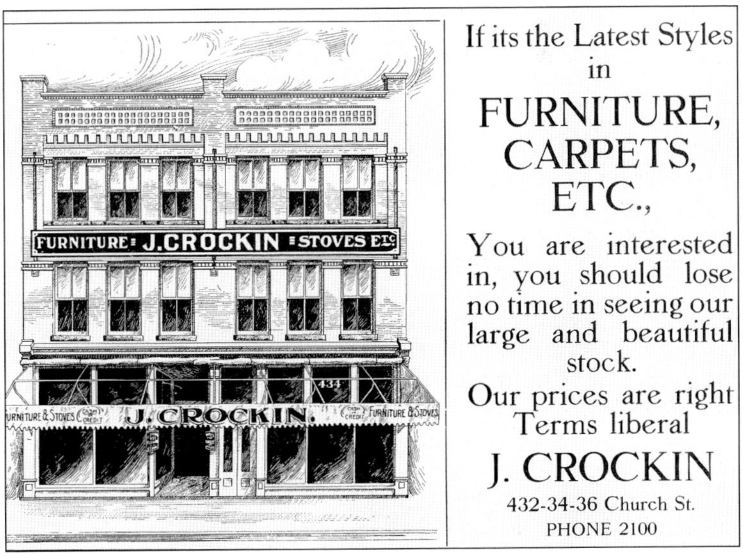

When this advertisement for J. Crockin was published in 1910, his furniture and stove establishment had only been in operation for eight years. Located at 432-434-436 Church Street, seven doors above Charlotte Street, J. Crockin had succeeded in developing a fine trade and a large, growing patronage of those interested in purchasing fine quality furniture and stoves. He occupied a three-story brick building which was 50 by 150 feet in dimension. Crockin accepted cash and credit sales, and was well known for the progressive and liberal nature of his dealings.

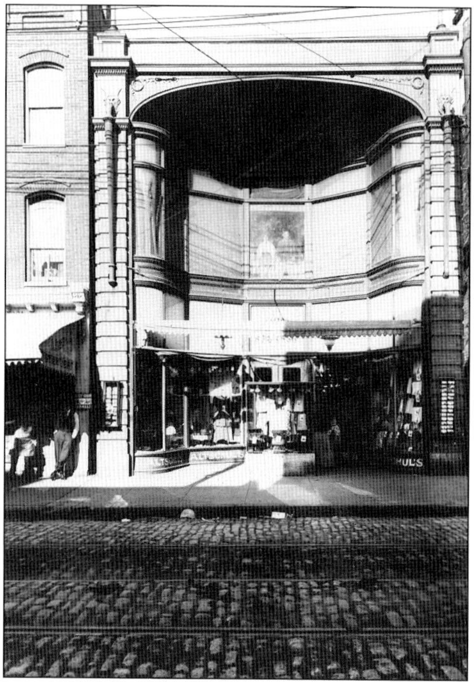

Altschul's operated from two department store locations during the clothier's history on Church Street, including this one at 534-536 Church Street. Harry C. Mann took this picture about 1908 as the fall season was getting underway. Benjamin Altschul opened in the location shown here in 1897 and continued there until June 1910, when the store moved to 310 Church Street. Altschul's stocked men's and women's clothing and household furnishings but, unlike some of his fellow merchants on Church Street, did not cater to credit sales. Benjamin Altschul did business in cash only in a low-rent district with low overhead. After Benjamin died, his wife became president of the company, ably assisted by the couple's two sons, Sylvan, who served as secretary and treasurer, and Herbert B., vice president. Altschul's left Church Street as it declined and customers favored Granby Street. Altschul's The Spot remains a clothing store fixture on Granby. (Courtesy of the Library of Virginia.)

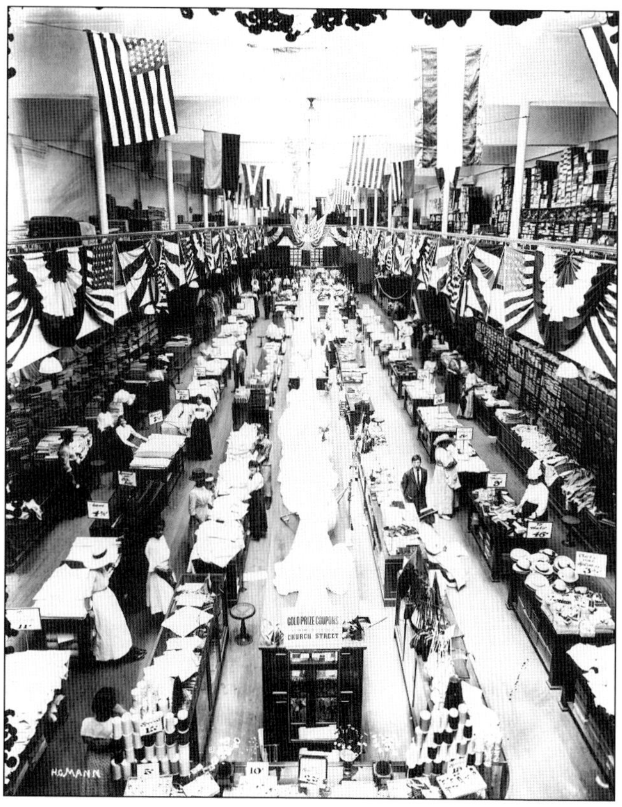

The interior of the Altschul's store at 310 Church Street, photographed during the city's annual sales week in the summer of 1912, demonstrated the ease with which Jewish merchants opened their establishments to white and African-American patrons. In this Harry C. Mann photograph, black and white patrons alike shop for men's and women's apparel and accessories. The sign on the center counter boasts, "You Can Always Buy It for Less on Church Street." (Courtesy of the Library of Virginia.)

March of Time: Jewish Women in Community Service

Formation of the Norfolk chapter of the National Council of Jewish Women was a significant step forward in the organization of benevolent institutions long associated with their beginnings on Church Street. Elise L. Margolius, chairman of the National Council's Norfolk section, remarked in 1945 to a gathering of Jewish women: "Give me a child before the age of seven—you know the rest—I lived in the house with my grandmother. It was in early 1905 that I, a little girl of three, peered through the banisters of our Holt Street home and wondered why I wasn't dining with that auspicious assembly gathered around the table discussing plans for the organization of the Norfolk Section, National Council of Jewish Women." On February 12, 1905, organization of the Norfolk section was complete, and meetings began to be held regularly at Ohef Sholom Temple to discuss furtherance of the best and highest interests in the fields of religion, social service, civics, education, and peace. The organization's first chairman, Ida Adelsdorf, requested that Rabbi Simon Cohen open his Bible study class to council members. In an effort to alleviate the shortage of adequate child care in Church Street neighborhoods, the Norfolk section provided two rooms at 82 Fenchurch Street in 1907 to house children of working parents. Known as Settlement House, the attendance of 444 children in one month led to a paid worker and a kindergarten. Children held a special place for the work of these dedicated Jewish women. One example was a child found in the woods, pinned with a note that read: "If found, please entrust to Jewish care." The baby was temporarily placed in a home and later named Ruth Virginia Cohen. Settlement House grew to six rooms plus a caretaker within a year of opening, expanding its mission to include a sabbath school for children of unaffiliated parents. The Settlement House moved in 1910 to Cumberland Street at which time Miriam Umstadter was engaged as a social worker to see to the needs of disenfranchised children.

There was no hiding the fact that Jewish immigrants faced hard times in early 20th-century Norfolk. Two immigrant Jewish men received deportation orders from the Bureau of Labor and Commerce in 1910 for rather minor reasons. One gentleman was without any money, the other ill, but in those days, these were justified reasons for deportation. Though the prospects for both men seemed poor, a reversal of fortune must have occurred because they were allowed to stay in the United States, marking a rare—and first—occasion that the bureau opted to change its mind. The bureau commissioner in Norfolk was Percy Stephenson. Immigrants were still arriving in Norfolk in fair numbers, compelling the Settlement House to teach English to foreign girls. This became the nucleus of the Maury Night School.

Reaching beyond the needs of their brethren in Norfolk, the ladies of the Norfolk Section proffered relief aid to victims and victims' families of the HMS *Titanic* disaster in 1912 as well as those of the famous Mississippi flood that year. It was in 1912 that strong feelings were voiced for creation of a Jewish Community Center. The Jewish community was forced to create places for its people to live, recreate, and worship, places, in large measure, apart from gentile institutions. By 1914, members of the Norfolk section were working with the Anti-Defamation League, and the ladies began taking hard looks at cases as varied as being poor to those of deportation, bigamy, seduction, runaways, and all manner of marital discord and broken homes. The transition from Old World to New had not been smooth for many of Norfolk's working-class poor. Within a year of their significant work with Anti-Defamation cases, the ladies moved the night school for foreign girls to the Holt Street School.

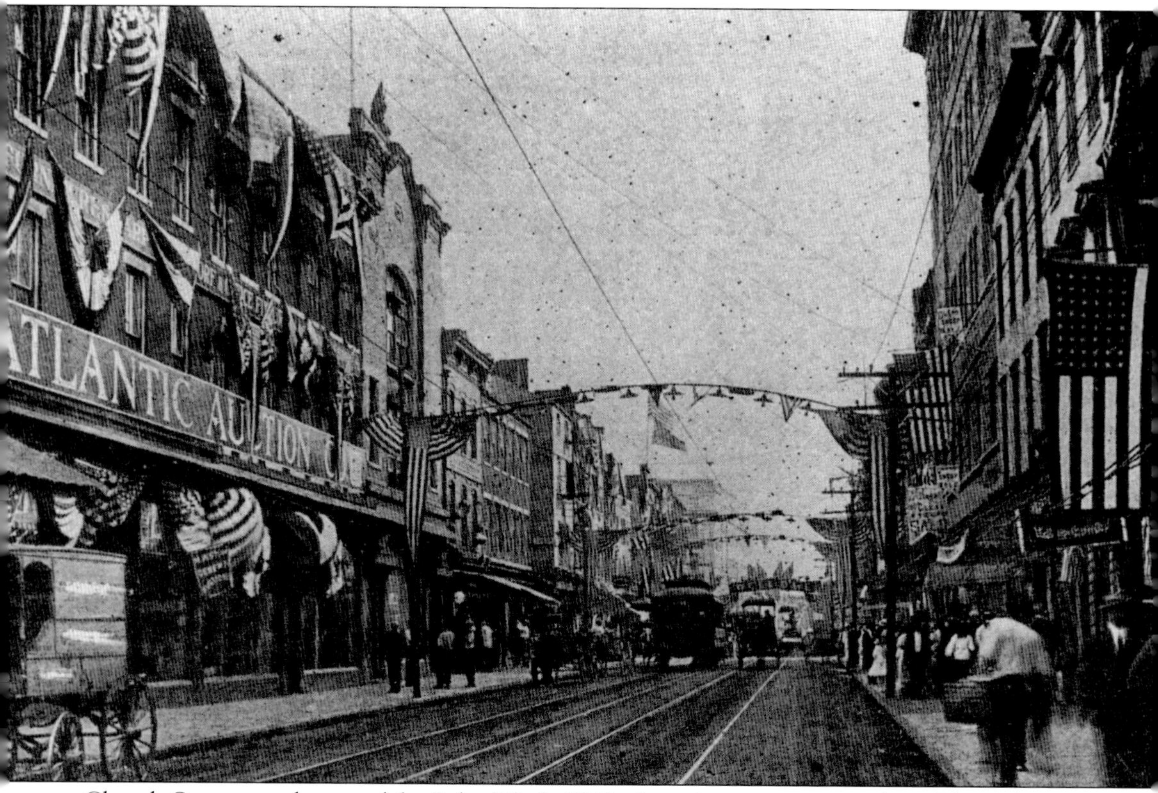

Church Street was decorated for Sales Week 1912 when this picture was taken. The Atlantic Auction Company, situated at 203 to 215 Church Street, is in the left foreground. The repair of Church Street, begun in late January of 1912 and finished in July, had just been completed. The inauguration of Sales Week was in celebration of the completion of the new paving and other street improvements. Having the street repaired was a blow to business and an eyesore for shoppers and merchants while it was underway, but a godsend once completed. Atlantic Auction Company occupied several large three-story buildings on the street. The business was established in 1900 by Morris Asher. (Photographer unknown. Courtesy of Kirn Library).

Four

Prosperity Built on Diversity

"But we are authors,
all of us,
concerned with beginning,
with making,
with sources and substance. And those possessions,
the objects of our desire for security
are results,
not causes,
in our lives. When we too much honor
them, we start weakening ourselves
and fear of loss
becomes even greater than the desire
for life."

—From *Greed, Part 4* "The Turtle," 1969
Diane Wakoski, American poet (1937–)

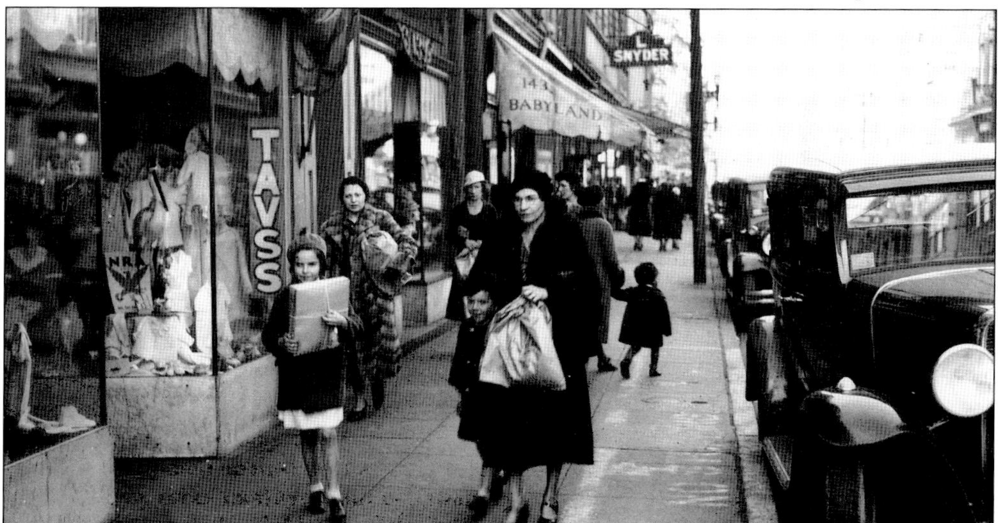

A mother and her children do their shopping on Church Street in proximity of Tavss' Infants' and Children's Clothing Shop, located at 135 Church Street where Bermuda intersects Church and L. Snyder's Department Store (151-153). The date was March 26, 1934. L. Snyder's Department Store was established in Norfolk in 1894. Mathew A. Tavss owned the infants' and children's store while Daniel A. Tavss operated a clothing store in the 300 block of Church Street on the same side of the street as A.J. Legum Furniture Company (327-331). (Charles S. Borjes, photographer. Courtesy of Kirn Library.)

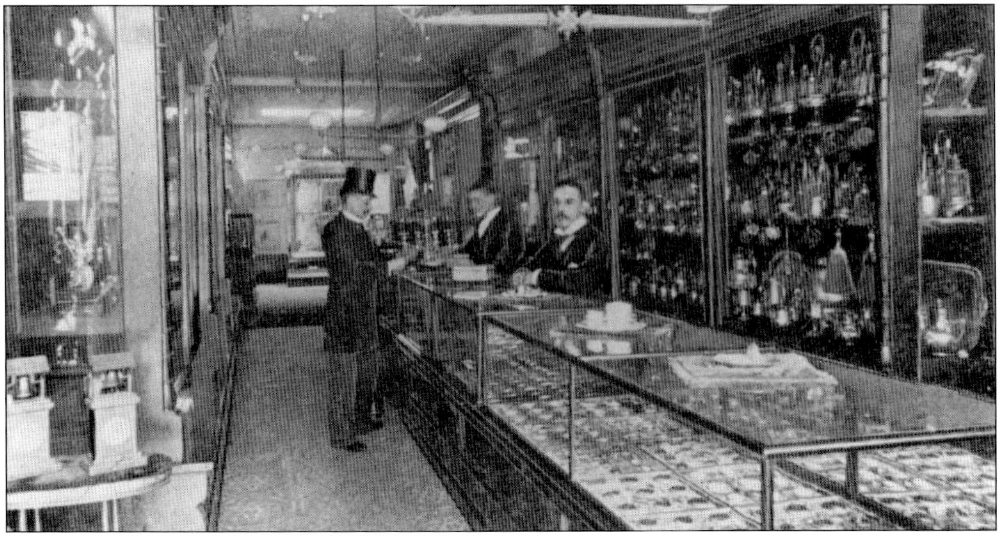

The interior of A. Spertner's Jewelry Palace, founded by Aaron Spertner and located at 106 Church Street, was photographed by an unknown photographer in 1893. Mrs. Fannie Spertner, widow of Moses, advertised her business enterprises as "Manufacturer of Regalias, Badges, Banners & Everything Belonging to Societies & Orders" at her 114 Church Street location (also known as the Beale Building). Edward Spertner was listed as a clerk at that time. Spertner's opened its doors in 1879, 14 years prior to the year this photograph was taken, and is still in business in the city of Norfolk. Located in Southern Shopping Center, Spertner Jewelers remains one of the oldest continuous business establishments in Hampton Roads.

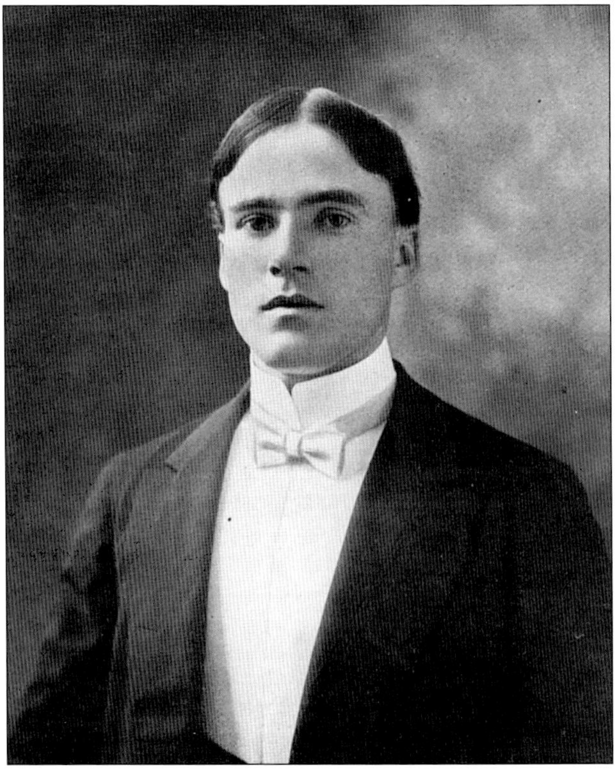

John A. Anderson Jr., a dealer in wall paper, but a decorator and painter by trade, had a store at 255 Church Street. He was the son of John A. and Sarah F. Anderson, natives of Norfolk County, and he was born in Norfolk on April 7, 1875, the only child of his parents. John Jr. married Lillian Midyett, a native of Pasquotank, North Carolina, on March 13, 1892. The couple reared two children, Thelma P. and Jennielle L. Since John Jr. was an Episcopalian and his wife a devout Methodist, he attended Saint Paul's Episcopal Church, where he sang tenor in the choir, and Central Methodist Episcopal Church, South, of Portsmouth, as well. He also attended Beth-El on Cumberland Street opposite Norfolk Academy for no other reason than his community interest.

The Fraternal Order of Eagles (F.O.E.), Norfolk Aerie No. 163, was established in the city in 1901. The year the F.O.E. started in Norfolk, they met the first and third Thursdays of the month at Elk's Hall, then located at the Academy of Music. The president of the Norfolk aerie at the time of its establishment was William B. Oberndorfer, and the secretary was William B. Langley. Though Aerie No. 163 in Norfolk is no longer in existence, there are two aeries on the southside of Lower Tidewater, Aerie No. 795 in Chesapeake, and Aerie No. 3204 in Virginia Beach. The Fraternal Order of Eagles is a fraternal, social, and humanitarian organization with thousands of member lodges, called "aeries," in most states of the United States and provinces of Canada. Aeries give millions of dollars each year, internationally and locally, to a wide variety of charitable causes. Incorporated in Seattle, Washington, in 1898, the Fraternal Order of Eagles was founded by a group of theatre owners who initially called the organization The Order of Good Things.

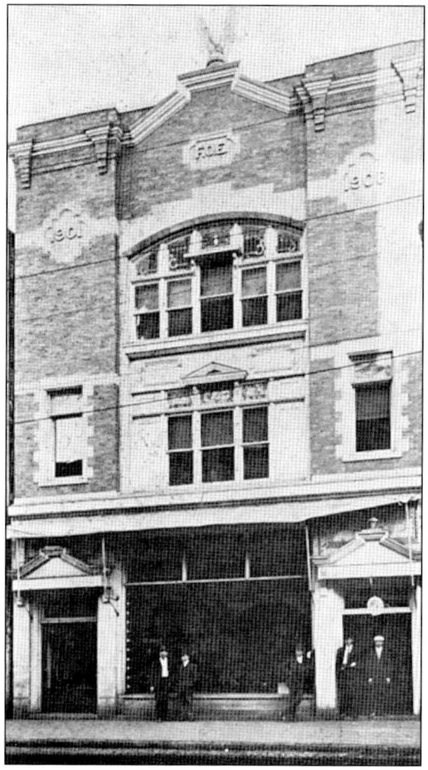

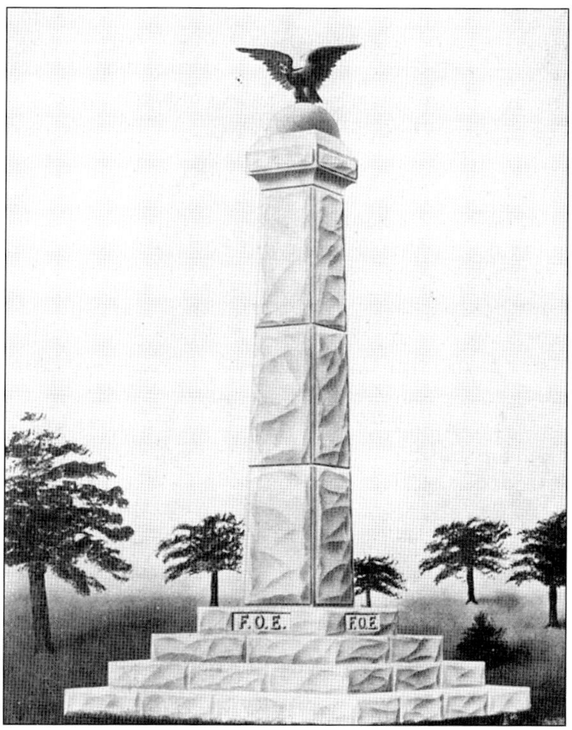

The emblem of the Fraternal Order of Eagles (F.O.E.) is the American bald eagle, clearly shown in the image of Norfolk Aerie No. 163's building 203-205 Church Street (above), taken in 1910, and the organization's monument in Forest Lawn Cemetery. By 1910, William R. Brown was president, Joseph E. Henley, secretary, and Robert E. Atkinson, treasurer. The bald eagle was adopted as a symbol at the turn of the century when most fraternal organizations were selecting animals as their symbols. Two additional symbols hold great significance to the F.O.E.: the Holy Bible, respected for its wisdom and moral teachings, and the flags of the countries in which there are aeries. The precepts of the Fraternal Order of Eagles are liberty, truth, justice, and equality.

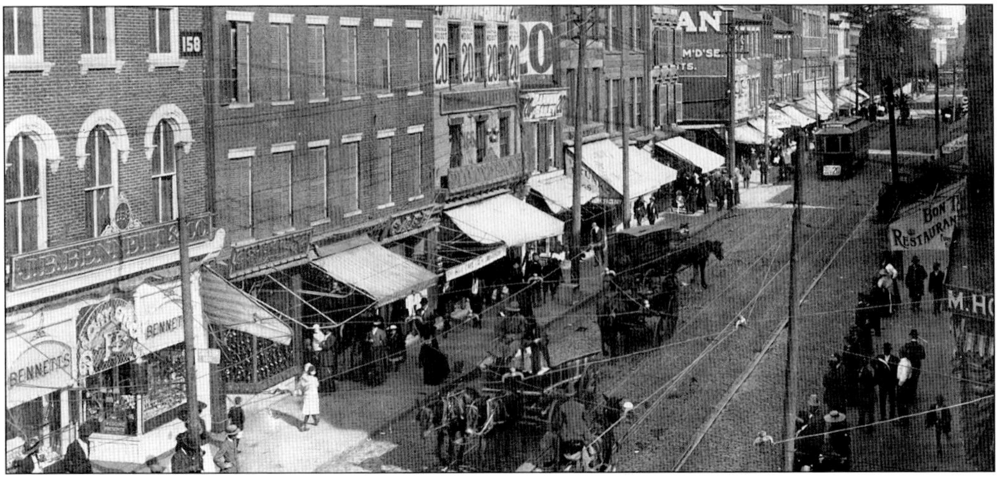

This is a view looking north on Church Street from Main Street in 1910. The building rising tall above the streetcar is the L. Snyder's Department Store, adapted from the same structure that once housed the old Odd Fellows Hall and Church Street Opera House. J.B Bennett & Company, a popular jewelry store, is at 158 Church Street (in the left foreground). St. Paul's Church is located where the trees are found in the picture. The Barnum & Bailey Circus was coming to town on October 20 according to the advertisements for "The Greatest Show on Earth" hanging from several of the buildings along the street. Everything from shoe stores, a trunk factory, restaurants, and general merchandise stores to cafés and candy stores dotted the landscape of the street in this picture. (Harry C. Mann, photographer.)

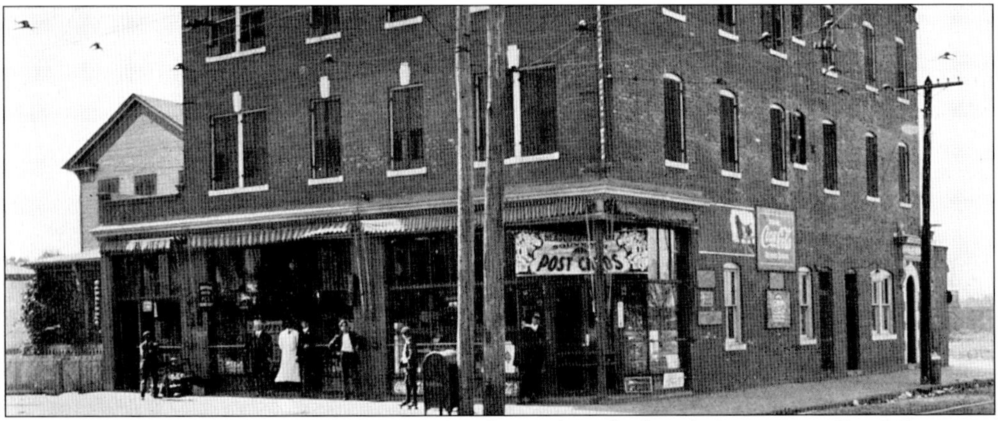

The Hague Hotel, situated at the corner of Eighteenth and Church Streets, proffered European plan to those seeking accommodations for reasonable prices. The European plan provided rooms ranging from $1 to $3 per day, according to location and the condition of the room. Gentlemen were served their meals as a matter of course, and at very reasonable prices, normally in a regular European dining room. The hotel derived its name from The Hague or Smith's Creek, which at one time wound its way around Elmwood Cemetery, cutting into Church to the south and north of the old burial ground. The Hague was advertised as being within a 15-minute trolley ride of Ocean View, and accessible to the piers and stations. J.W. O'Connor was the manager of The Hague when this picture was taken. There is a grocery store on the corner featuring souvenir postcards. The picture was taken in 1909. The Hague later became known as The Plaza, a hostelry owned by Bonnie and Graham F. McEachin, which catered to African-American entertainers coming to Norfolk to perform at the Attucks Theatre.

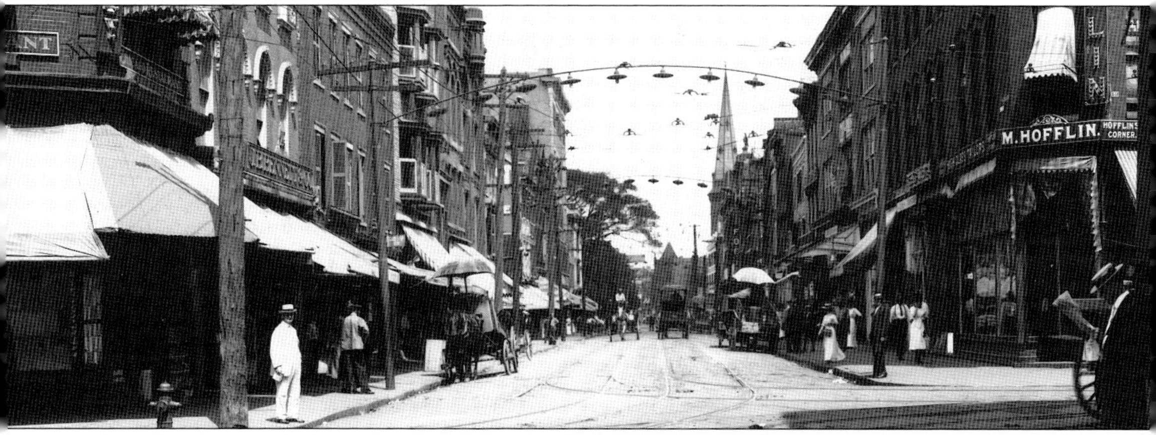

Harry C. Mann took this exceptional picture of Church Street looking north from Main Street *c.* 1910. Identifiable establishments on the left side of the street, starting at the corner of Main and Church Streets are the Chicago Restaurant, managed by Jung Hong; J.B. Bennett & Company at 158 Church, owned and operated by Jonas B. Bennett; J.E. Land, shoes (160); Mrs. Pauline Ries, milliner (162); M & M Café Company (164); Metropolitan Loan Office (166); A. Fox and Lee Sims, shoemakers (168), both of whom lived on Church Street in Huntersville; Marx Shapiro, clothier (170); Wagner Shoe Company, Jack D. Cherry, proprietor (174); Norfolk Electric Shoe Repairing Company (176); and Star Shoe Store (178). On the right side of Church Street before its intersection with Plume Street was M. Hofflin, men's clothier on the corner of Main and Church; Tony's Shoe Store (161), founded in 1898 by Antonio LaGiglia; Frank Driesell, jeweler (163); Gunter Sewing Machine Corporation (165); Bon Ton Restaurant, Samuel Lavine, proprietor (167); Owl Drug Company, Arthur R. Greene, proprietor (171); Berry & Shannon, liquors, owned by Richard W. Berry and Edgar Shannon, and William H. White, furniture rooms, both businesses sharing 173 Church Street; John F. Sheahan, saloon, pool & billiards establishment (175); and George J. Eichhorn, barber (177). From its intersection at Plume Street to Bermuda Street was an equally interesting mix of businesses, social clubs, and service industries. Continuing down the left side of the photograph, keeping in mind that there were vacancies in the storefronts, there was Barney Nicholson's pawn brokerage (186) and Ralph Kanter's dry goods business sharing a storefront with the Virginia Tailoring Company at 188 Church Street. Down the right side of the picture, much of which is obscured from view, was D.B. Cain's saloon (181); the American Restaurant (183); David Singer's pawn shop (185); Norfolk Furniture Manufacturing Corporation (187); and N.B. Joynes' saloon (191). From the intersection of Church Street with Bermuda Street looking north, there was Joseph F. Jones & Company, purveyors of fine shoes and two rooms for rent (192); G.L. Saffy & Company, dry goods (194); C.H. Swink, men's furnishings, and the Automobile Exchange & Repair Company sharing 196 Church; P.N. Wright, dry goods (198); S.E. Simmons Shoe Company (200); Louis Snyder's dry goods emporium (202-204); Odd Fellows Hall (206); L.P. Lathrop, baker, and Rosario Rugieri, physician (208); Harvard Hat Store (210); Model Confectionary (212); Grand Union Tea Company (216); R.E. Gornto, shoes (218); Underhill & Company, druggist (220); and on the right side of the street, W.D. Boyett's saloon (195); Mrs. Maggie Wicks (197); George Eddy, shoemaker (199); Bernard Lilienfeld, pawn broker (201); Fraternal Order of Eagles (203-205); N.S. Horton & Company, grocer (217); Clingman Hodges, barber (219); and I X L Restaurant (221). From the intersection of Church and Cove proceeding north, one would have found Watkins Grocery (229); Whitehead & Riley, furniture (231-233); Novelty Furniture Company (235); and St. Paul's Episcopal Church (236-242), and eventually, along the right side of the street, old Christ Church. The trees to the left indicate St. Paul's churchyard. (Courtesy of the Library of Virginia.)

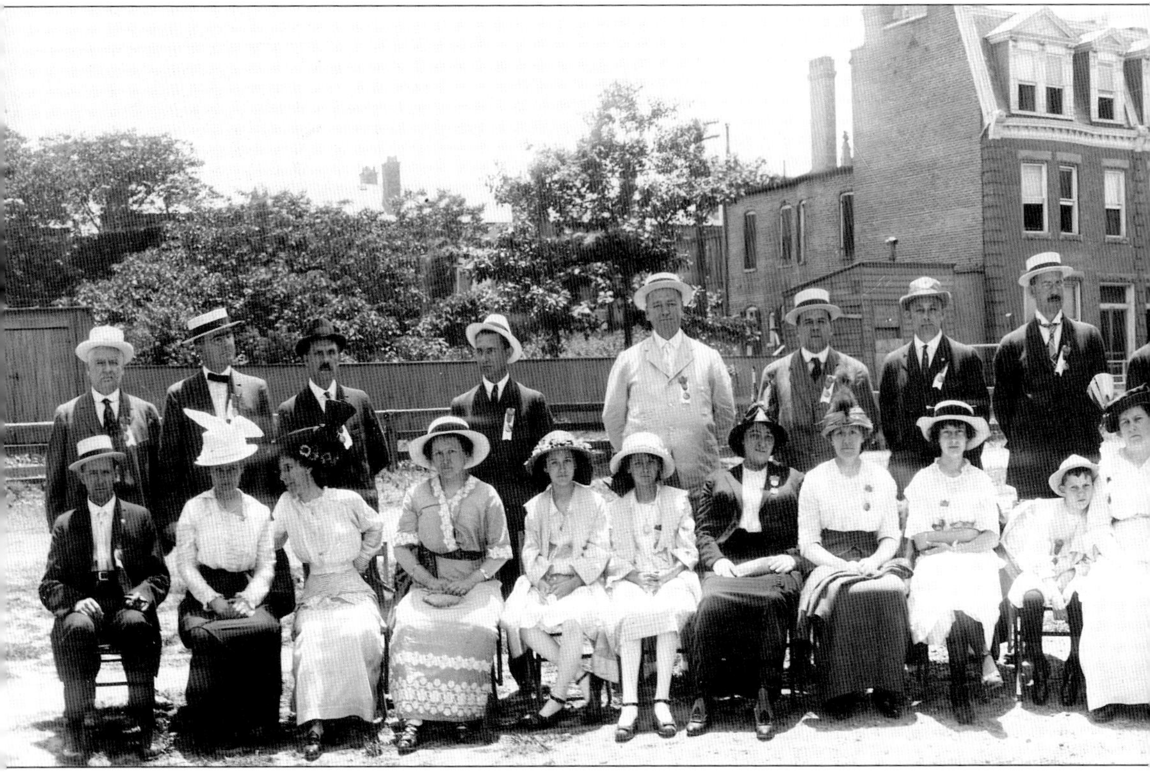

The conventioneers in this panoramic photograph had their picture taken by photographer Harry C. Mann in front of the Norfolk Academy building in the spring of 1912. The group is

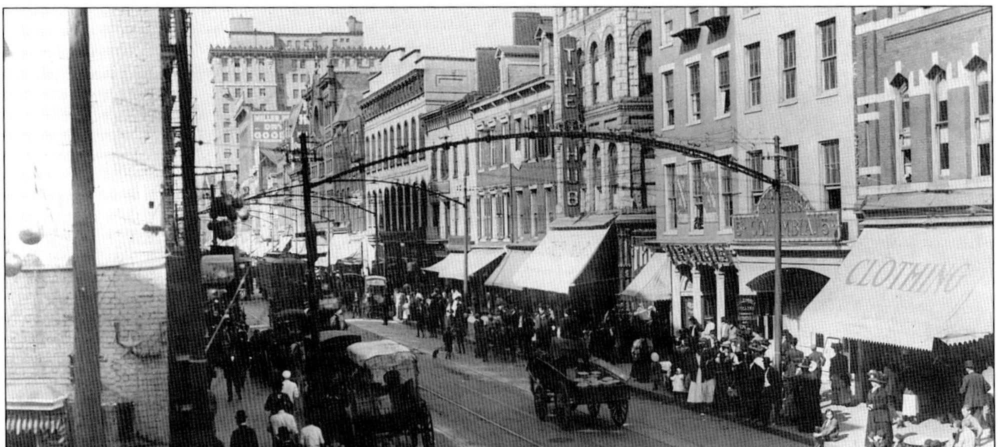

In this photo, taken by Harry C. Mann in 1911 looking west down East Main Street from the corner of Church Street, it is easy to see how Church Street was at the center of activity in early Norfolk. The intersection point of the two streets was also the convergence of culture for the city, as the black and white children sitting on the curb at the horse trough in the lower right corner of the picture or the finely dressed African-American men and women standing on the left (Church Street corner) looking across Main Street attest. The Columbia Theatre, a popular vaudeville and movie house, sits directly to the right of the horse-drawn cart on the street. Two storefronts to the left of the Columbia was The Hub clothier.

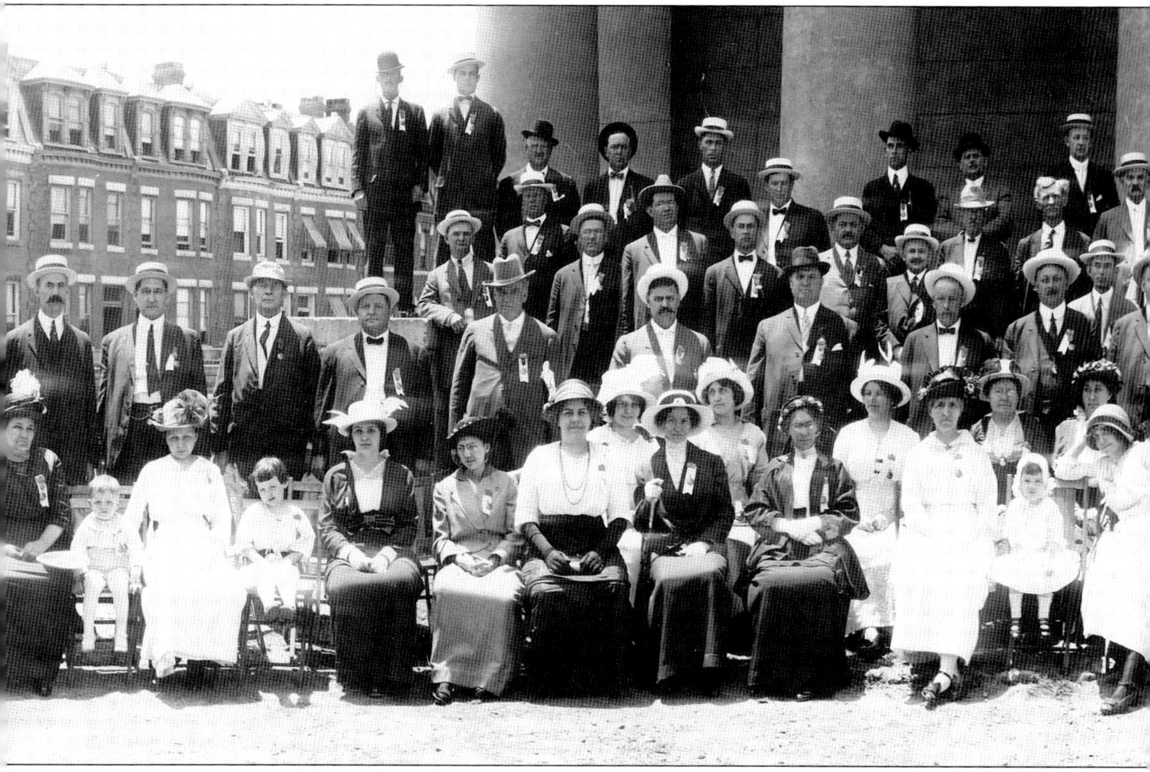

facing Cumberland Street, one block off Church Street. The spire of Freemason Street Baptist Church is visible beyond the townhomes in the left foreground, and Charlotte Street is clearly

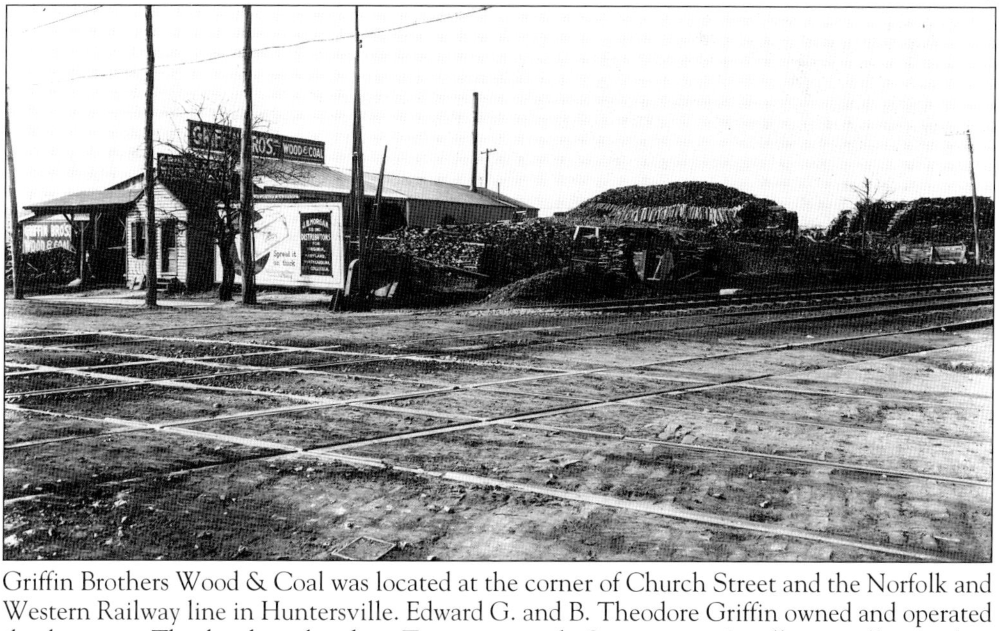

Griffin Brothers Wood & Coal was located at the corner of Church Street and the Norfolk and Western Railway line in Huntersville. Edward G. and B. Theodore Griffin owned and operated the business. The brothers lived at Twenty-seventh Street near Gazelle in Villa Heights. The picture was taken about 1915. (Harry C. Mann, photographer. Courtesy of the Library of Virginia.)

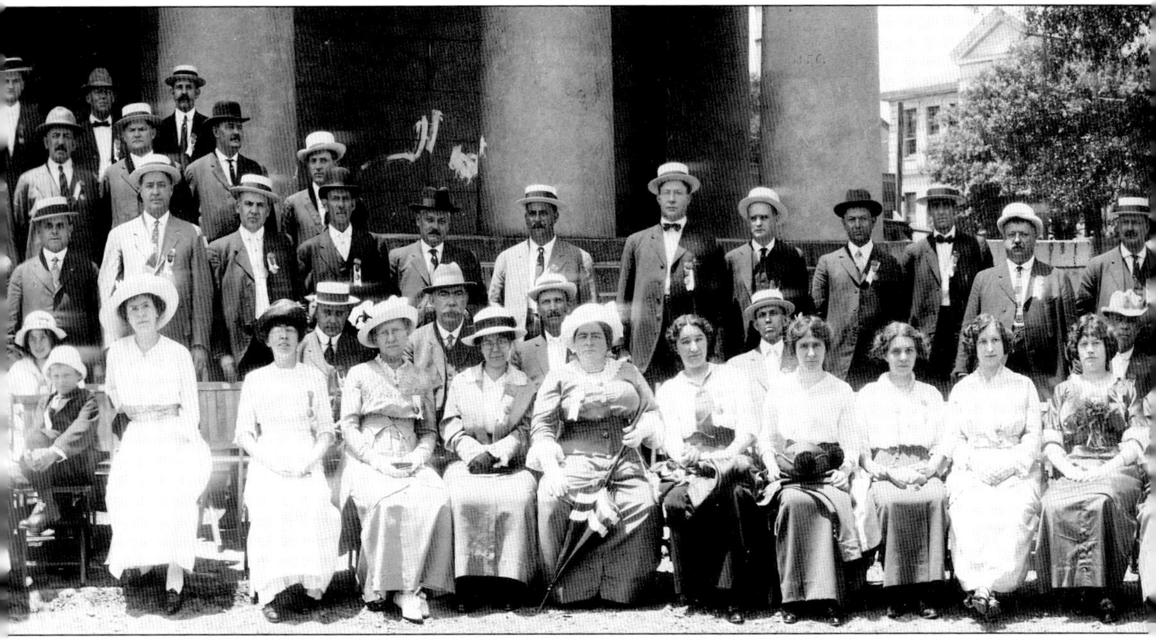

shown running along the right side of the picture. The public school on the corner of Bank and

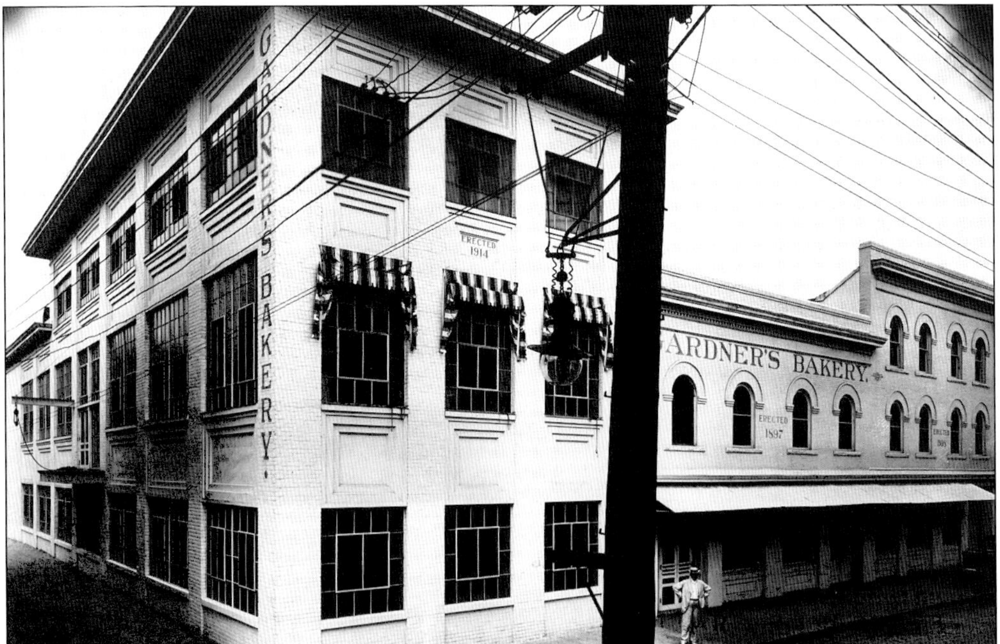

Gardner's Bakery, located at 30-32-34 Cumberland Street, one block off Church Street, was begun in 1897 in the center building in the photograph (directly behind Mr. Gardner). He added on to the business in 1908 with the building attached to the far right and, again, in 1914, with the three-story building on the left. Harry C. Mann took the picture in 1914 to commemorate the bakery's second major expansion. Gardner ran the premier bakery in Norfolk in its day, supplying hotels, restaurants, and grocers with an impressive diversity of breads, cakes, and confections. (Courtesy of the Library of Virginia.)

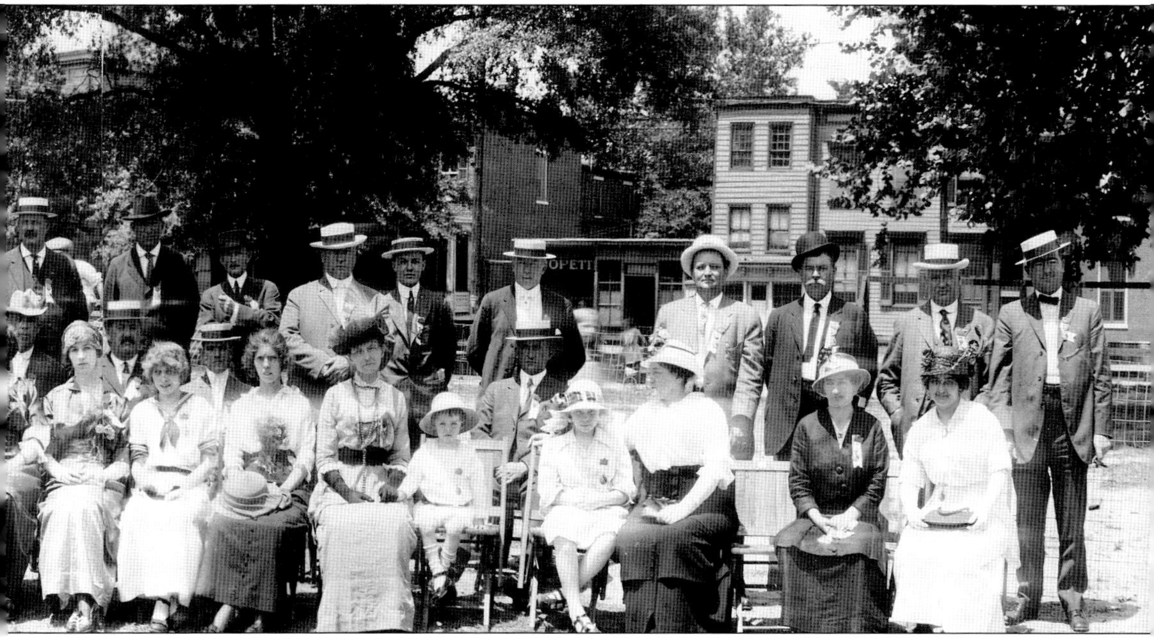

Charlotte Streets is also noticeable behind the large oak tree on the right side of the image.

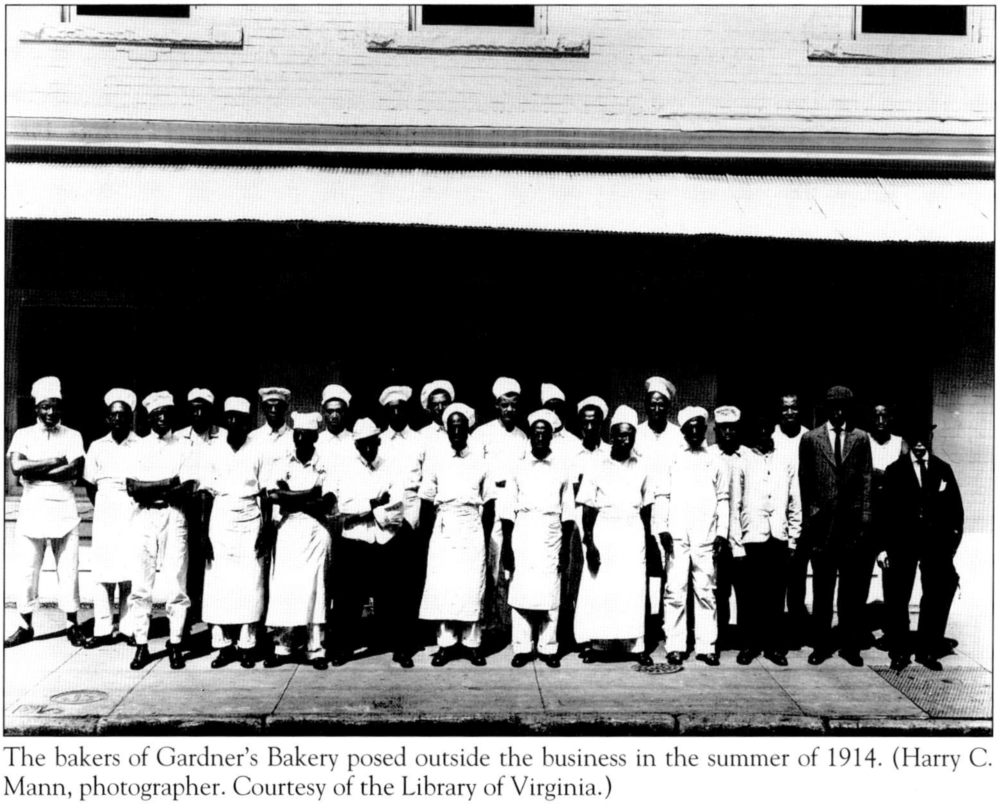

The bakers of Gardner's Bakery posed outside the business in the summer of 1914. (Harry C. Mann, photographer. Courtesy of the Library of Virginia.)

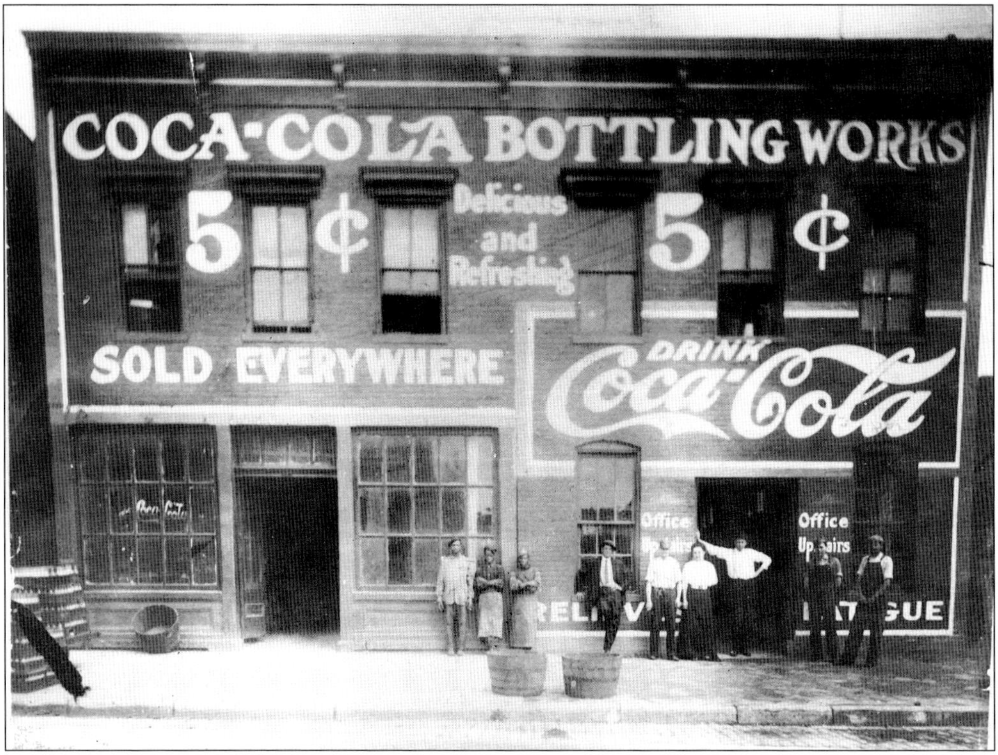

The Coca-Cola Bottling Works, formerly located at 390 Chapel Street, was the subject of this photograph, taken *c.* 1910. Alonzo F. Cathey managed the bottling works, and W. Egbert Cathey worked as foreman. The Catheys lived at 238 Reservoir Avenue. (Courtesy of Kirn Library.)

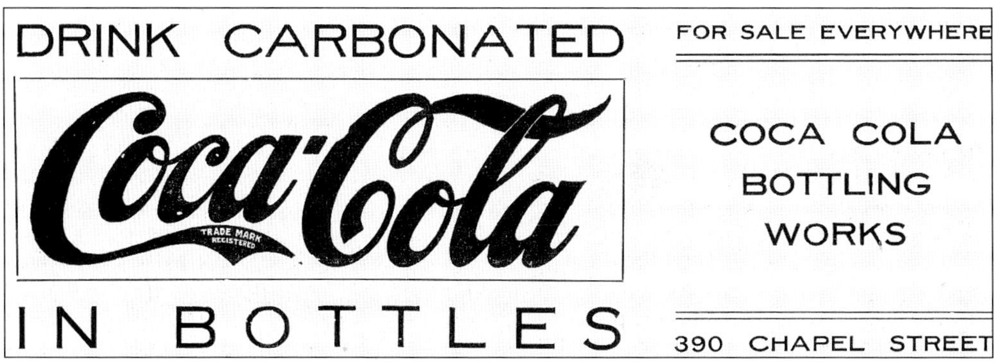

This advertisement for the Coca-Cola Bottling Works ran in 1910.

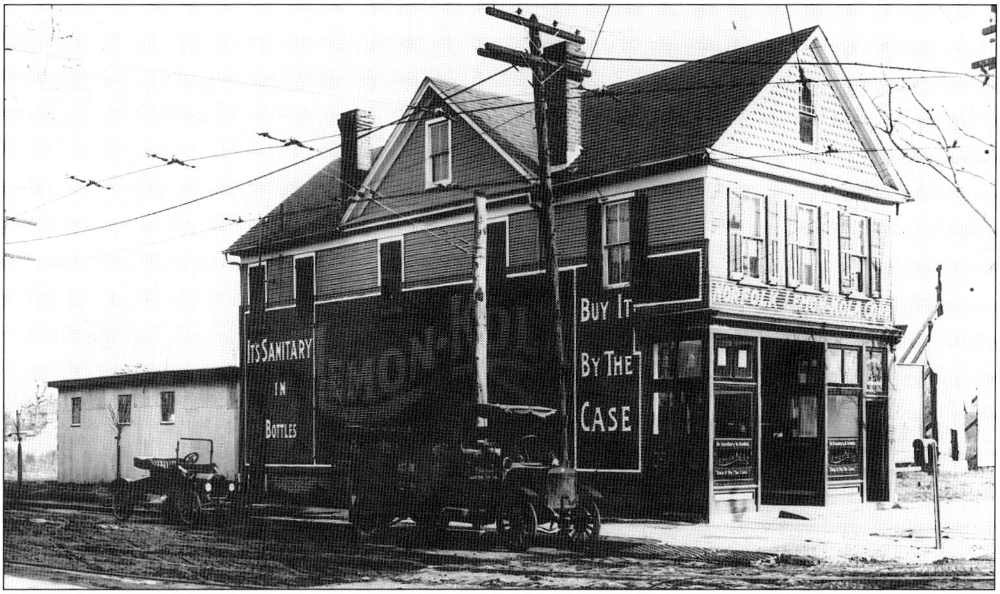

The Lemon-Kola Bottling Company, located at 2536-2538 Church Street, was photographed by Harry C. Mann in 1915. Operated by T. Bent Young and Walter R. Reamey, this was to be one of several bottling works to locate in Norfolk. Walter Reamey maintained a home in Roanoke, Virginia, while Young lived in the Goffigon Apartments in Norfolk. (Courtesy of Kirn Library.)

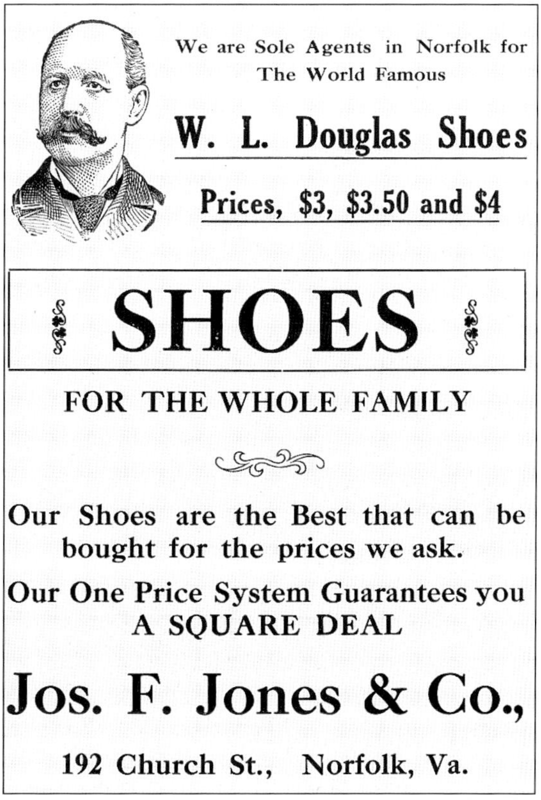

Joseph F. Jones & Company, Inc., advertised as "The Reliable Shoe Store," was located at 192 Church Street. Joseph F. Jones opened his retail shoe establishment in 1901 and incorporated it on January 1, 1912, two years after this advertisement ran. Jones, president and treasurer of the company, was a native of Baltimore, Maryland, and he came to Norfolk the year he founded his business. He began his enterprise on Church Street by carrying a wide array of high-grade footwear, and employed a respectable number of clerks to wait on customers. Everyone paid the same price for a given shoe under Jones's strict rule, "one price to all."

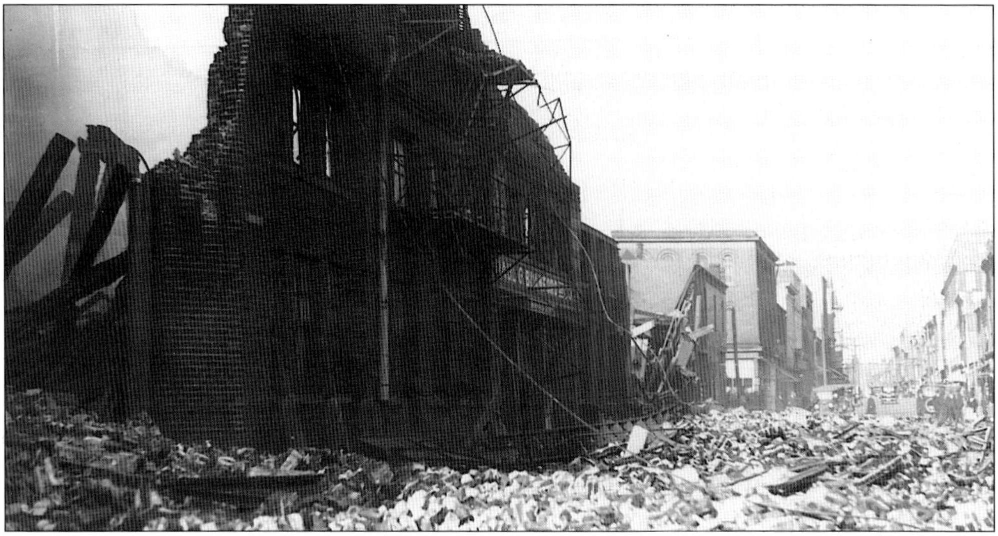

Church Street was in shambles near the Marine Equipment Company building (left) after a major fire burned most of the buildings along the street to the ground. The date was December 18, 1921. The Marine Equipment Company, marine supply dealers, occupied a six-story structure at the corner of Church and Water Streets. Firemen from Company No. 5 responded to the night-time blaze, which gutted the building owned by Tidewater Securities Corporation, of which Paul White was president. The top floor of the building occupied by the Eastern Hide and By-Product Corporation, on the lane adjoining the three-story building occupied by Thomas M. Cashin, barrel and metal dealer, at 600-602 Water Street, was crushed by falling brick and debris from the fire in the two buildings between the lane and Church Street. The fire spread rapidly through the buildings around the Marine Equipment Company, resulting in the considerable destruction evidenced in the photographs. At the time of the fire, S. Lloyd Drake was president and treasurer of Marine Equipment Company, and A.J. Bohannan was vice president and secretary. Both men resided in Portsmouth. (Charles S. Borjes, photographer. Courtesy of Kirn Library.)

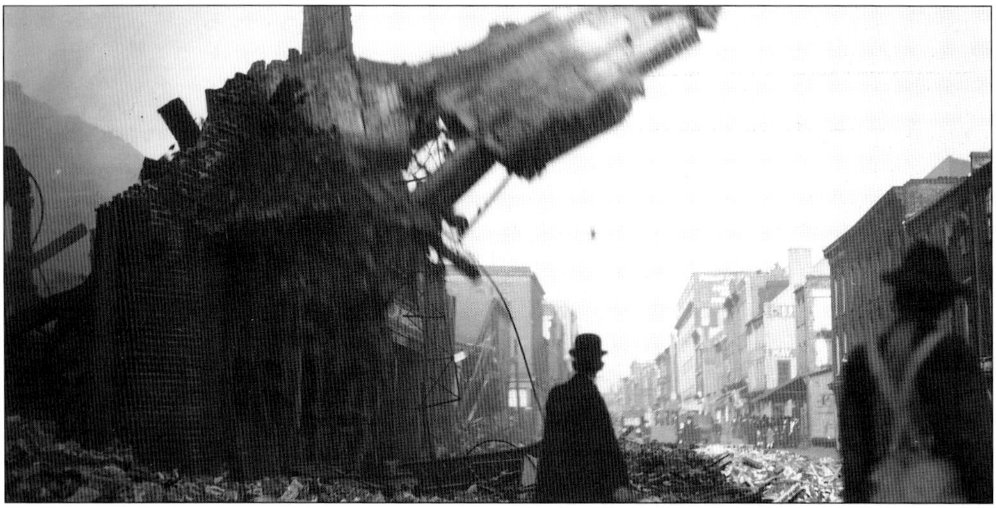

Charles S. Borjes captured the drama of the fire on December 18, 1921, as the remaining portion of the Marine Equipment Company collapsed into the street after the conflagration had been extinguished. (Courtesy of Kirn Library.)

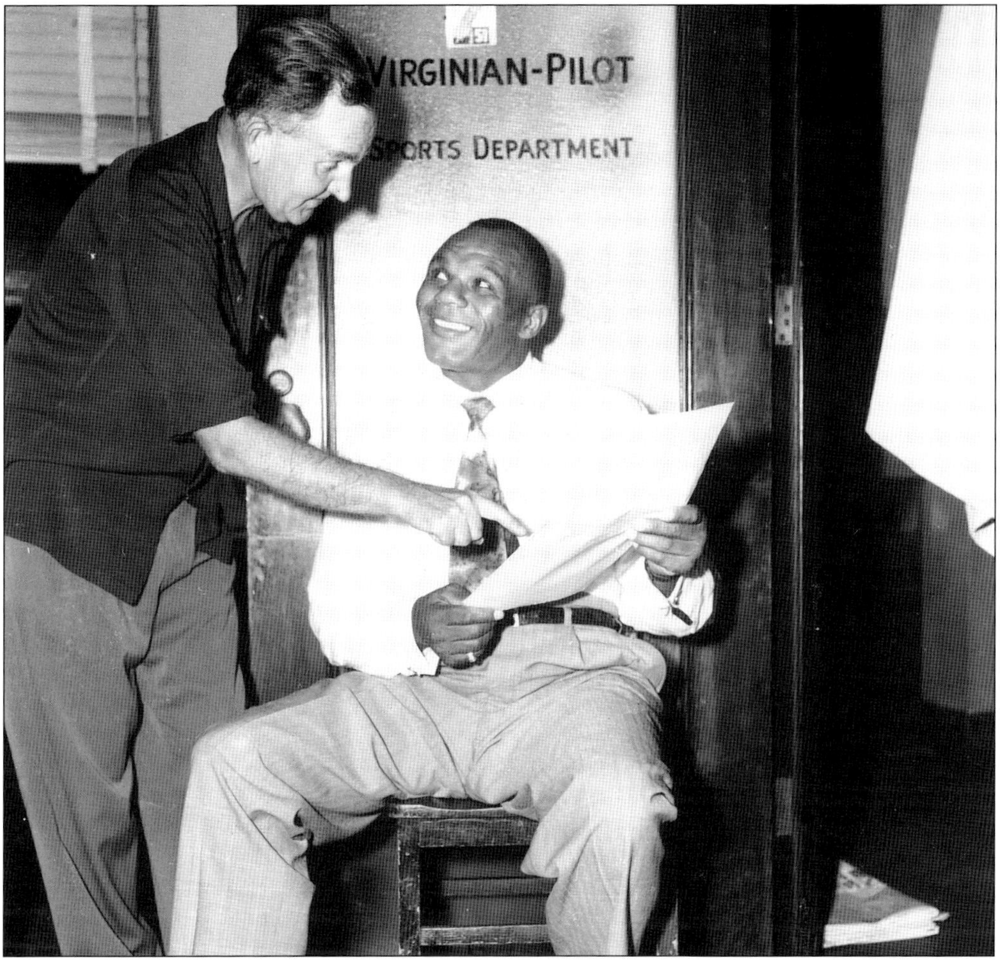

Virginian-Pilot sports editor William N. Cox points out a story to boxer Joe "Jersey Joe" Walcott, August 15, 1931. Walcott was the world heavyweight champion from 1951 to 1952, retiring in 1953. "Jersey Joe," whose real name was Arnold Raymond Cream, began his boxing career in 1929. A proficient and intelligent fighter in the ring, but hardly of the caliber of a Max Schmeling or Gene Tunney, Walcott fought Joe Louis for the World Heavyweight Championship at Madison Square Garden on December 5, 1947, and lost. Though Walcott was actually winning the fight against the defending world champion, the fight was ruled in Louis's favor. Louis knocked out Walcott in the 12th round of a subsequent match at Yankee Stadium on June 25, 1948, but Louis had begun to show his age in the ring. Walcott had been in the fight business for 20 years when he took on Ezzard Charles for the vacant heavyweight title in Chicago, June 22, 1949. Charles, considered one of the best light heavyweights of all time, was in his prime when he met "Jersey Joe" in the ring, the first of five matches the two would fight, and defeated him. Walcott finally defeated Charles for the title on July 18, 1951, in Pittsburgh. At 37 years of age, he finally garnered the World Heavyweight Championship. After having retired four times from boxing, and having been rejected for a boxing license in New Jersey eight years before because of his age, Walcott had finally gotten the win. He held on to the title until beaten by Rocky Marciano in Philadelphia's Municipal Stadium on September 23, 1952. "Jersey Joe" became an important part of boxing history and was the oldest man to win the heavyweight title before George Foreman broke his record in 1994. (Charles S. Borjes, photographer. Courtesy of Kirn Library.)

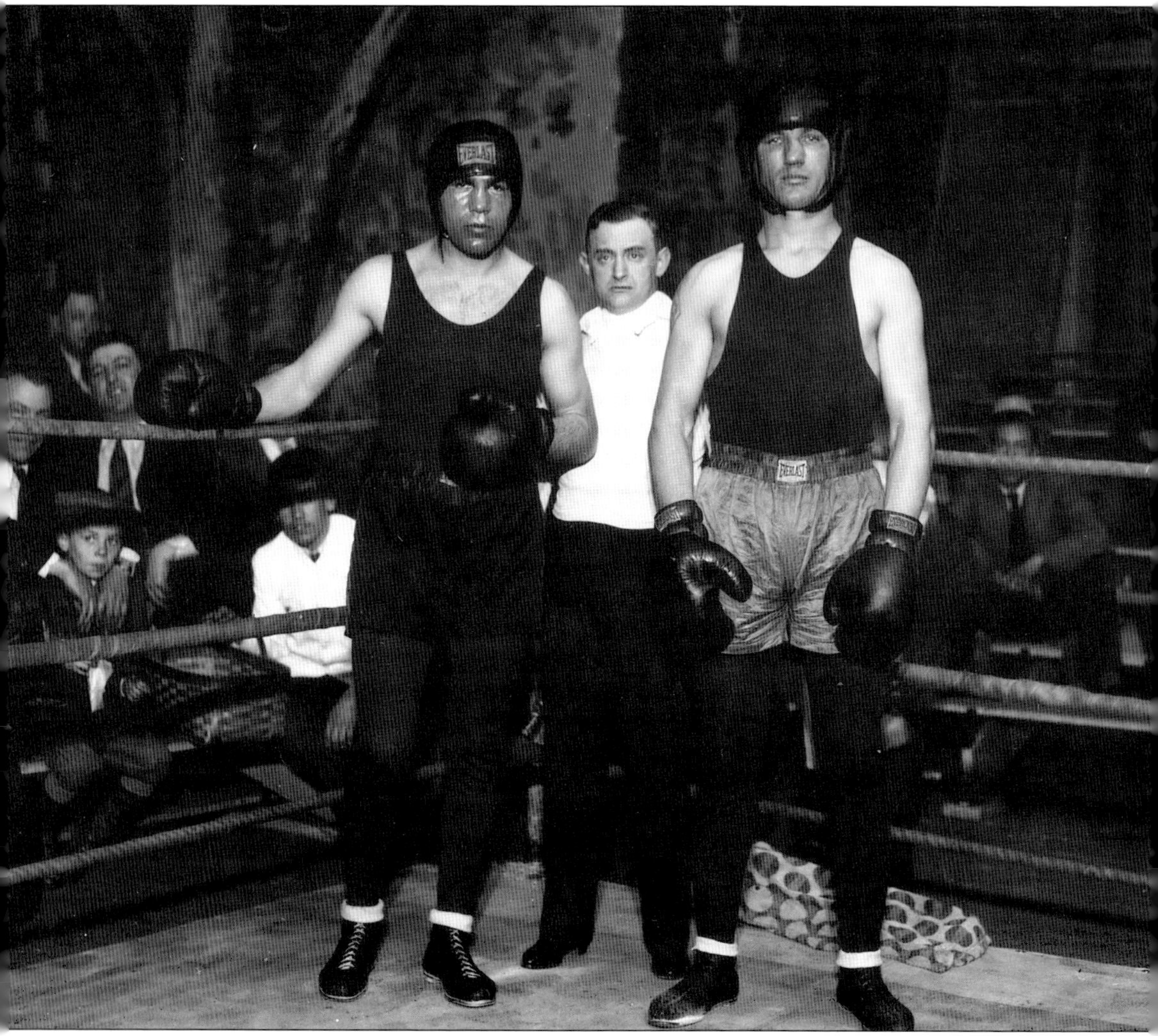

German boxer Max Schmeling, his manager, Joe Jacobs, and Jack Shore (left to right) were photographed in Norfolk during a bout Schmeling won on April 13, 1932, at the Colonial Theatre. Schmeling's fight in Norfolk occurred in the heat of the Lindbergh kidnapping, so the anti-German sentiments in the United States were running at an all-time high, even in Norfolk. The 193-pound Schmeling boxed to row upon row of empty seats in a three-round exhibition against a 200-pound Jack Shore, a native New Yorker. After winning the match, Schmeling, his face covered in vaseline, took off his head-gear and addressed his small audience in good English mixed with a touch of better German: "I cannot make a speech. I thank you for coming to see me." His smile caught a few at ringside by surprise, winning them over, but the champion's work was lost to those who opted to pass on the performance. Schmeling's Norfolk appearance punctuated the prejudice and suspicions people across the nation felt toward ethnic and racial groups. Though Schmeling stayed in the Cavalier Hotel and played a round of golf while in town, he received a less than warm welcome. (Charles S. Borjes, photographer. Courtesy of Kirn Library.)

Schmeling was born in Klein Luckow, Germany, on September 28, 1905. He went on to become the first boxer of European extraction to win the boxing heavyweight championship in the 20th century on June 12, 1930, though it was won on a foul his opponent, Jack "The Gob" Sharkey, committed in the fourth round—a low blow. Schmeling retained the title upon beating Young Stribling in Cleveland, Ohio, on July 3, 1931. On June 21, 1932, a couple of months after the fight in Norfolk, Schmeling fought Jack Sharkey a second time and lost the World Heavyweight Championship. He remained active, and some would say, controversial, as a boxer from 1924 to 1948. The most controversial portion of his career began in the late 1930s when Nazi Germany used Schmeling as a poster child for Arayian propaganda campaigns, particularly after Schmeling beat Joe Louis (1914–1981), the great "Brown Bomber," in the 12th round of a bout in June 1936. Louis trained hard and fought fiercely following his loss to Schmeling, and on June 22, 1938, "The Brown Bomber," reigning world heavyweight champion, defeated Schmeling in the first round of a non-title match at Yankee Stadium, defeating the one boxer to whom he had ever lost a fight. This was perceived as much a loss for Nazi Germany as a personal defeat for Schmeling, who was far from being a Nazi and has been wrongly associated with Naziism over the years. Louis struck Schmeling so hard he broke his spine in two places, so in many ways, he paid a greater price for the loss to Louis than anyone could ever have imagined, particularly at that time. Schmeling recovered from his injuries and continued to fight for another ten years. The German ended his career with 56 wins, ten draws, and four defeats, with 37 knockouts.

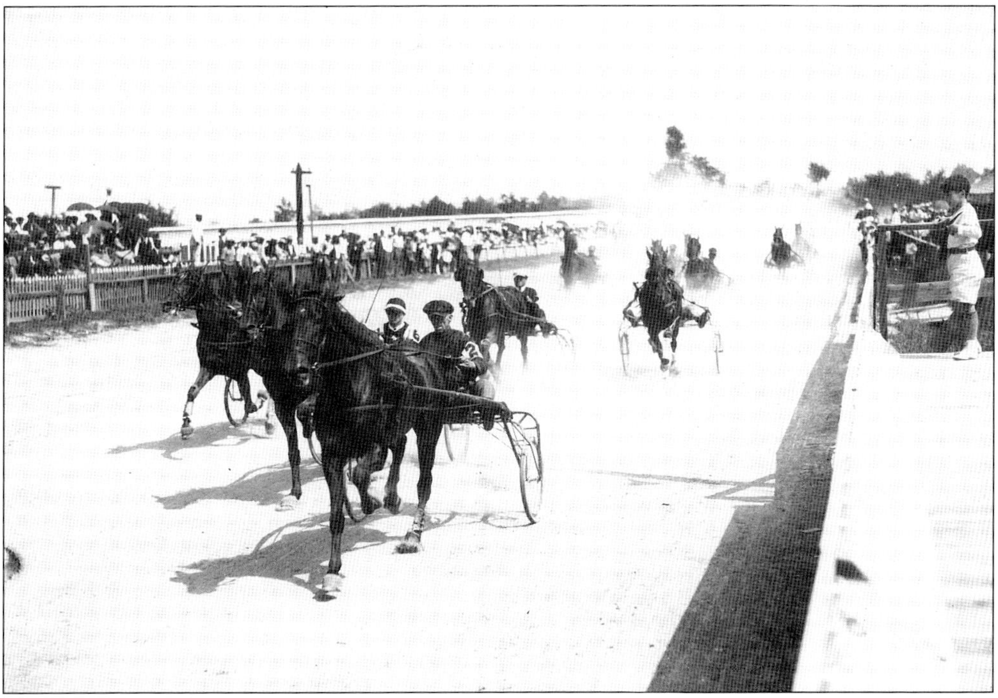

Norfolk's harness racing season, held annually at the old fairgrounds in conjunction with the Norfolk Fair, opened on September 6, 1926, the day this picture was taken. There were about 150 fast-stepping thoroughbreds in the stables for the races, each anxiously awaiting the bell of the starter. The entry list in 1926 was the largest in the fair's history, most of the entrants coming from Virginia and North Carolina. The fairgrounds were located off Church Street. (Charles S. Borjes, photographer. Courtesy of Kirn Library).

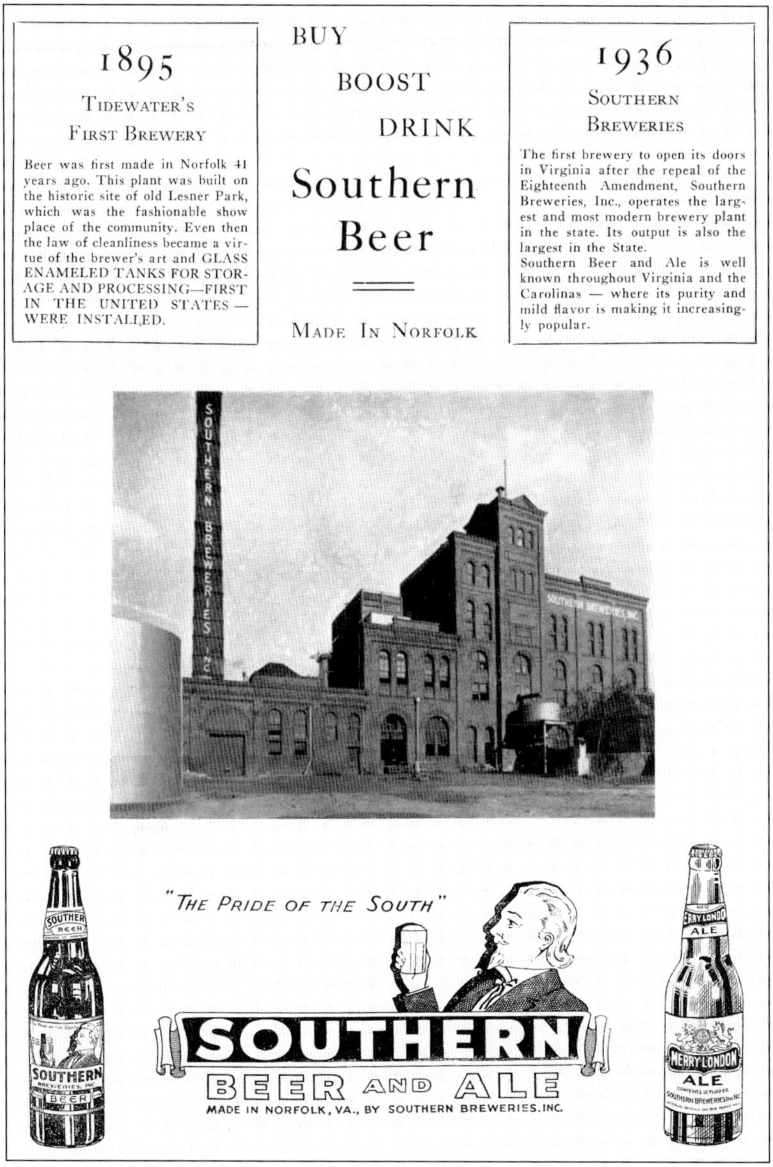

Consumer's Brewery established a plant on the site of John A. Lesner's old Maplewood Park (or Lesner's Garden) in Huntersville at 710 Washington Avenue. Norfolk's only brewery moved to the location in 1895. With the advent of Prohibition in 1916, the Consumer's Brewery plant manufactured fruit beverages and acted as a truck storage facility for neighboring manufacturing plants. When the Eighteenth Amendment was repealed in 1933, Southern Breweries purchased the property and reconditioned the buildings, including the purchase of new brewery equipment. In the spring of 1934, the plant began merchandising their primary product—Southern Beer and Merry London Ale. Southern Breweries' predecessor, Consumer's Brewery, had been the first brewery in the United States to install glass-lined tanks and maintain a laboratory for control of plant methods. Southern Breweries continued Consumer's tradition of public health safeguards through pioneering state-of-the-art brewing techniques. The picture shown here of the Southern Breweries' plant on upper Church Street was taken in 1935. David T. Gallo was the brewery's general manager at that time.

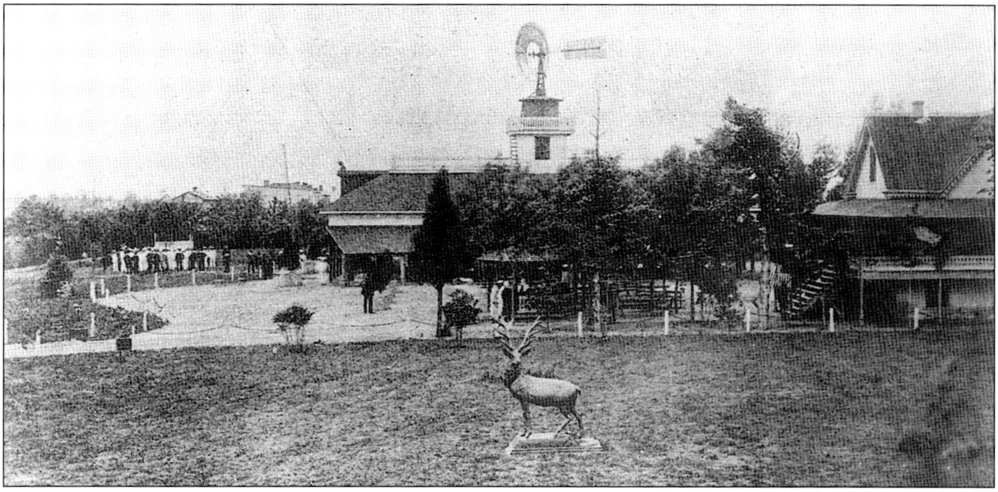

Maplewood Park or Lesner's Garden was located off Church Street at Washington Avenue in Norfolk's Huntersville section. A popular resort more often remembered as Lesner's Garden, the park was a zoological and flower garden where visitors could wander among the trees, fountains, ponds, flowers, and shady bowers, or gaze in wonder at the line of cages filled with wild animals. The old resort, brainchild of John A. Lesner, was located at the neck of Church Street, which once skirted Smith's Creek near the cemetery. The picture shown here was taken in 1885. The Consumer's Brewery and, later, Southern Breweries (see opposite page), took over this location for their respective bottling plant operations. (Courtesy of Kirn Library.)

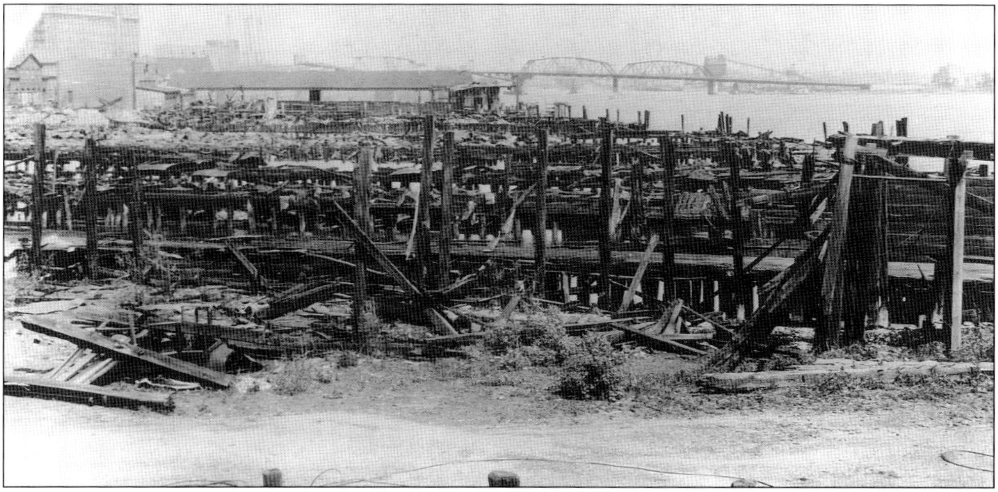

Fire visited Norfolk again the afternoon of June 7, 1931. A fuel barge exploded while tied to a pier at the foot of Church Street, setting off a fire which held the potential of burning down most of downtown Norfolk. The fire spread as it was fanned by 24-mile-per-hour winds. Fire companies from as far away as Elizabeth City, North Carolina, responded to this devastating blaze. In the end, the fire destroyed over $1 million in pierage, buildings, and vessels. The burned out pier shown here belonged to Old Dominion Steamship Line. Old Dominion continued to operate from their Lambert's Point facility, but the loss of steamship companies and cargo handlers at the foot of Church Street's southern terminus forever changed the complexion and usage of the southern end of the street. The large building to the left in the photograph is Union Station. The Berkley Bridge runs above the wrecked pier, and the Berkley section of Norfolk is the land mass to the far right. (Courtesy of Kirn Library.)

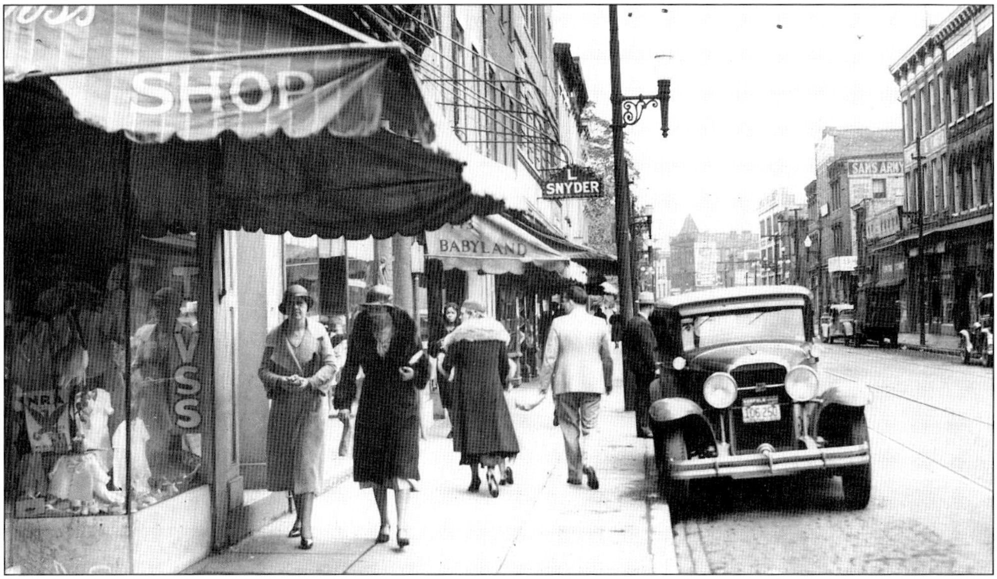

Shoppers once filled a thriving Church Street, as this scene, taken March 26, 1934, demonstrates. (Charles S. Borjes, photographer. Courtesy of Kirn Library.)

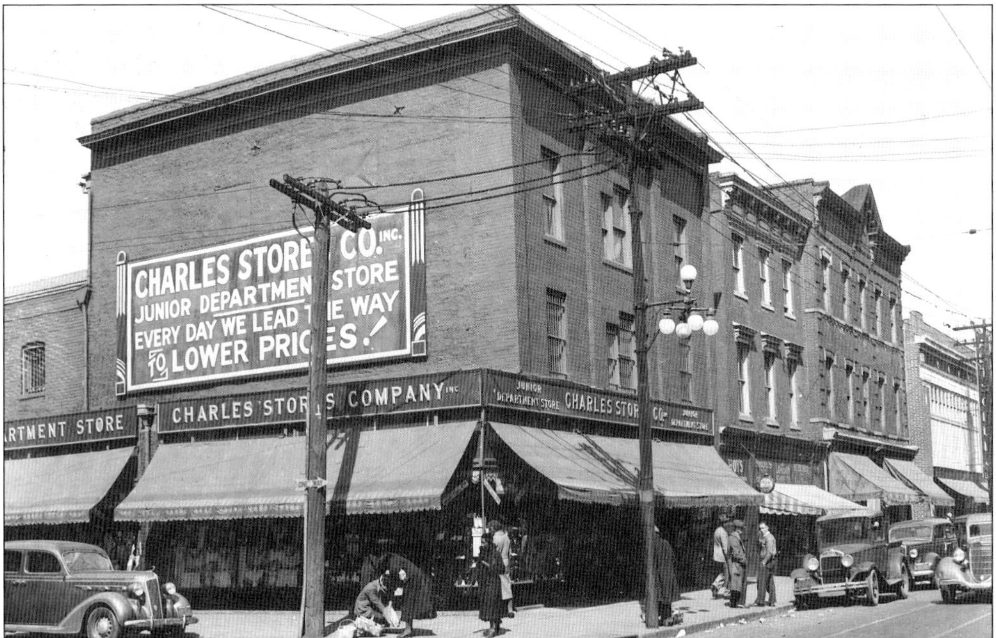

The Charles Stores Company Junior Department Store, located at the corner of Church and Holt Streets, was photographed by Charles S. Borjes on March 10, 1937. The Charles Stores Company in Norfolk was part of a national chain of junior department stores that sold ready-to-wear garments, novelties, and house furnishings on a strictly cash basis. At the time this picture was taken, the store had been in business in the city since 1922 at the same location, 301-303 Church Street. The parent corporation was re-organized in 1937. B.S. Hornstein and K. Ray Katz had become president and vice president, respectively, of the New York-based retailer. F.R. Close was manager of the Norfolk store. (Courtesy of Kirn Library.)

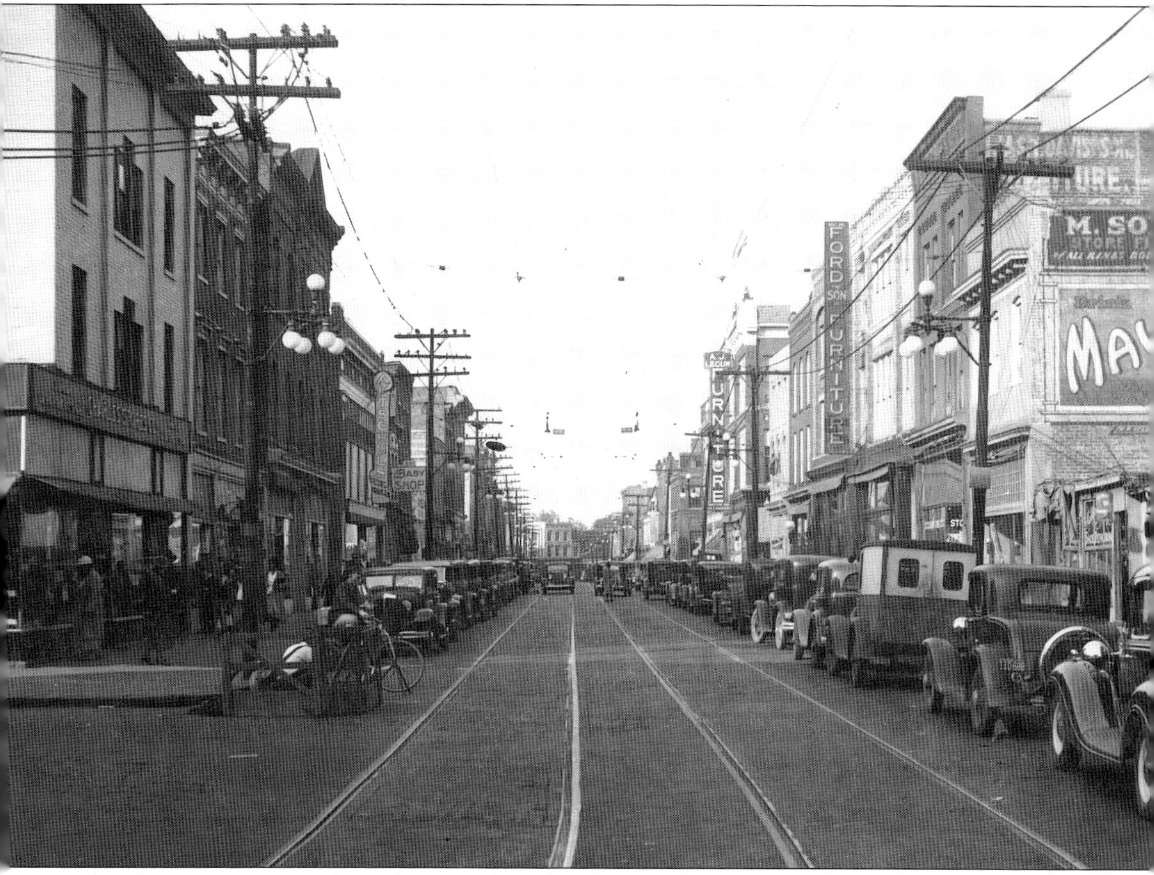

Church Street thrived throughout its long history on the merchant class, who filled both sides of the thoroughfare with their shops and services. From butchers and bakers to tailors and sailmakers, Church Street earned a reputation as one of the best streets to shop. This picture was taken on March 10, 1937, shortly after merchants had formed the Church Street Improvement League. On Church Street, a shopper could find luxuries as well as standard merchandise. Luxury items might have been jeweled, dainty bottles of perfume, large lockets on heavy chains, jeweled pendants or large blocks of jade, broaches and rings, kid leather gloves or woolen mittens, some worked with "M" for Maury and "W" for Wilson High Schools. At Christmastime, Santa might have made a stop on Church Street to pick up Dutch dolls, toy firemen and policemen, or a set of miniature cowboys and Indians for diehard cowpokes. The Church Street Improvement League aggressively marketed the fineries and the ordinary available on their street. When the league was established, Ben Paul Snyder was its first president; Herbert B. Altschul, vice president; Louis Bartley, secretary; J.G. Madden, treasurer; A.J. Legum, publicity chair; and I. Wahrman, membership chair. Wahrman managed the Exchange Furniture Store, located at the corner of Main and Church Streets, in 1937. Exchange Furniture's original location was 262 Church Street when the store opened for business in 1917. The store specialized in factory samples, sold at lower cost, though still of high quality. The "exchange" in the name meant the store took old furniture in trade for relatively new pieces. A.J. Legum, on the other hand, opened his furniture company in 1920 at 805 East Liberty Street in Berkley and moved to Church Street in 1933. A relative newcomer to the thriving merchant district, Legum's company offered a complete line of everything for one's home and maintained one of the largest furniture stores in the city at that time, selling for credit and cash. (Charles S. Borjes, photographer. Courtesy of Kirn Library.)

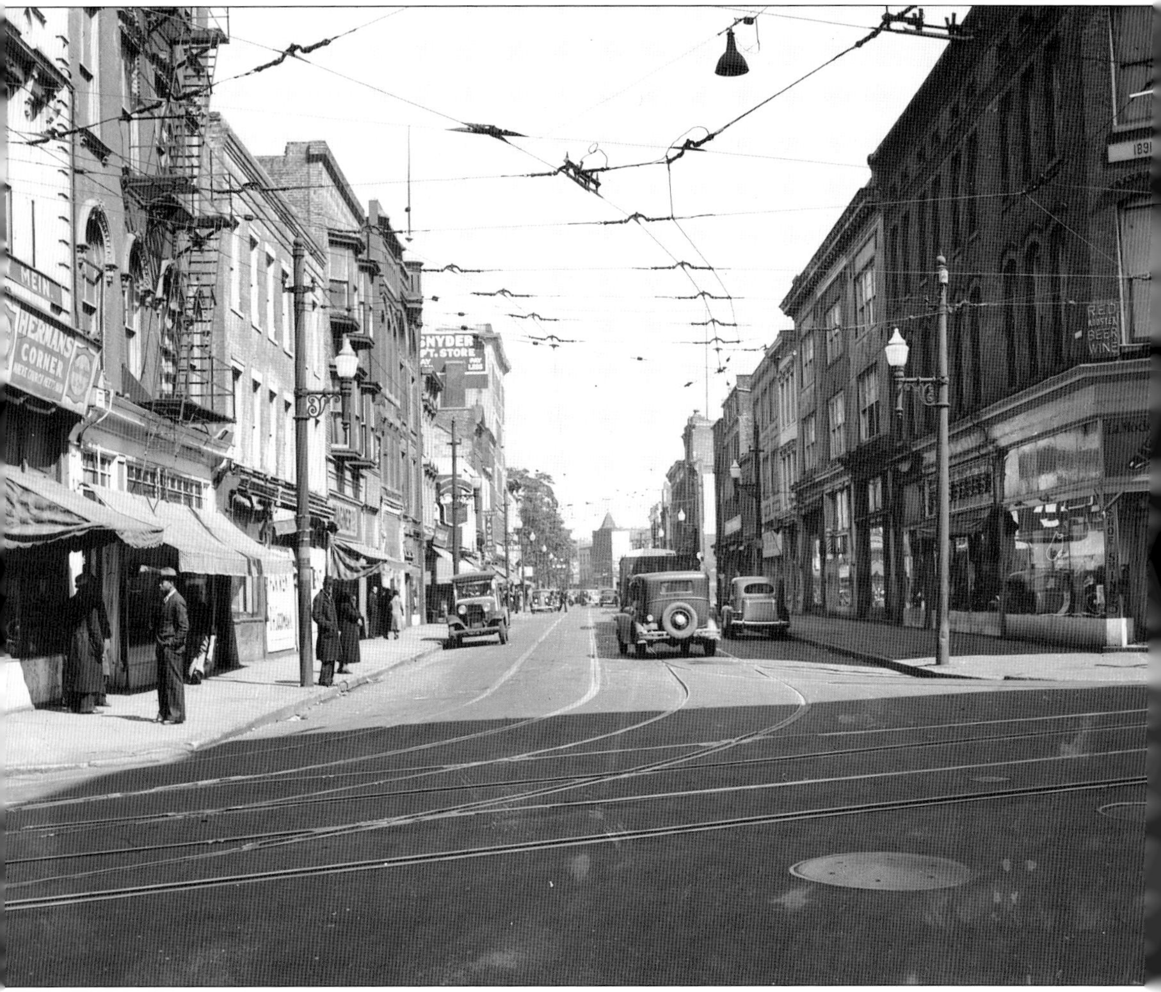

This image is quite a departure from the Harry C. Mann image, taken from the same perspective looking north on Church Street from Main Street in 1910. Charles S. Borjes took his picture on November 21, 1938. Much had changed, including the numbering sequence along city streets and the elimination of key thoroughfares, and though some of Norfolk's favorite establishments remained in business, the majority of them had already closed their doors for the last time. From the intersection of Main and Church Streets moving north, one would find Marx Shapiro, clothier (117); The Lorraine Press (120); Rosenberg Cleaning & Dye Works (122-126); Hofheimer's, Inc., shoes (127); Nat Liebman & Company, purveyor of wholesale notions (128); and H.B. Forrest Furniture Company (130-132). Upon reaching Bermuda Street and looking down Church Street, Mathew A. Tavss was still in the children's clothing business at 135 Church Street; Samuel Snyder, seller of women's wear (139); Mary K. Leventhal, owner of a children's wear store (143); Sidney's, women's wear (145); Fraternal Order of Eagles (148); L. Snyder Department Store (151-153); H. Comess Furniture Exchange, owned and operated by Harry and Morris B. Comess (158); The Bargain Store, clothing (157); Capitol Millinery Outlet Store (159); Pearl Kofsky's shoe repair business (162) came next; Capitol Dress Shop (163); Manhattan Shoe Repairing Company (165); Fleming Shoe Company (167); and crossing City Hall Avenue, there were new landmarks blended with the old. At 200 Church Street was an Army & Navy Store, and next to it at 201-203 was St. Paul's Episcopal Church. The street tended to thin in number of businesses, a marked contrast with the scene Harry C. Mann photographed in 1910. Passing the intersection of Market and Church Streets, one could find the likes of Thomas Thomas and Terkel Terkelsen at 242 Church and Isaac Jacobson's restaurant at 244, a rather odd pairing. Moving up to Holt and Church Streets, there were interesting and diverse business enterprises worthy of mention, including Charles Stores Company Junior Department Store (301-303); The Victor, apartments (302); Altschul's (317-319); W.P. Ford & Son Furniture (324-326); and Sid's Restaurant (328). It is interesting to note that Antonio LaGiglia was still active in his shoe stores, Tony's Shoe Stores, in 1937. His son Joseph had joined his father in the business, operating out of two locations, one on Church and the other on Main Street. W.P. Ford & Son was founded in 1919 by the late Captain W.P. Ford, who had resigned at that time as Norfolk's chief of police. He had been in business at the same location on Church Street for 18 years when this picture was taken, selling a complete line of furniture and expanding his operation to include two warehouses. Ford's wife was president of the company in 1937, while the couple's sons, W.P. Ford Jr. and Chesley A. Ford, managed the store and warehouse operation. (Courtesy of Kirn Library.)

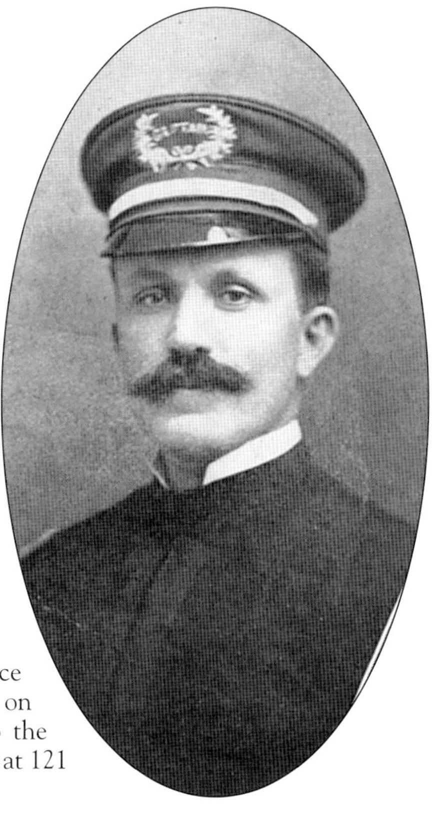

W.P. Ford, then first captain of the Norfolk Police Department, was photographed in 1909. Born on November 2, 1873, Ford was first appointed to the police department on October 24, 1904. He lived at 121 Windsor Avenue.

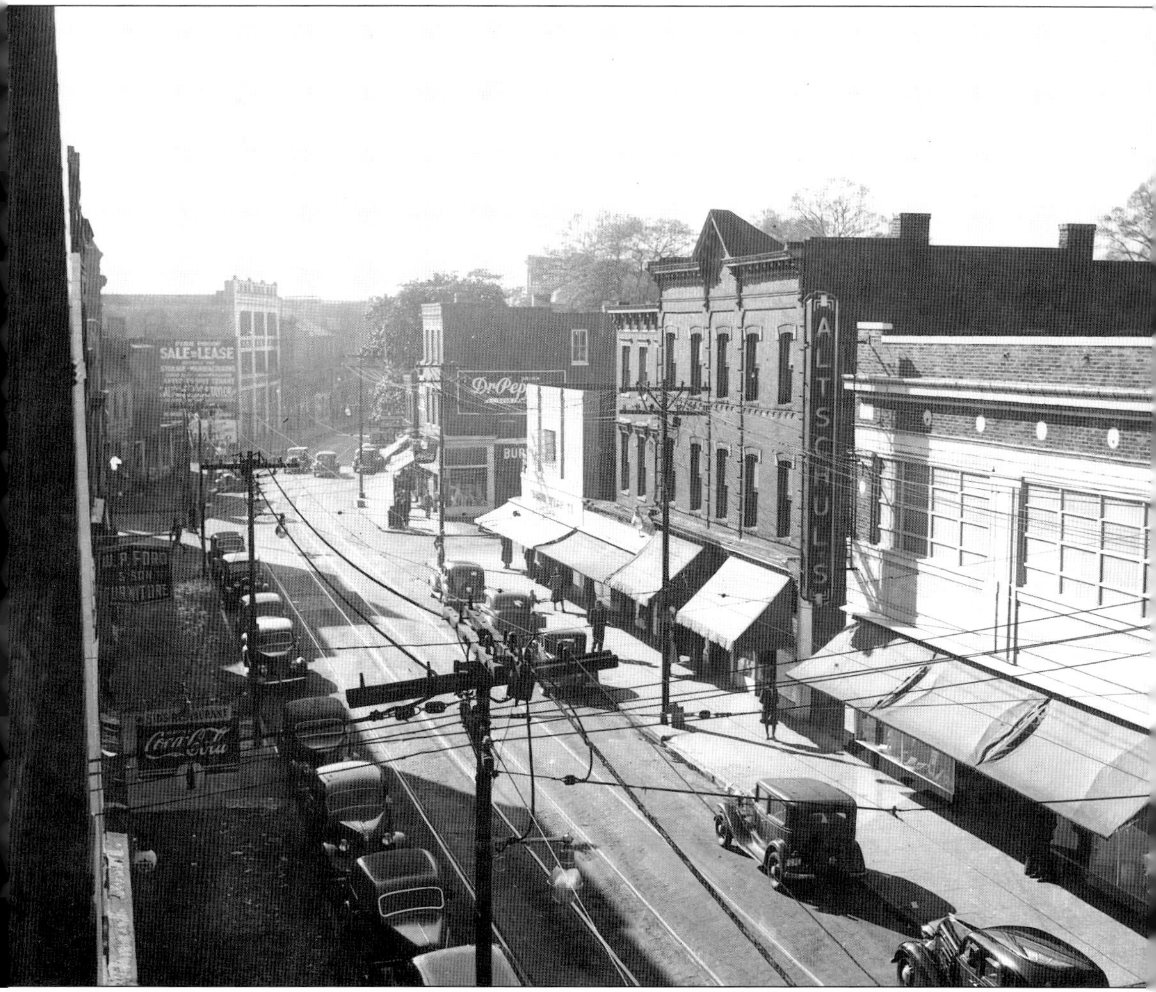

Church Street, looking south from the three-hundred-block demonstrates the evolving diversity of the oldest street in Norfolk's history. Chin Dick Laundry (560 Church Street) sits in the center, right foreground, north of Saint Paul's Episcopal Church, pinpointed by the patch of stately old trees beyond the Dr. Pepper sign. This picture was taken on Tuesday, October 10, 1939, a date that set a record for warm temperatures for Norfolk at that time: 92 degrees. The unseasonably hot weather lasted less than a week. (Charles S. Borjes, photographer. Courtesy of Kirn Library.)

Five

Norfolk's Harlem

"Droning a drowsy syncopated tune,
Rocking back and forth to a mellow croon,
I heard a Negro play.
Down on Lenox Avenue* the other night
By the pale dull pallor of an old gas light
He did a lazy sway . . .
He did a lazy sway . . .
To the tune o' those Weary Blues."

—From *The Weary Blues*, 1926
Langston Hughes, American poet (1902–1967)

*Lenox Avenue is a major street in Harlem.

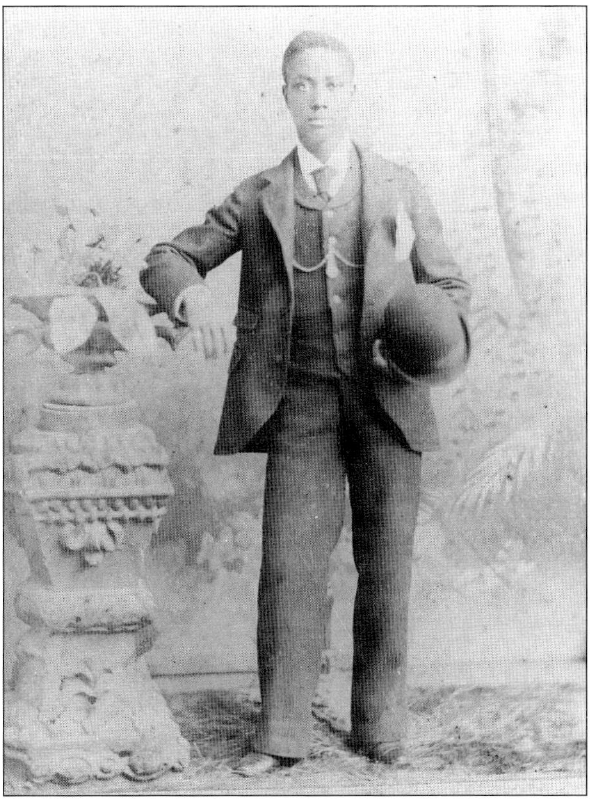

Taken *c.* 1892–1893, this photograph was made at the Richmond Art Gallery of Norfolk. The Richmond Art Gallery was located at 156 Main Street. The finely attired gentleman's identity is regrettably unknown. (Courtesy of Kirn Library.)

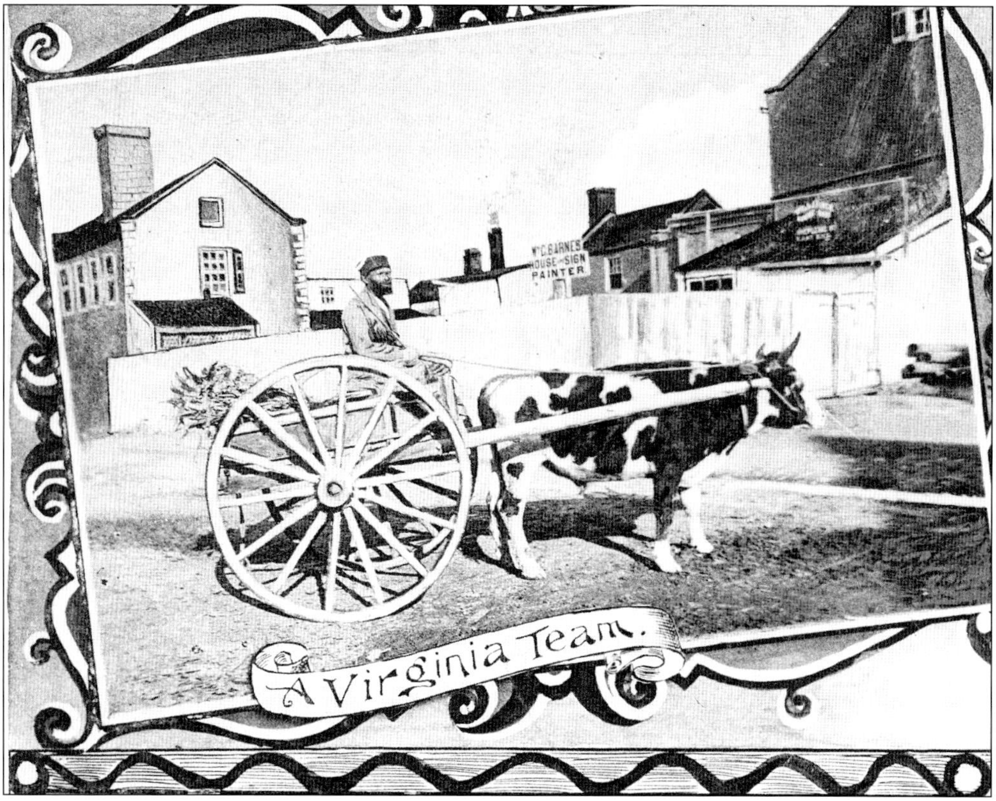

This photograph was taken in 1900 of a finely attired African-American laborer taking goods to market. The picture was taken behind a row of storefronts on Church Street. William C. Barnes, a house and sign painter, had a shop located directly behind the cow and cart.

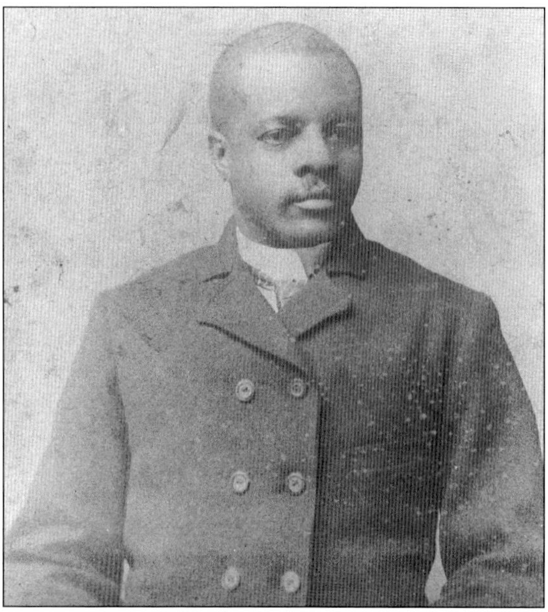

J.J. Faber took this picture c. 1900. Again, the identity of the subject is not known. (Courtesy of Kirn Library.)

A photographer named William Clinedinst at the Norfolk Photographic Studio took this lovely portrait of an unknown African-American woman *c.* 1900. Clinedinst also managed the studio, located at 314 Main Street. (Courtesy of Kirn Library.)

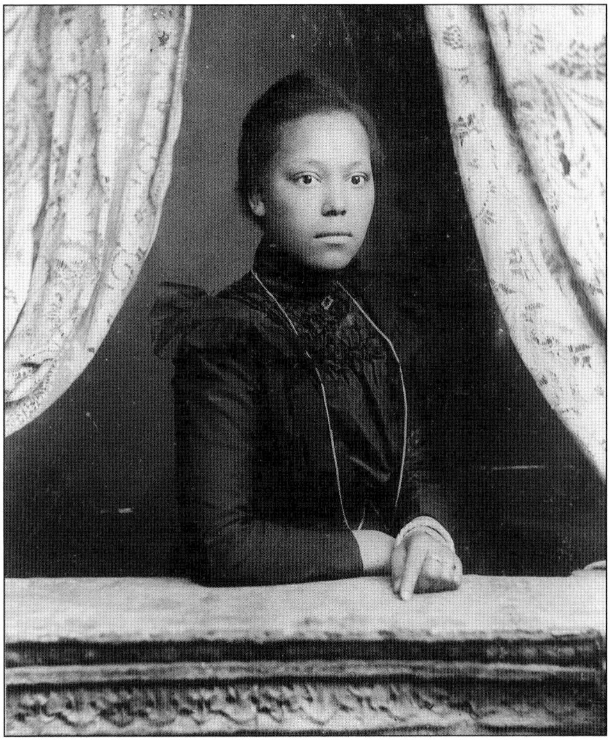

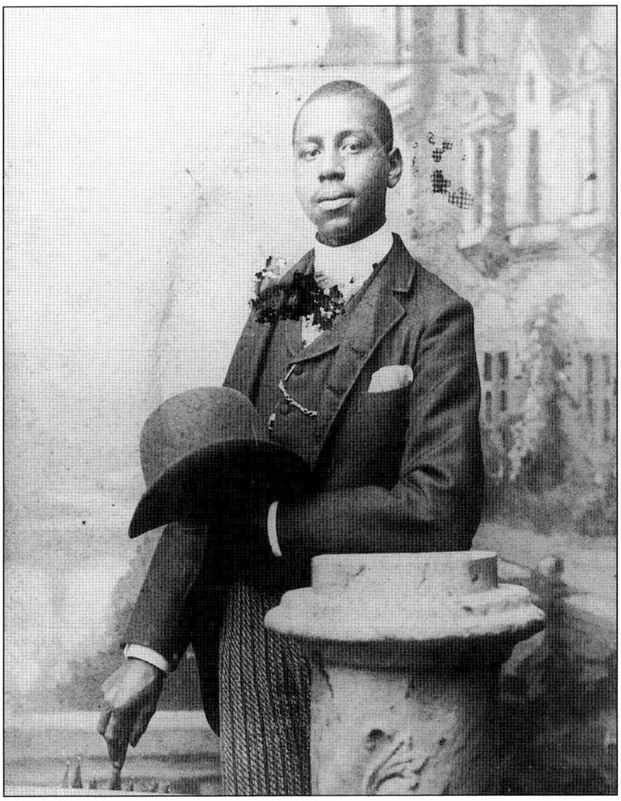

J.J. Faber's studio was responsible for some of the most distinctive portraits of prominent Norfolk residents both before and after the turn of the century. Though some of the city's finest photographic studios would not take pictures of African Americans and immigrants of Asian and Hispanic extraction, Faber's did. The African-American gentleman in this portrait, his identity unknown, was photographed *c.* 1900. (Courtesy of Kirn Library.)

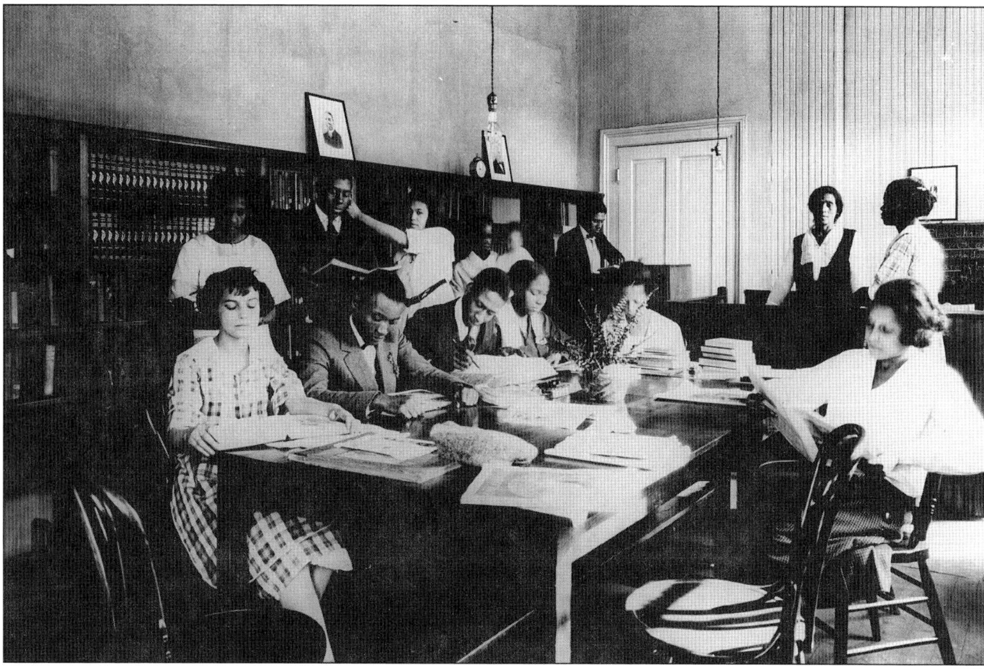

The Blyden Branch Public Library was photographed by an unknown photographer in 1921. Located on Chicazola Street, the library became an important centerpoint of the community. (Courtesy of Kirn Library).

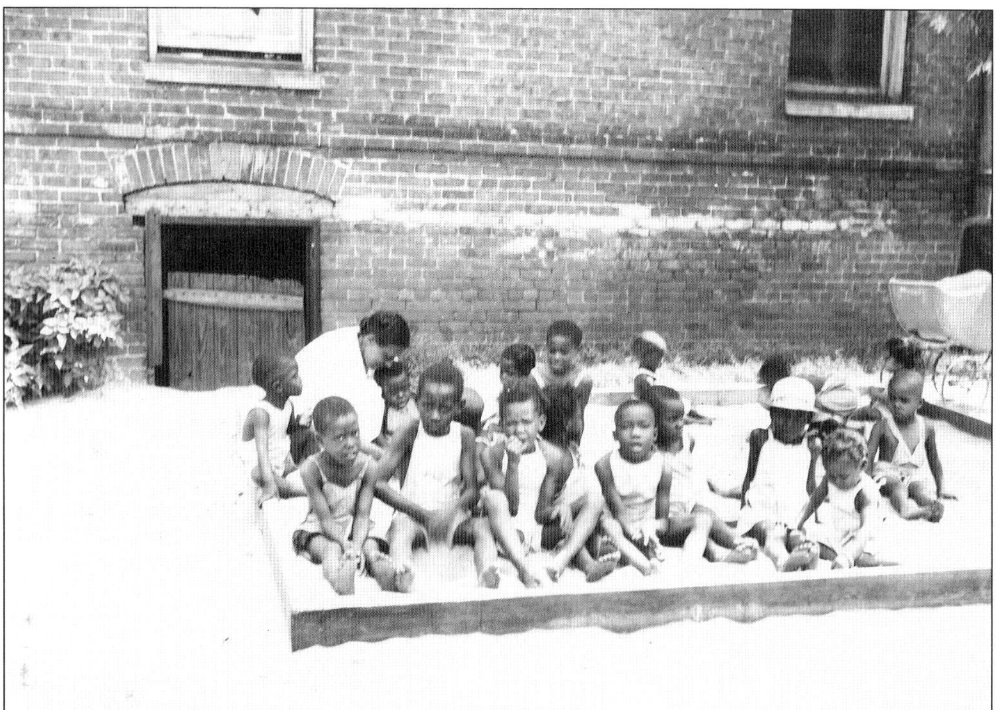

Children play in the sandbox of a day care facility on Chapel Street, July 7, 1939. (Charles S. Borjes, photographer. Courtesy of Kirn Library.)

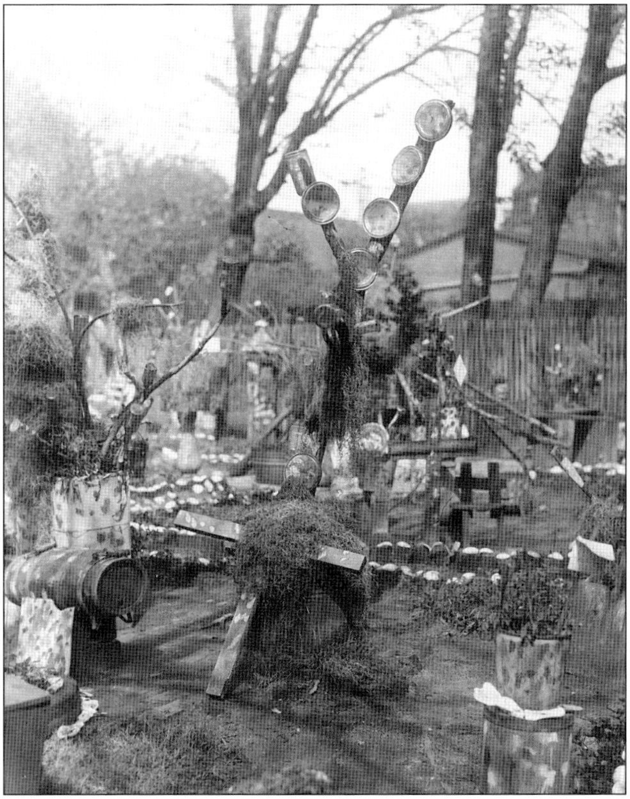

Aunt Sarah's Prayer Garden was located one block off Church Street at the corner of Cumberland and East Freemason Streets. The pictures shown here offer both general and detail views of this once-popular attraction, *c.* 1930.

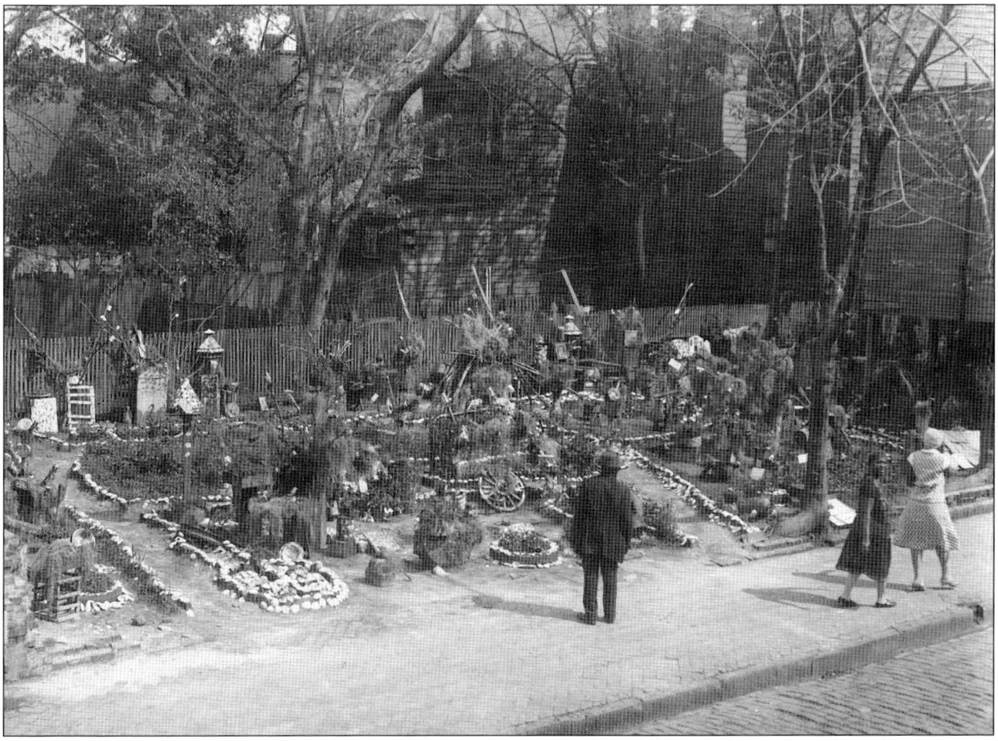

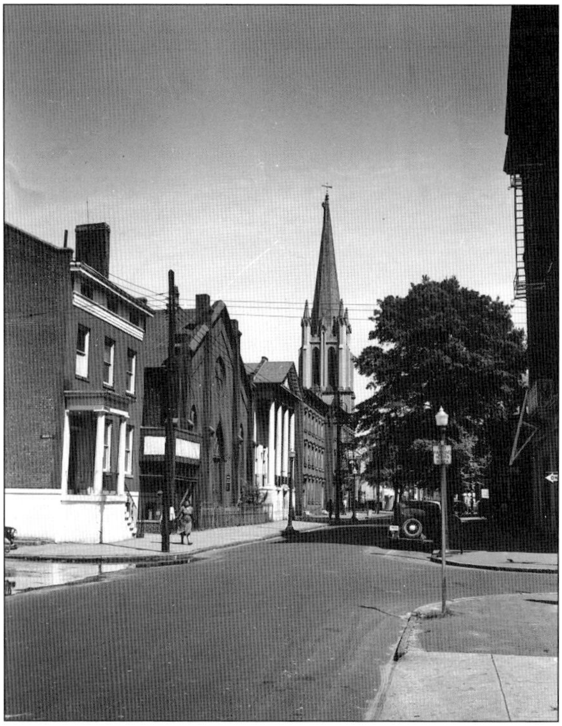

Freemason Street at Brewer Street caught the eye of photographer Charles S. Borjes in 1940. The Freemason Street Baptist Church looms prominently in the center of the picture. The second building on the left, located at 306 Freemason Street, was the Chinese Baptist Church. The local Chinese Baptist Church was admitted to the Portsmouth Association in 1931, and in 1935, it moved into the building formerly occupied by the First Christian Church. Reverend Sidney Quong, a longtime member of Freemason Street Baptist Church, became the church's pastor in May of 1947. The church was not listed in city directories after 1948, presumably due to the building being targeted for demolition in the first phase of the city's redevelopment and housing initiatives in the late 1940s and early 1950s. (Courtesy of Kirn Library.)

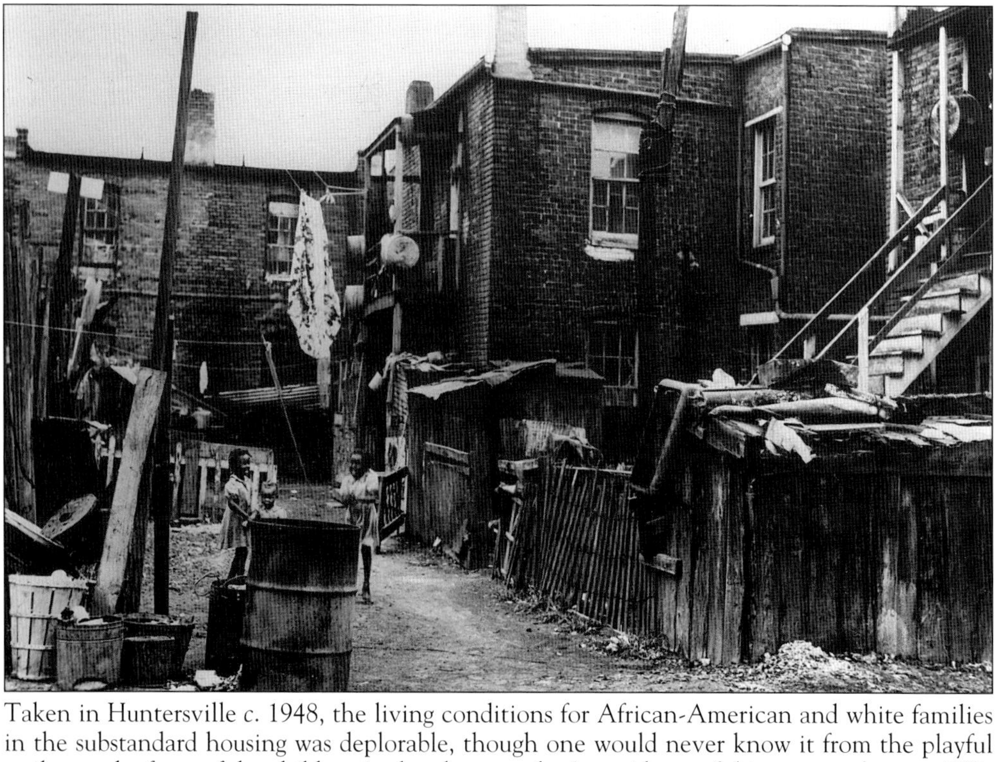

Taken in Huntersville *c.* 1948, the living conditions for African-American and white families in the substandard housing was deplorable, though one would never know it from the playful smiles on the faces of the children in the photograph. As residents of this area used to say: "We were so poor, we didn't know we were poor."

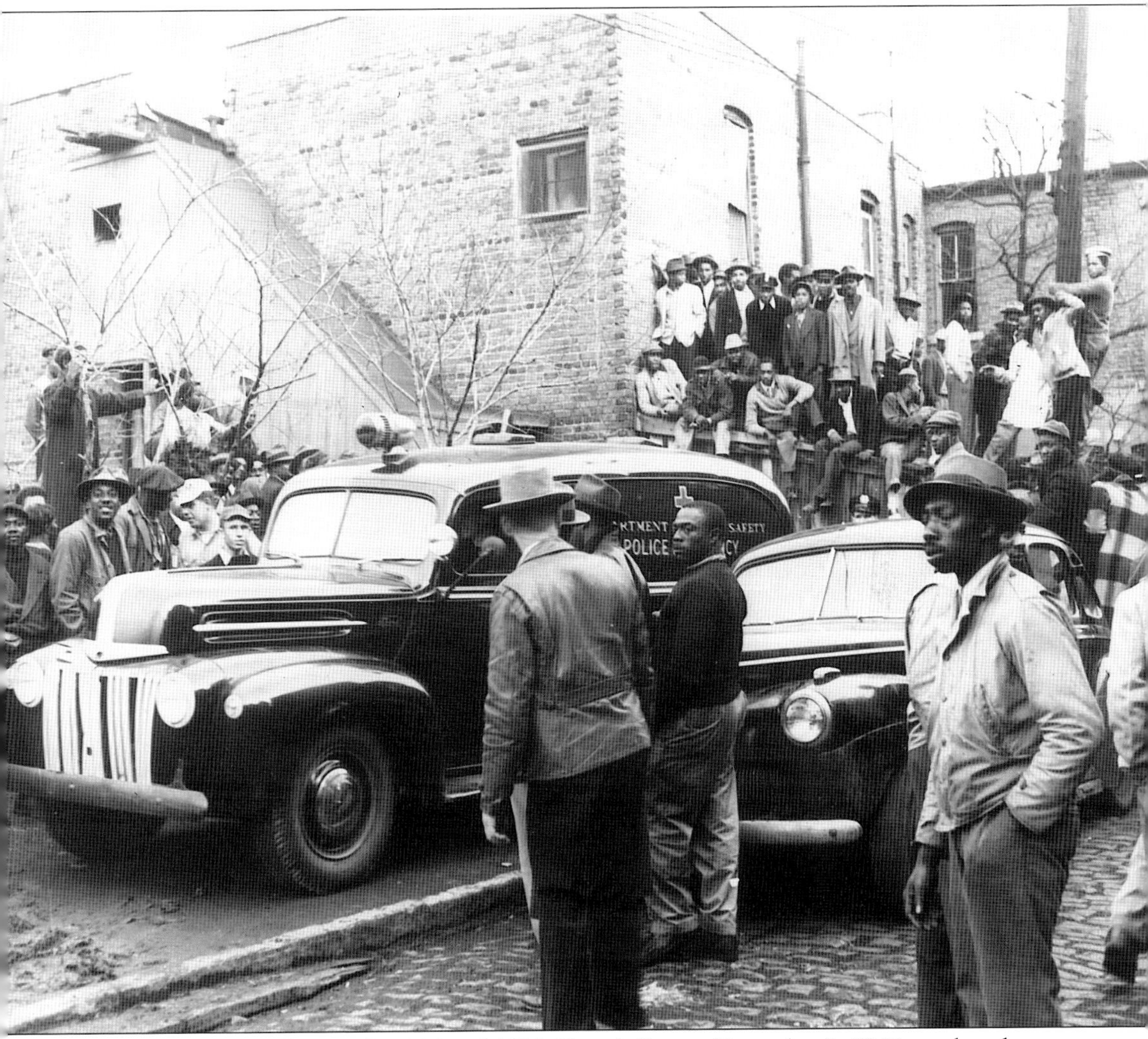

A coordinated numbers raid at 926 and 1007 Church Street, December 2, 1948, produced many onlookers and yielded a respectable number of arrests; 130 to be exact. Those arrested were charged with gambling in a numbers racket. The raid was led by Captain of Detectives Claude J. Staylor, who joined 11 other plainclothesmen he quickly divided into two groups, and entered the two gambling establishments simultaneously to avoid a tip-off. Staylor's group raided 926 Church Street, and the second group, led by Sergeant Everett G. Watts, raided 1007 Church Street. The 926 Church Street location was the largest and most highly organized gambling establishment in Norfolk at that time. The police seized thousands of numbers tickets, seven adding machines, eight telephones, one wheel of fortune, and a little over $3,000 in cash, all of which provided ample evidence of the crime. Fifteen white men, all of whom were known to have been involved in running the racket, were among those arrested; the rest were African American. Police quickly identified the key operators of both establishments. John McGowan, an African-American man, and Shep Miller and Raymond L. McHorney, both white, were charged with operating gambling establishments or devices. McGowan and Miller operated the 1007 Church Street gambling house, and McHorney the one at 926. It should be noted that the raid that took place at 1007 was literally across the street from the Attucks Theatre at 1008 Church Street. (Charles S. Borjes, photographer. Courtesy of Kirn Library.)

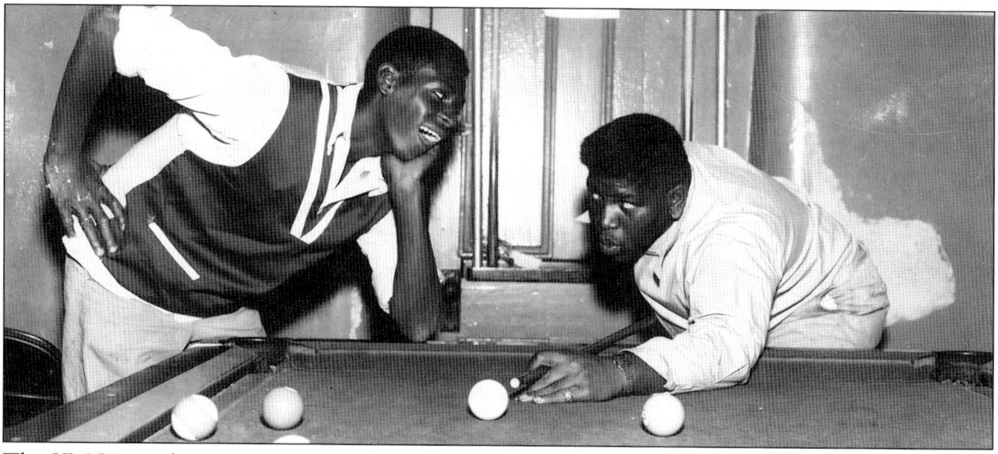

The YMCA took in young men such as the two pictured here to provide guidance and care for a segment of the population that received little attention from society. At the time the picture was taken, the Hunton YMCA had 45 beds and cared for an average of 280 men a week, not nearly enough space to meet the demand. Although about 25 percent of the men who stayed at the Hunton YMCA had family elsewhere, in Norfolk they were classified as unattached. The YMCA was a place these unattached men, usually in dire need of a place to stay and employment, could go. An unattached man might have been a migratory worker, merchant seaman, serviceman, waterfront worker, or mechanic. At the YMCA, he could get a clean shower, have his clothes laundered, play pool, ping-pong, basketball, checkers, dominoes, or use a reading room, piano, television, or radio. Both these young men, unattached, took time out of their day to shoot pool at the Hunton YMCA on Church Street, a Red Feather agency of the Community Chest. This picture was taken on October 8, 1953. (Charles S. Borjes, photographer. Courtesy of Kirn Library.)

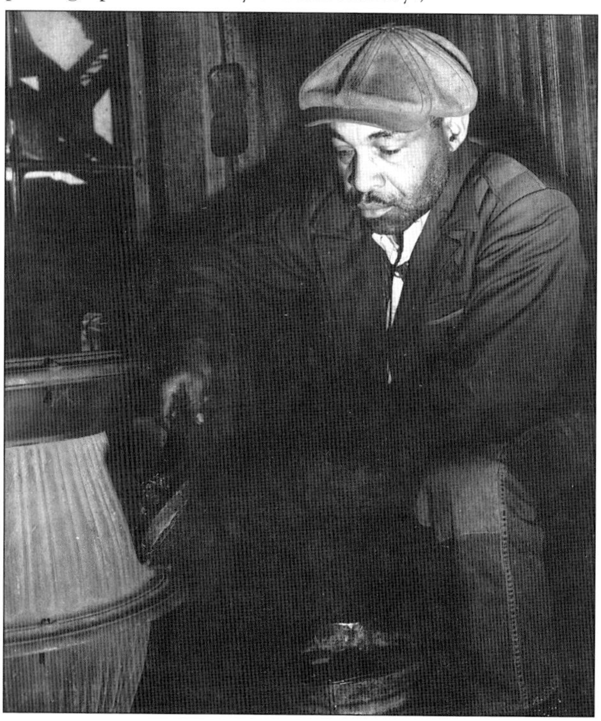

Stoking his stove, the man in this photograph seeks warmth during a cold wave that brought a low temperature of 17 degrees to Hampton Roads the morning of November 25, 1950, the day the picture was taken. The November 25 low temperature went lower than the previous low for the date—26 degrees—set in 1917, and gave residents their first look at snow, though it was only in the form of flurries. Severe cold temperatures nipped a budding Christmas shopping season, as potential shoppers chose to remain at home. (Charles S. Borjes, photographer. Courtesy of Kirn Library.)

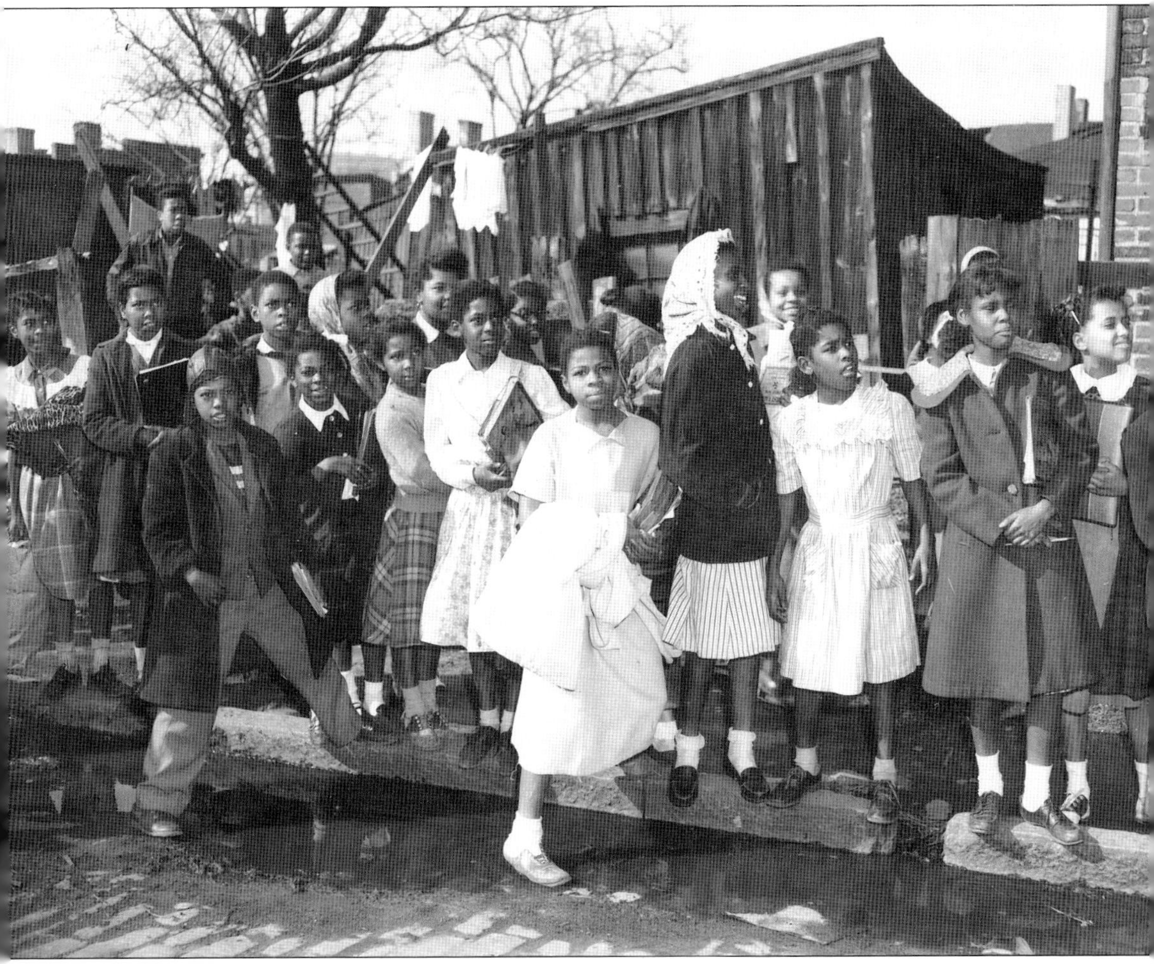

Just about the time school ended on March 27, 1952, two Norfolk firemen touched off a kerosene-fed fire in a two-story brick house at 712 Saint Paul Street (not yet a boulevard). One of the children making his way home from school shouted: "Look at the man settin' that house on fire! Boy, we gotta see what this is all about! Fireman doin' it with his own hands." Within minutes of setting the fire, the 50-year-old building was engulfed in flames. As black smoke billowed over Brambleton Avenue, a large crowd gathered, mostly children mesmerized by the fire practice. Lawrence M. Cox, executive director of the Norfolk Redevelopment and Housing Authority, provided the 1902 house for the fire department's use, but others were also used for fire practice in the authority's plan to rid the city of dilapidated housing. Live fire drills on Norfolk's slum housing was another way of clearing the properties under the city's redevelopment program. The day after the house on Saint Paul Street was cleared by fire, 722 Smith Street met the same fate. The house on Smith Street was reputed to be the headquarters of the notorious Belle Brown, who, in the words of some of the older male residents of Norfolk, ran an establishment that catered to the "carriage trade." One gentleman, who declined to be identified for obvious reasons, remarked at that time that "It was a very well known place. There was a maid on the front door and a lot of pretty entertainers. There were about forty rooms in the place and several parlors, if my memory is correct. I remember when I was a young man we would catch the old Queen Street streetcar to get there. Very fancy establishment." (Charles S. Borjes, photographer. Courtesy of Kirn Library.)

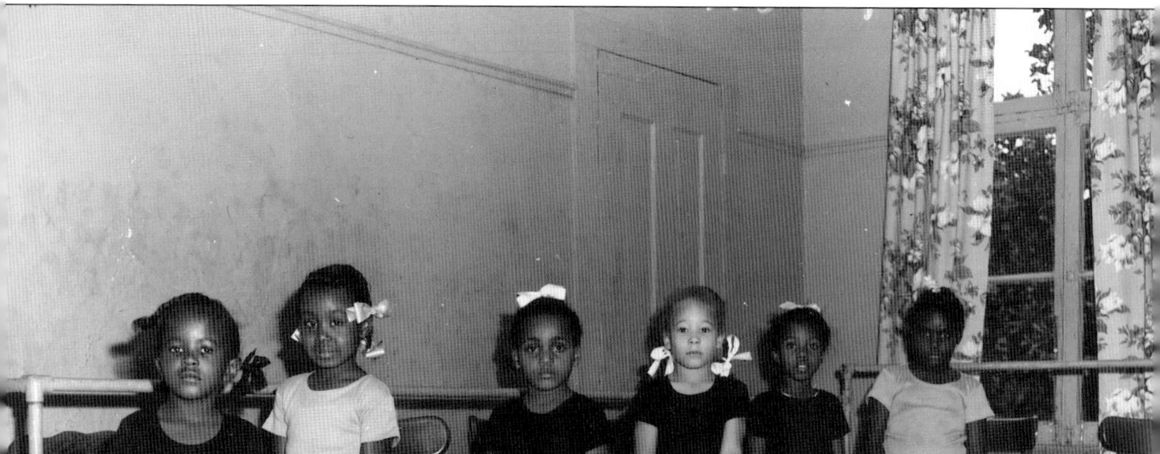

These little ladies pose in ballet's first position, pausing from their ballet class at the Phillis Wheatley Branch Black Young Women's Christian Association (YWCA), October 9, 1953. Ballet and tap lessons were given every Friday morning at 729 Washington Street, home of the YWCA. The YWCA provided programs designed to make teenagers better citizens, tiny tot classes, such as the little ballerinas in the picture, and civic and social activities for women from the African-American community. The house on Washington Street was abandoned by the YWCA shortly after this picture was taken, as the Phillis Wheatley Branch shifted its activities to the 40-room Mary Ballentine Home.

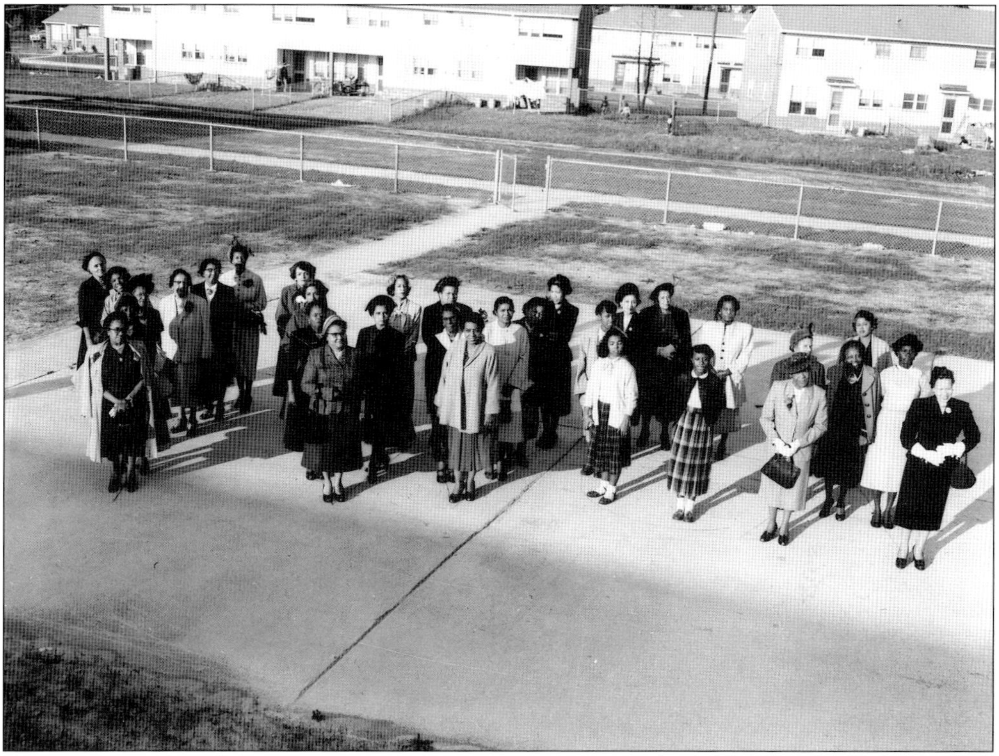

Pictured are the Phillis Wheatley Branch Black YWCA board of directors on Princess Anne Road, October 10, 1953. The YWCA was named for Phillis Wheatley (175?–1784), brought to America from Africa by slave traders, where she was sold on the Boston slave market in 1761. Taught to read and write by the daughter of Susannah and John Wheatley, Phillis soon began to write poems and had 39 of her poems published in 1773 as *Poems on Various Subjects, Religious and Moral.* This was likely the first book ever published by an African American in the United States. Wheatley is considered the first important African-American poet, though she died in nameless poverty in Boston at the approximate age of 30. (Jim Mays, photographer. Courtesy of Kirn Library.)

Mom's Day Out

Paid for by the Community Chest Fund, the Washington Street YWCA provided mothers with a well-earned respite from their little ones, offering organized activities for toddlers to pre-school-aged children. Women rounded up their children and coaxed them down Church Street to begin the day. Fashioned like the "mothers day out" we know today, as soon as a mother shooed the children up the porch and into the main room of the house used by the YWCA, she was joined by other mothers, waiting, gossiping, chatting, and smiling in anticipation, as day care providers took the children and the mothers socialized. While the children played upstairs, mothers started the day with a lecture on how to plan parties for their children, dressmaking, cooking, and saving money, progressing to a luncheon and hobby time. Mothers' activities aside, it was not so much what they did while at the YWCA, it was the change of pace. Gone for the day were the depressing tenement walls, the kitchen with broken fixtures and appliances, and other stark reminders of poverty for African Americans living in a Southern city before desegregation. The Phillis Wheatley Branch of the YWCA brightened the lives of women through its presence in the community, giving women, young girls, and small children a place of fellowship and dreams.

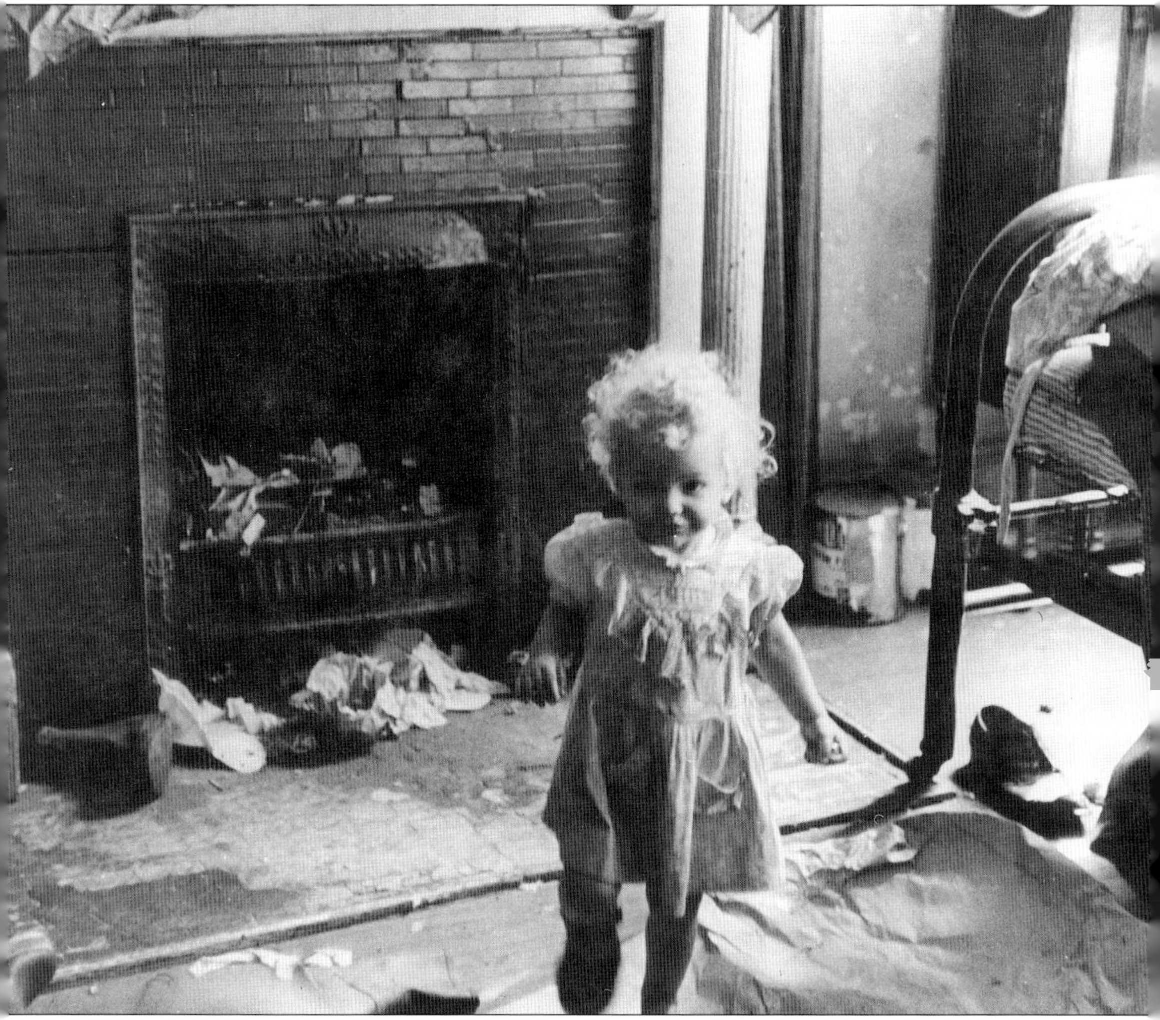

The way we were was not always the way we would like to remember. This child was photographed by an unknown photographer in the slums of Norfolk on Lincoln Street near Church Street in 1955. Norfolk Redevelopment and Housing Authority was created after WW II for the purpose of ridding the city of slums and replacing them with affordable housing. When the Federal Housing Act of 1949 was enacted, Norfolk became the first city in the nation to complete an application for funds from the program to begin its redevelopment projects. Norfolk embarked on an extensive plan to clear slums such as the one pictured here, homes that were largely rat-infested, and dilapidated structures without heat or proper sanitary conditions. The authority began with the area north of Brambleton Avenue and west of Church Street in 1951, and continued through such areas as Atlantic City from Front Street north along Colley Avenue to the medical center complex.

Six

THE APOLLO THEATRE OF THE SOUTH

"Naught but a slave was Attucks,
And yet how grand a hero, too.
He gave his life for freedom,
What more could royal sovereign do?

Well may we eulogize him!
And rear a monument of fame.
We hold his memory sacred;
We honor and revere his name.

A century has vanished,
Yet, through the years still rolling on
We emulate his bravery
And praise the deed he nobly done.

Then write in glowing letters
These thrilling words in history—
That Attucks was a hero,
That Attucks died for Liberty."

—From *Crispus Attucks*, 1899
Olivia Ward Bush-Banks, American poet (1869–1944)

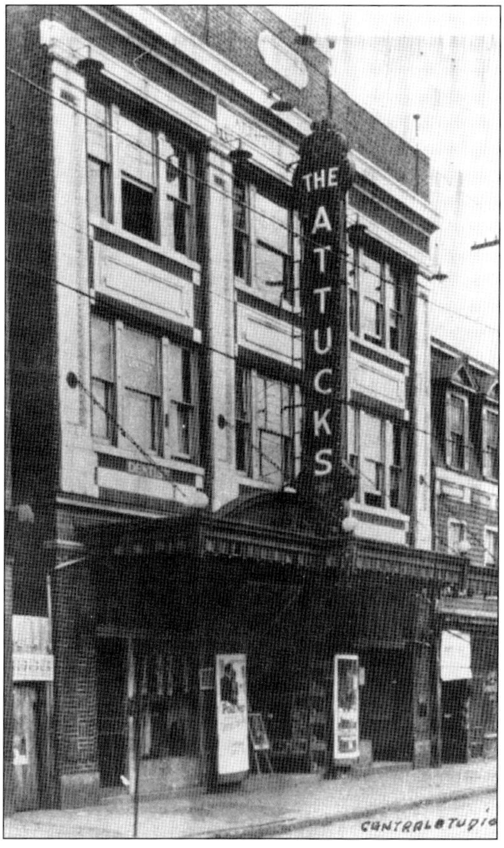

The Attucks Theatre was photographed by the Central Studio *c.* 1927. The Central Studio had a storefront at 923 Church Street and was owned by Mrs. Fannie E. Wainwright. Wainwright lived on Maple Avenue. Harvey Johnson, the Attucks' architect, was 25 years old when he designed the theatre. Johnson's architectural legacy to Norfolk included the Queen Street Baptist Church, the Union Commercial Bank, and Second Calvary Baptist Church. Though the Attucks was renamed the Booker T in December 1933 in honor of Booker T. Washington, the theatre continued to serve as the center of African-American culture and community into the early 1950s. (Courtesy of Crispus Attucks Cultural Center.)

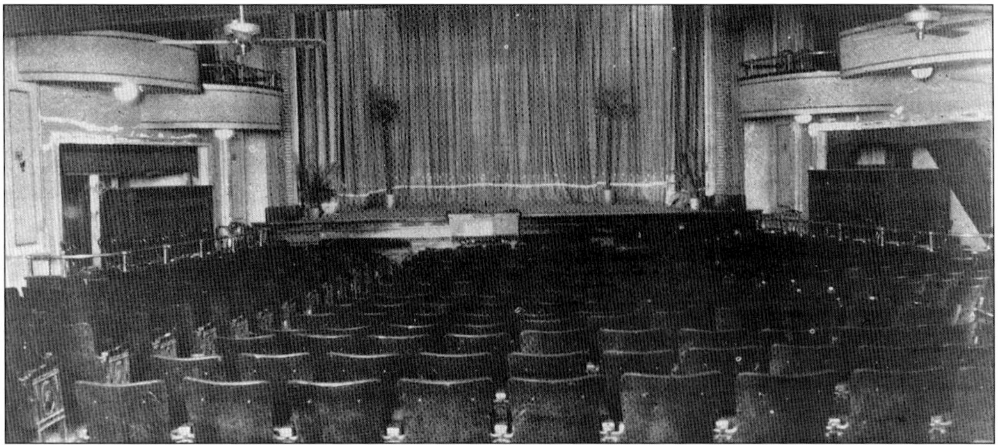

The interior of the Attucks Theatre, pictured as it appeared c. 1927, once seated 600 and featured the nation's most prestigious African-American performers, including Marian Anderson, Redd Foxx, Louis Armstrong, Erroll Garner, Count Basie, Lionel Hampton, Moms Mabley, Ruth Brown, Sarah Vaughan, Nat King Cole, Duke Ellington, and Slappy White, in addition to those mentioned below. The theatre headlined an incredible string of performers until 1952, after which the Attucks Theatre was no longer in business. (Courtesy of Crispus Attucks Cultural Center.)

The Apollo Theatre of the South

Located at 1008 Church Street, the legendary Attucks Theatre has long been a source of tremendous pride in Norfolk's African-American community. The old vaudeville and movie house is named for Crispus Attucks, the first colonist killed in the American Revolution. One of the most memorable aspects of the interior of the building is the large asbestos fire curtain portraying the scene of the Boston Massacre in which Attucks was killed along with several other Bostonians. Built in 1919, the building was a center of black culture in the "black downtown" of the city. The grand old theatre once had 600 seats and has often been compared to Harlem's Apollo Theatre in New York City as a Southern showcase for leading black entertainers and personalities who came to Norfolk on their tours. Among the great entertainers to grace her stage were Cabell "Cab" Calloway III, Bessie Smith, Ethel Waters, Dinah Washington, Little Jimmy Reed (born Leon Atkins), child star Smokey Robinson, The Flamingoes, The Orioles, LaVern Baker, Jackie Wilson, and Clyde McPhatter, a rock-and-roll legend who went on to form The Drifters. There were even local talent shows that featured now renowned rhythm-and-blues singer Gary U.S. Bonds, who became famous with a string of hits in the 1950s and early 1960s.

The three-story structure is also historically significant because it was designed by an African-American architect of importance, the late Harvey N. Johnson. The Attucks was also financed and constructed by African Americans, making the theatre wholly unique among black entertainment facilities in the United States. The Attucks Theatre has been listed on the National Register of Historic Places since 1982 and is currently owned by Norfolk Redevelopment and Housing Authority. The theatre holds the unique distinction of being the only original building left standing in the Church Street Business District.

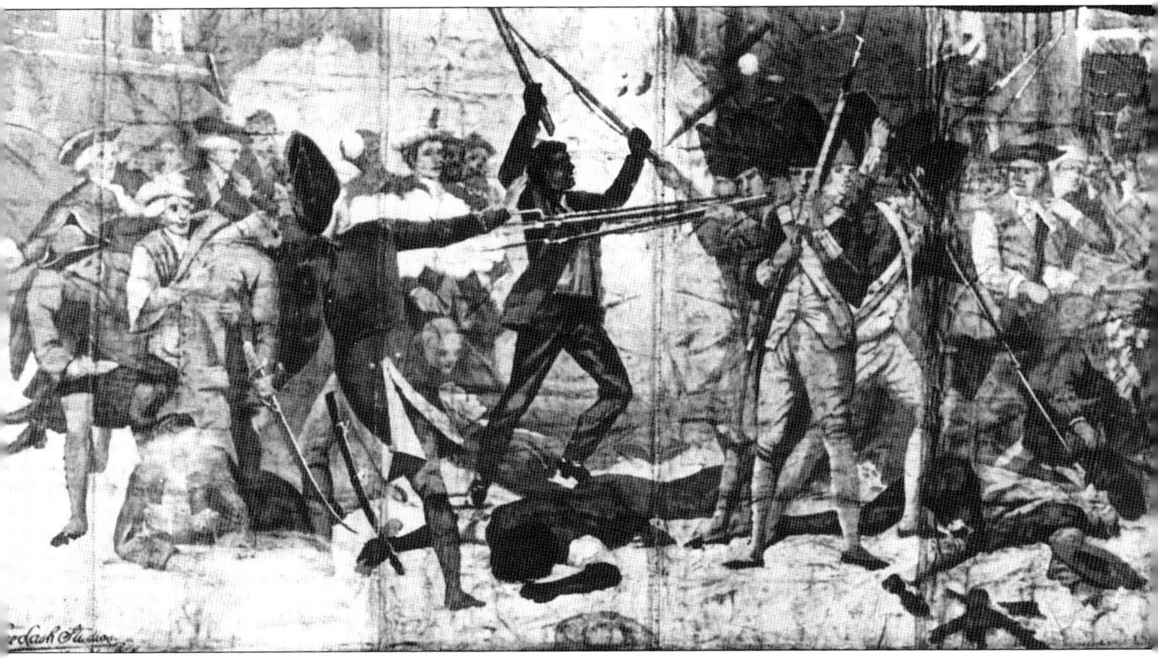

The fire curtain in the Attucks Theatre, depicting the death of African-American patriot Crispus Attucks at the Boston Massacre, is pictured here in a c. 1997 photograph. Crispus Attucks was born in 1723 and grew to manhood as a slave. His father was Prince, an African shipped to New England to become the slave of Colonel Buckminster of Framingham, Massachusetts. Prince married Nancy, a Natick Indian and the mother of Crispus, Phebe, and another boy who died in infancy. By the age of 16, Crispus was sold to Deacon William Brown, also of Framingham, and it was during his time in the ownership of Brown that Crispus furtively applied for a job as a whaler. In the fall of 1769, he returned to Boston, safe in the knowledge that 20 years had passed since he had escaped slavery, and no one was looking for him anymore. Attucks escaped slavery at the age of 27 and came to Boston where he became a whaler. On the night he was killed, March 5, 1770, Attucks was leading a group of approximately 30 sailors armed with cudgels and sticks against a British sentry they ascertained had beaten a young apprentice senseless. British troops came to the defense of their own, and Attucks was subsequently killed in the fray that ensued. Called "the Molatto who was shot," Attucks's future as an American hero was in serious question immediately after the events of March 5. Samuel Adams called Attucks the leader of "a motley rabble of saucy boys, negroes and mulattoes, Irish teagues and outlandish jack tarrs" out to pick a fight. This would make Attucks's motivations on the evening in question less than patriotic or noble. Several decades of American history would pass before Attucks was called a true American hero. Harriet Beecher Stowe, author of *Uncle Tom's Cabin*, wrote in 1855: "It was not for their own land they fought, not even for a land which had adopted them, but for a land which had enslaved them, and whose laws, even in freedom, oftener oppressed than protected. Bravery, under such circumstances, has a peculiar beauty and merit." (Millard Arnold, photographer. Courtesy of Norfolk Redevelopment and Housing Authority.)

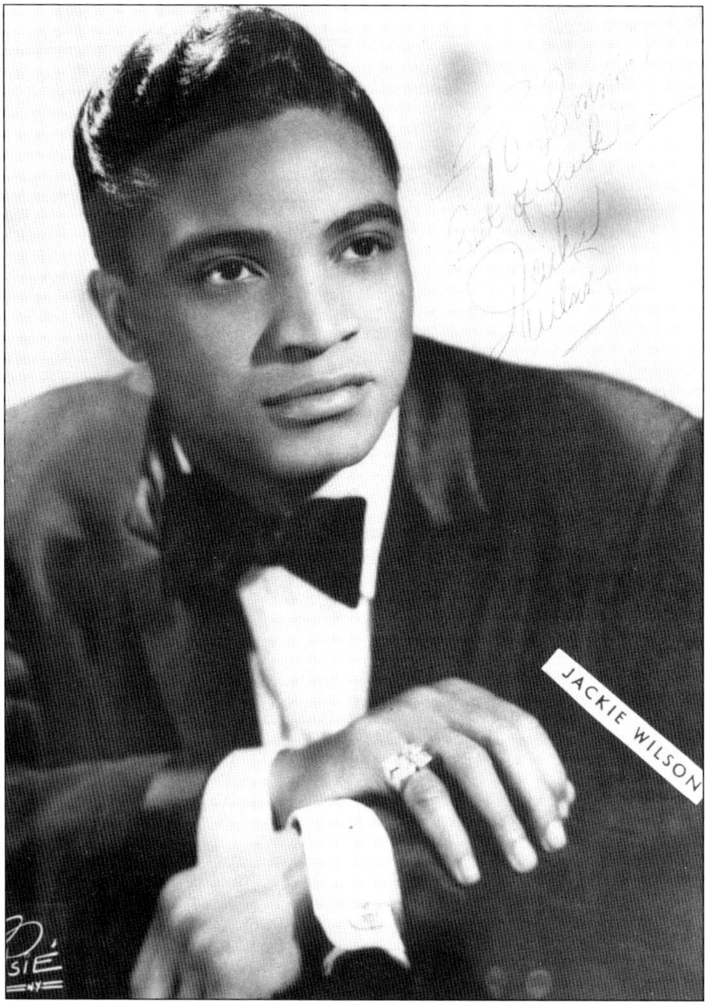

Jackie Wilson was born in Detroit, Michigan, on June 9, 1934. The photograph shown here, given to Bonnie McEachin *c.* 1952 while Wilson was in Norfolk for a performance at the Attucks, shows Jackie Wilson before he departed Billy Ward and The Dominoes for a successful solo career. Billy Ward discovered Wilson at the age of 18 in Detroit's Fox Theater. Ward was trying to replace his departed lead singer, Clyde McPhatter, and Wilson fit the bill. Before leaving The Dominoes for good, McPhatter trained his replacement, leaving a profound influence on Wilson's style and vocal performance. Wilson produced an astonishing range of rhythm-and-blues and pop hits in the late 1950s and early 1960s. While his singing career flourished, his private life became his undoing. While staying in a New York City hotel in 1961, he was shot and gravely wounded by one of the women he dated. Wilson lost a kidney and nearly his life, but despite this setback, he continued to sing and record hit songs. Jackie Wilson, known for two decades as "Mr. Entertainment," suffered a stroke and collapsed on stage while performing his signature song, "Lonely Teardrops," in Cherry Hill, New Jersey, on September 29, 1975. The stroke left him bedridden and mentally incapacitated until he died on January 21, 1984, in Mount Holly, New Jersey, of pneumonia. His life ended in indignity when Wilson was buried in an unmarked grave in his native Detroit, an affront that was ultimately corrected three years later. (Courtesy of Crispus Attucks Cultural Center.)

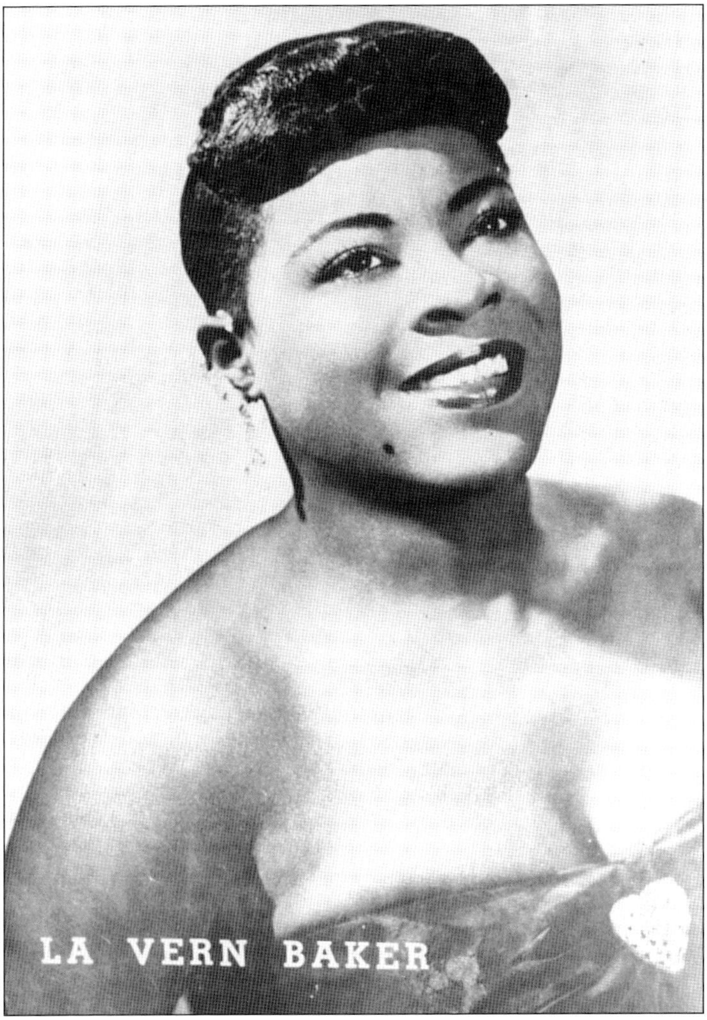

Born Delores Williams, LaVern Baker was considered one of the most talented and versatile vocalists to meld the sweet sounds of rhythm-and-blues with jazz and blues, and later, rock-and-roll. Baker came by her singing ability naturally. The niece of Memphis Minnie, Baker had a powerful voice and someone to encourage her early in life. She began her singing career under the stage name Little Miss Sharecropper when only a teenager, recording songs by that name and others until finally settling on LaVern Baker. Baker recorded with Atlantic Records from 1953 to 1962, cutting half a dozen singles that went high on the charts: "Tweedle Dee" and "Jim Dandy," and it was during this period that her career took off. Like most African-American performers of this period, Baker's greatest hits were covered by a white singer, Georgia Gibbs, whose versions of songs outsold Baker's own. Radio stations adhering to racist principles refused to play black recording artists like Baker in favor of the white vocalists who were popular with mainstream listeners. As radio stations began to let go of their racist policies, Baker's music thrived on the rhythm-and-blues chart. She had an enormously popular hit, "See See Rider," in 1962. While entertaining troops in Vietnam in 1969, Baker contracted pneumonia and was treated in the Philippines where she remained in residence for nearly 20 years before returning to the United States. (Courtesy of Crispus Attucks Cultural Center.)

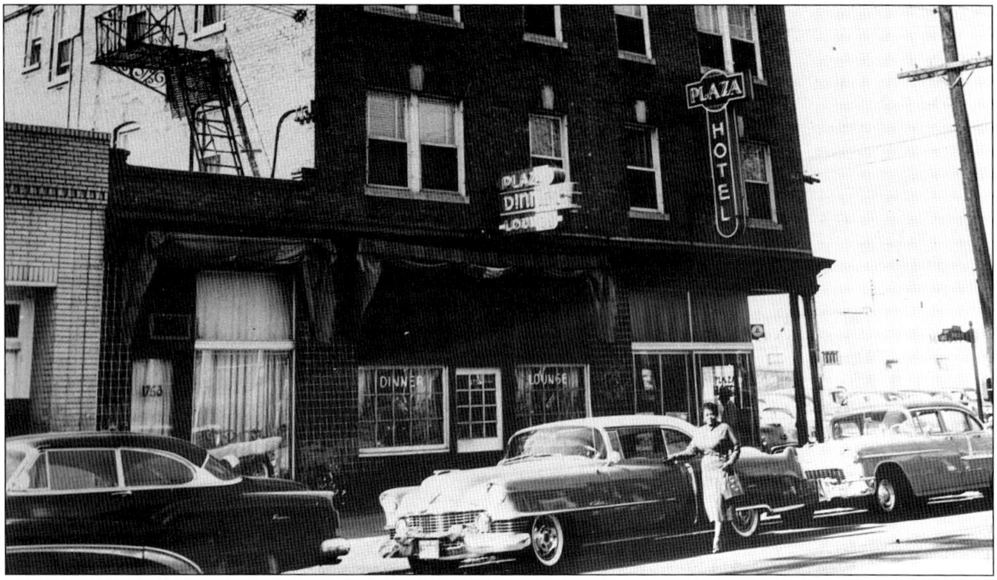

The Plaza Hotel, located at the corner of Eighteenth and Church Streets, was the only hostelry in which African-American entertainers and personalities appearing at the Attucks Theatre could stay while they were in Norfolk. Owned by Bonnie E. McEachin, who passed away in 1997, the Plaza held many memories of a time long ago when Church Street jumped to the sounds blues and jazz, and some of the country's best musicians and singers entertained crowds in the Attucks and nearby nightclubs. In the photograph shown here, taken *c.* 1955, Bonnie McEachin posed in front of The Plaza, known as The Hague when it originally opened near the turn of the century. (Courtesy of Crispus Attucks Cultural Center.)

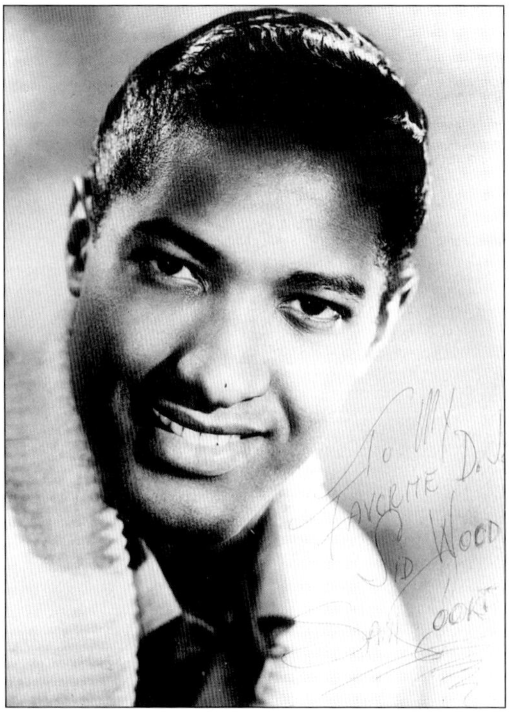

Sam Cooke, born January 22, 1931, began his singing career with a gospel group called the Soul Stirrers, but was let go from the group after recording a secular song. Cooke's unmistakable string of hits included "You Send Me," "Only Sixteen," "Wonderful World," "Another Saturday Night," "Chain Gang," and "A Change Is Gonna Come." Sam Cooke started his own record label, SAR, with J.W. Alexander in late 1959. Sadly, Cooke was shot to death during an argument at a motel in Los Angeles, California, after a woman accused him of attacking her. The date was December 11, 1964. The photograph shown here was given to Sid Woods in Norfolk *c.* 1950. (Courtesy of Crispus Attucks Cultural Center.)

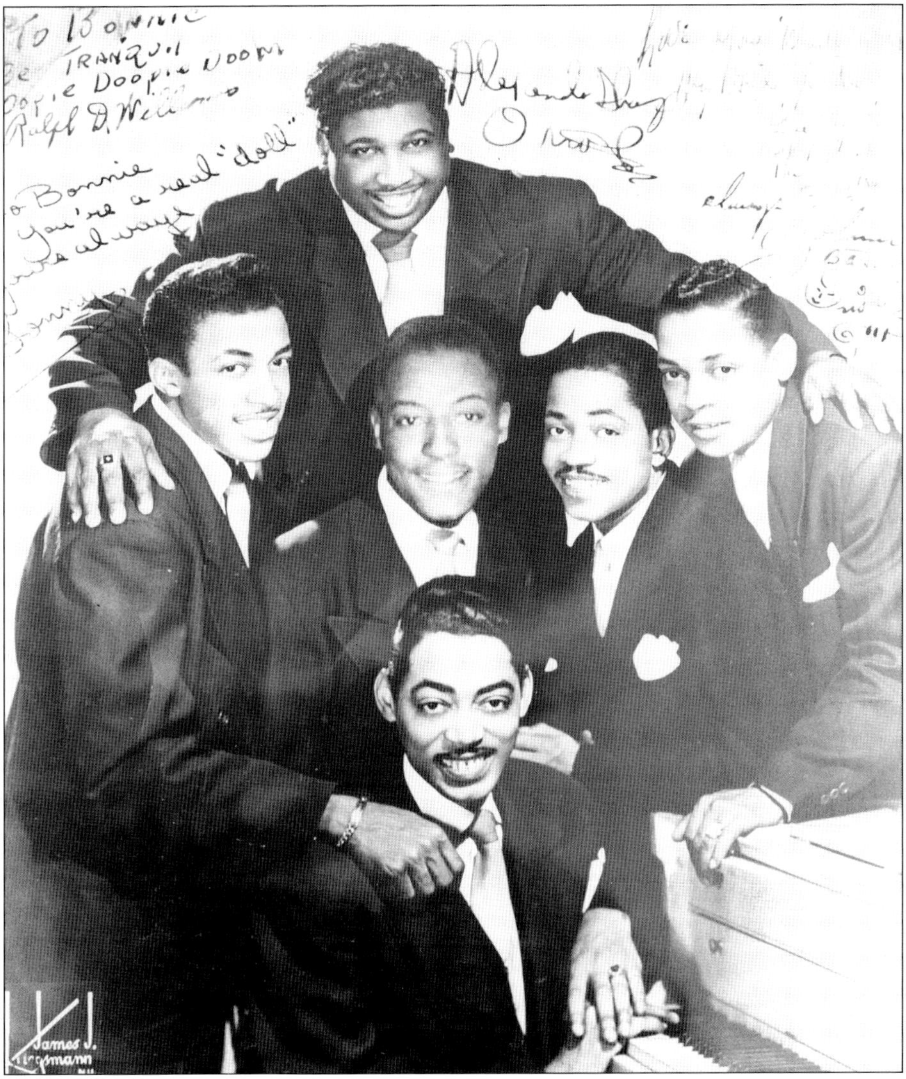

The Orioles, shown here c. 1950, performed at the Attucks in their heyday. The original Orioles are regarded as the first vocal rhythm-and-blues group. They formed in 1947 as the Vibranaires, in their hometown of Baltimore, Maryland, but changed their name to the Orioles, Maryland's state bird, and soon thereafter began performing at Harlem's Apollo Theater and Arthur Godfrey's talent show. It was the Orioles who established the doo-wop sound, wordless harmonies encompassing the tenor vocals of Sonny Til (born Earlington Carl Tilghman) and George Nelson. The group had three No. 1 singles in the late 1940s and early 1950s: "It's Too Soon To Know," "Tell Me So," and "Crying in the Chapel." The original Orioles were known for purely vocal music, accompanied only by Tommy Gaither on guitar. A tragic automobile accident in 1950 took the life of Tommy Gaither and seriously hurt George Nelson and Johnny Reed. Soon after Nelson and Reed recovered and Gaither was replaced, the Orioles recorded their best record, "I Need You So," a tribute to Gaither. Between 1948 and 1954, the Orioles had cut 121 sides for their record label—Natural/Jubilee—including the classics: "You Belong to Me," "Hold Me, Thrill Me, Kiss Me," and "I Need You So." The group broke up in 1954. (James J. Kriegsmann, photographer. Courtesy of Crispus Attucks Cultural Center.)

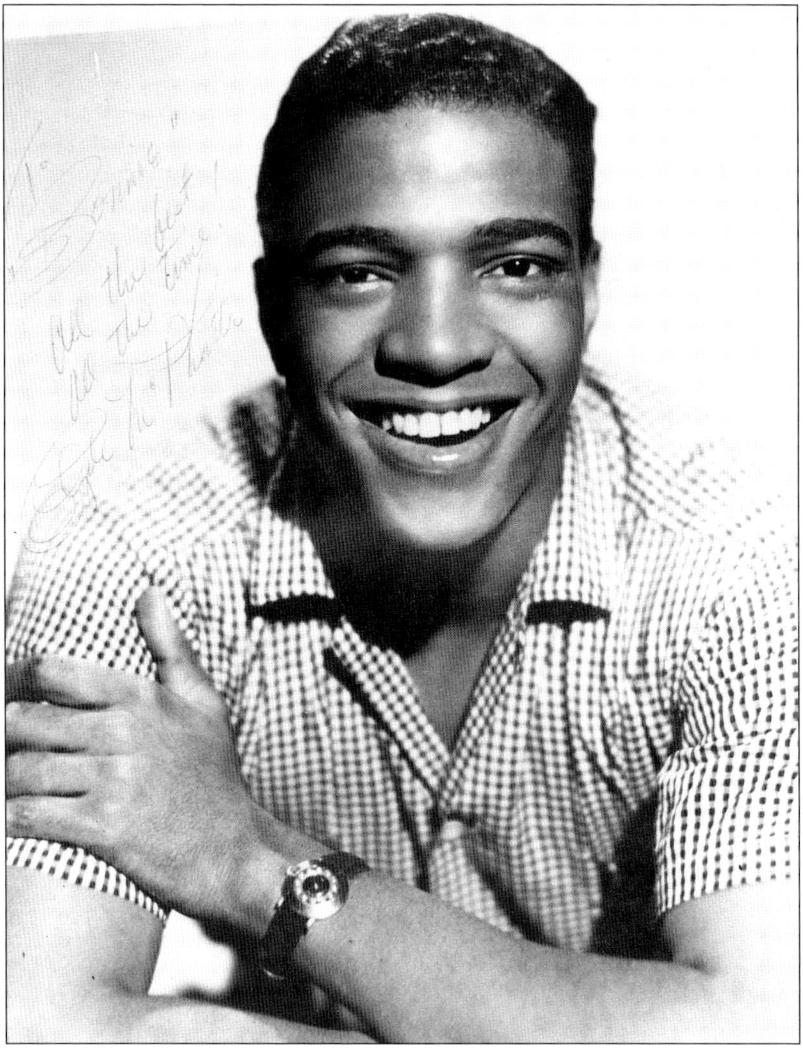

Clyde Lensley McPhatter was born in Durham, North Carolina, in 1932, son of a preacher who moved from Durham to New Jersey when Clyde was a boy. Clyde met Billy Ward and joined The Dominoes in 1950. After nearly three years of successful recordings, McPhatter left the group to form his own—The Drifters. The Drifters' "Money Honey" became an instant classic in 1953, reaching No. 1 on the rhythm-and-blues chart. The Drifters enjoyed another No. 1 "Honey Love" and hits like "Such A Night" and a doo-wop version of "White Christmas" before McPhatter was drafted by the United States Army in 1954. Though the group continued to record more hits into the 1960s, Clyde never rejoined them. After his discharge from the army in 1956, he launched a solo career, and by 1958, he had the biggest hit of his entire career, "A Lover's Question," the quintessential blending of doo-wop and rhythm-and-blues. This success eventually led to another—"Lover Please"—a top forty pop song in 1962. McPhatter was headlining at the Attucks Theatre *c.* 1952, when the photograph shown here was presented to Bonnie E. McEachin. Clyde McPhatter waged a personal war with alcoholism most of his adult life. He died of a heart attack at the age of 40 on June 13, 1962. (Courtesy of Crispus Attucks Cultural Center.)

Seven

Life on the Street

"And hard day-objects of the street
Grow soft, in the long light, and sweet.
Noon's hot fortissimo still clings,
Muted in many murmurings;
And with the lingering light o'erspread
My thoughts are all new garmented.
Far down the block in yellow ease
Behind a row of gold-tipped trees . . ."

—From *City Evening*, 1929
E.B. White, American essayist (1899–1985)

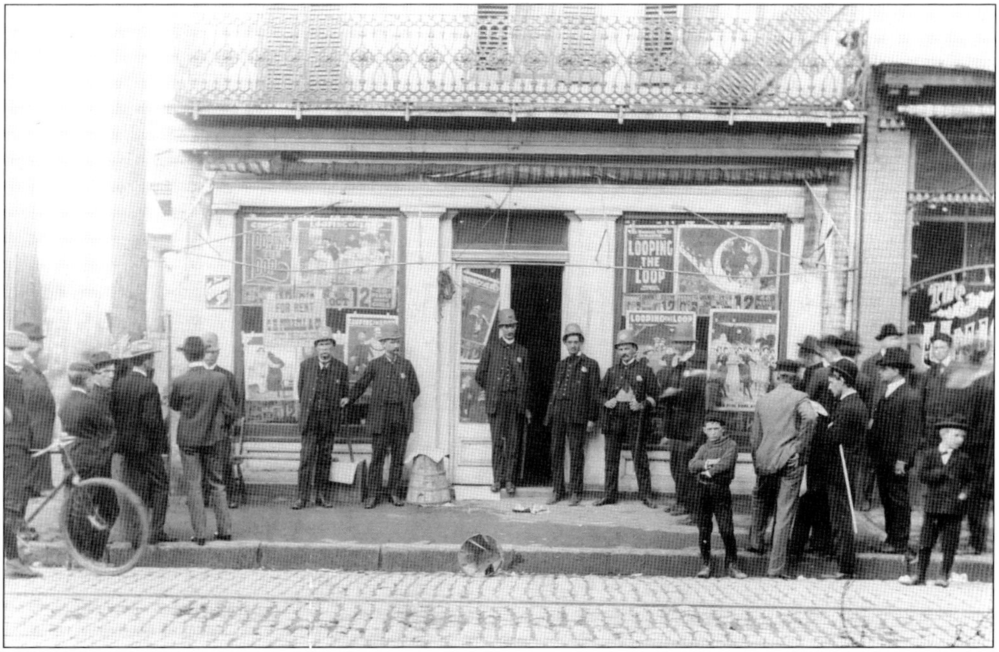

Election day at the northeast corner of Fenchurch and East Main Streets looks like a scene from a Keystone cops silent film. The picture was taken on October 13, 1903, during primaries. A voting area has been set up in a storefront for rent, and the policemen seem to be on hand to quell any disturbances, which were quite common during the days of Old Ring politics in Norfolk. Before the ward system died the first time in the city, in 1918, Old Ring city management was a carefully orchestrated plan: make the city flow freely with liquor, gambling, gaming, prostitution, and election tampering. Mobs often gathered at the polling areas, chasing away discordant voters. The gentleman with the cane in the right foreground is J.M. Arnold, later commonwealth attorney for Norfolk in the early 1930s.

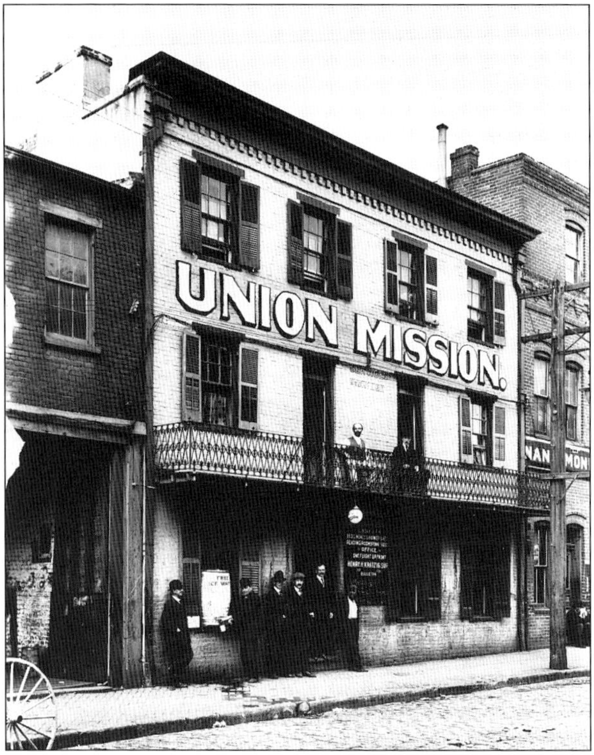

Norfolk's Union Mission was under the supervision of Reverend Henry H. Kratzig when Harry C. Mann took this picture c. 1915. The Union Mission, found at 51 Church Street, was under Kratzig's tutelage from 1915 through 1920. Kratzig had taken the reigns of the mission from longtime director Reverend J.R. Monica. The Union Mission was established in Norfolk in 1892, and held religious services every evening as well as a Sunday school for Chinese children. The mission provided room-and-board for men down on their luck, tending to their physical and religious betterment. An industrial school housed within the mission taught countless men carpentry skills and a shoemaker's trade. The library and reading room were places for those in need of quiet contemplation. (Courtesy of the Library of Virginia.)

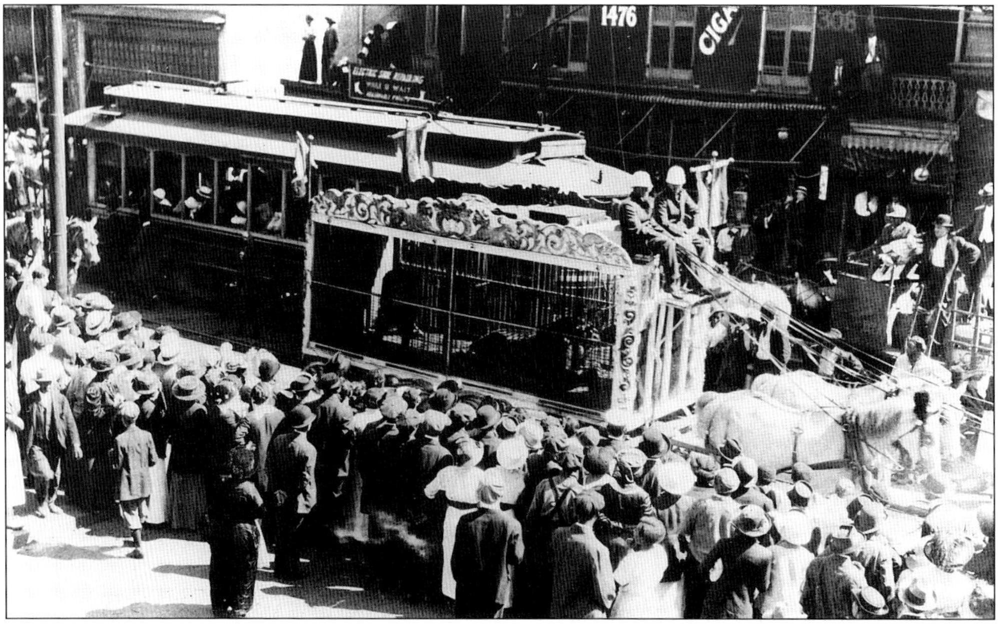

A circus parade, moving between Holt and Mariner Streets, enthralled crowds, especially the children, as it passed. The year was 1915, and this is one of the earliest photographs of a circus parade in Norfolk. The photographer is unknown. (Courtesy of Kirn Library.)

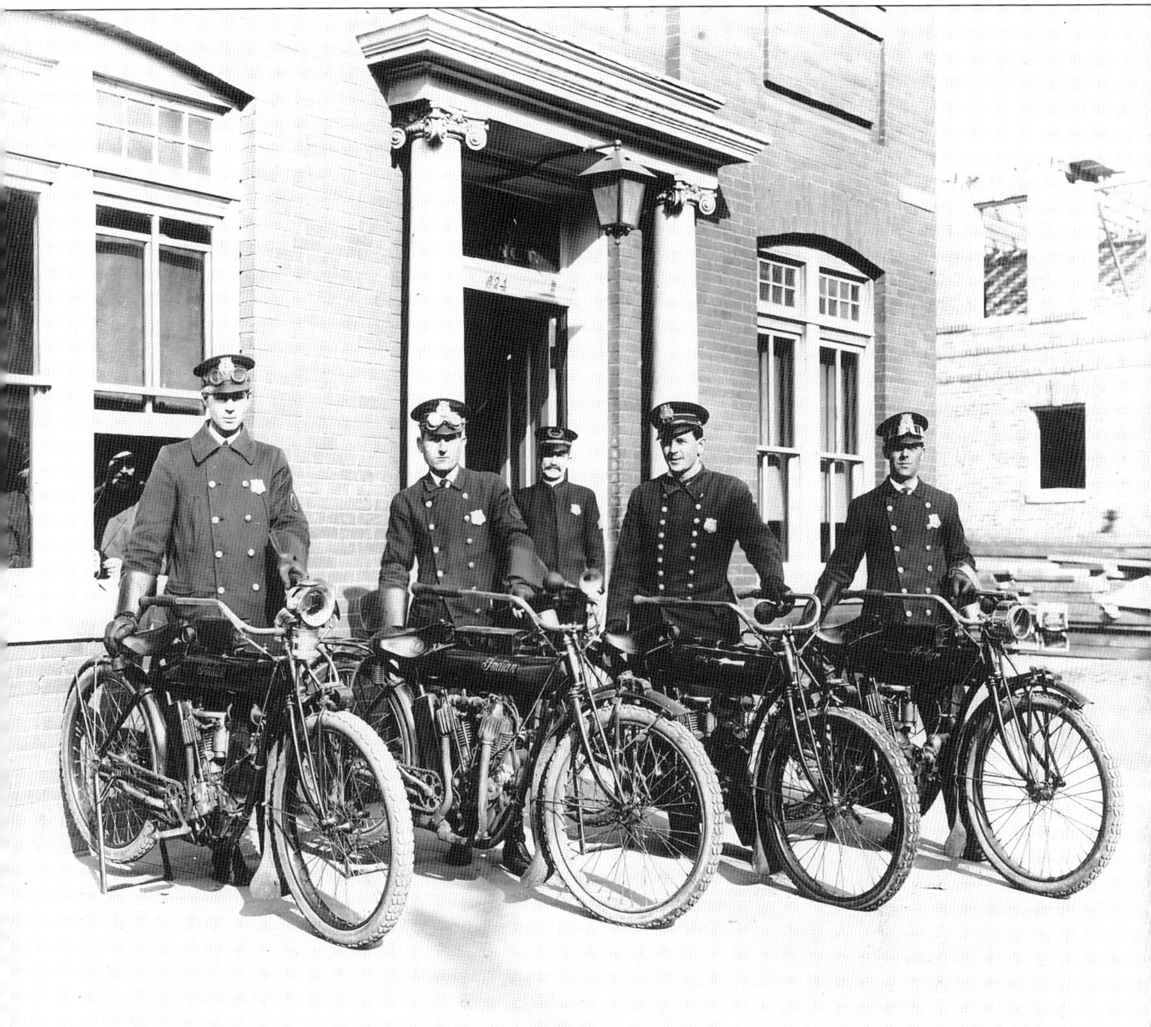

This 1913 photograph by Harry C. Mann depicts Norfolk's first motorcycle police patrol. Riding early Indian motorcycles, these officers patrolled the second precinct (in front of which they are posed). The motorcycles on either end have the old carbon lamps for illumination, and each of the Indians has rubber bullhorns. The officers standing with their motorcycles in this photograph are from left to right: Patrolmen William T. Allen, Cary D. Freeman, and an officer believed to be T.C. Sanderlin. The fourth motorcycle officer is unidentified. The sergeant standing in the doorway of the precinct house is believed to be Seventh Sergeant J.T. Godfrey. Freeman resigned from the Norfolk police force in 1916 with the onset of Prohibition. He went to work for the federal government's alcoholic tax unit, but was subsequently shot and killed by a bootlegger in the line of duty. The Indian Motorcycle Company of Springfield, Massachusetts, located in the Winchester Square section of Springfield, manufactured the motorcycles purchased by the Norfolk Police Department. Notice that Sanderlin's motorcycle has a flat tire.

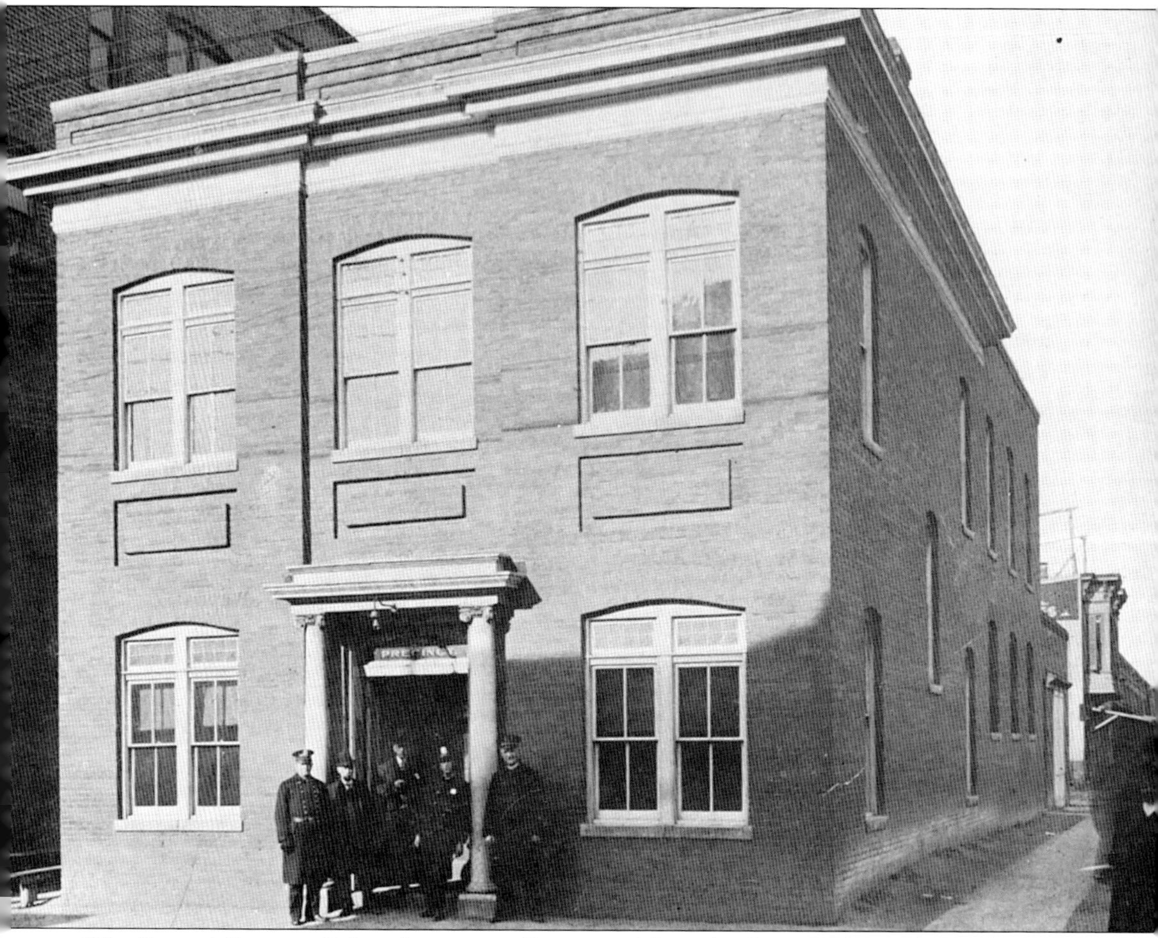

The Second Precinct Police Station, at Queen and Lincoln Streets (shown here, above, in 1910), was completed and opened on February 15, 1904. Major Charles G. Kizer, chief of police, sent Captain George L. Cuthriell from headquarters to command the new station. Cuthriell, born on October 24, 1847, was appointed a police officer on July 21, 1880, and lived at 161 Wood Street. The precinct was built in the section of Norfolk where the largest population of African Americans resided. All of the precinct's officers were, of course, in those days, white. The station was built to handle disturbances and crimes in what came to be called the "black belt" by officers in the second precinct. Most of the officers working the second precinct, including Patrolman J.J. Allen (pictured here, top right next page), wielded significant power over residents in the "black belt." Well into the 1950s, former Church Street residents recalled that no matter what a disturbance was about, who was right or wrong, the black person was nearly always arrested or told to move on. There are retired and former police officers from the turn of the century through the 1960s who, over a period of time, recorded their personal feelings about these often contentious days. Stanley Hurst, a former Norfolk city councilman and a white police officer on Church Street in the 1950s, told *Virginian-Pilot* reporter Tony Wharton, in 1997: "The laws back then were different. Rights were stepped on mightily. People were hurt." Hurst continued: "Officers were quick to act. A guy could say something and get hit with a billy club." At the time these pictures were taken, Cuthriell had four sergeants and one acting sergeant, two detectives and one patrolman detailed as a detective, two bicycle officers, two mounted patrolmen, two turnkeys, one cemetery officer, and 32 patrolmen.

Pictured here is Patrolman J.J. Allen, 1910.

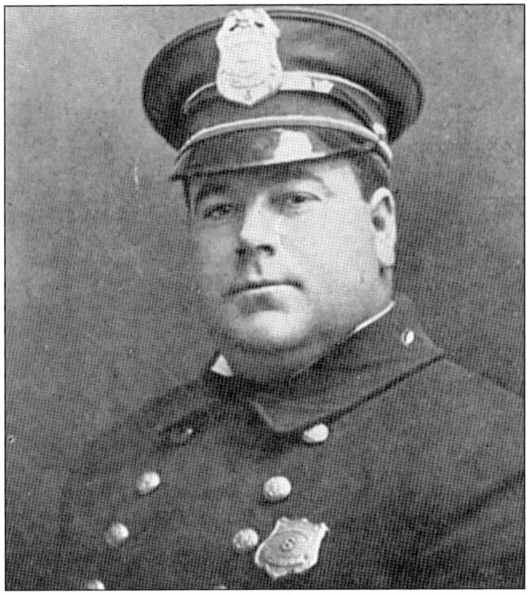

A Murder in the Black Belt

Patrolman John McNerney walked a beat in the second precinct, which at that time encompassed much of Church Street and its surrounding neighborhoods. Near midnight the evening of September 22, 1904, McNerney was alerted by two boys that a burglar was inside Bonney's store at the corner of Cumberland and Bute Streets. The patrolman told the boys to run fast to the precinct, located at the corner of Queen and Lincoln Streets, and send help. He then proceeded to the store where he found an African-American dentist in the street, who quickly informed him that he had just notified the police station that a burglar was, indeed, in the store.

Snapping the lock on the door to the store, McNerney entered in search of the burglar, even though the dentist had cautioned the patrolman to wait for help. There was no light to guide McNerney in the store, so as the patrolman struck a match to light a lantern, the intruder stood up from behind the counter and fired a shot which struck McNerney near the heart. The officer reeled a few steps into the street where he crumpled to the ground, bleeding profusely from his wound. The intruder got away in all the confusion.

By the time McNerney had been shot, the boys reached Samuel Davison's saloon and asked the proprietor to call for more patrolmen since they heard a shot ring out as McNerney entered Bonney's. Davison made the call, but by that time, the dentist had also called the station from call box No. 53, located on the corner of Cumberland and Queen, and notified the desk sergeant that McNerney had been wounded by the burglar. Every policeman on duty in the second precinct that night rushed to McNerney's aid, and even Davison, McNerney's friend, made a mad dash to help. Reaching the downed patrolman first, Davison held him in his arms and talked to McNerney, but the only response he received from the dying officer was a gurgling sound as he breathed his last breath and expired. As Davison turned in response to a commotion coming down the street, he reeled around to see the entire squad from the second precinct stopped in their tracks, each having heard the rattling sounds of a dying man's last gasp of air echoing down the cobblestone street. Patrolman John McNerney was declared dead at St. Vincent's Hospital [St. Vincent DePaul] and his body taken in a patrol wagon to his house where McNerney's wife and five children were told of the way he died. Though the police had a solid suspect, there was not enough evidence to make an arrest. His killer was never brought to justice.

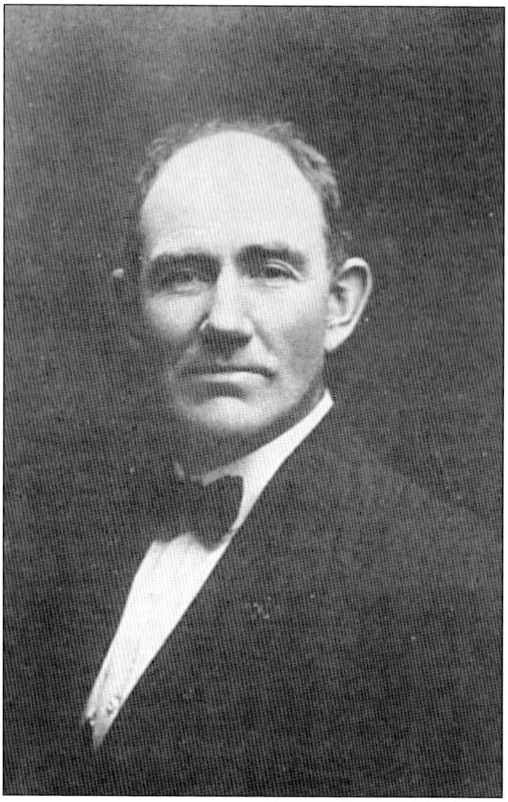
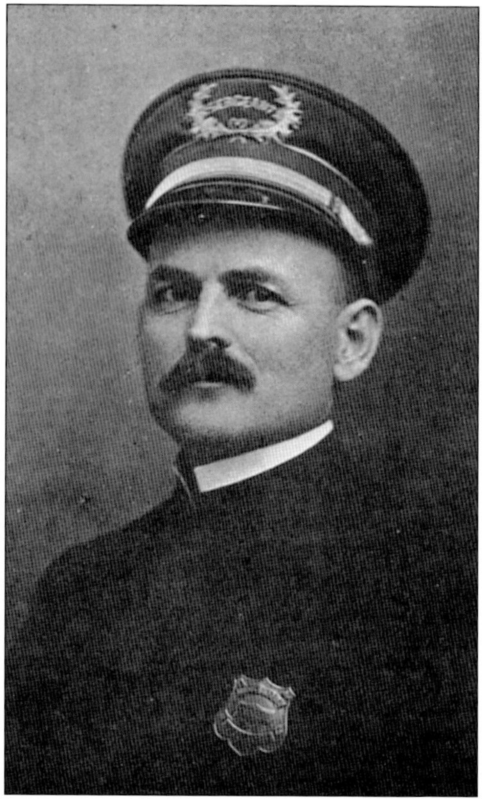

Detective T.L. Stevenson (pictured here, left) came upon a little nine-year-old boy curled up asleep alongside the railroad track near Church and Nineteenth Streets on a freezing cold night in the winter of 1909. "Well, what do you think of that?" Detective Stevenson asked himself, as he bent over the boy. It was shortly before midnight on an evening as cold as anyone could remember, but the child was snugly asleep. "Come, wake up, little fellow," said the detective, "what are you doing out here at this hour of the night. Ain't you frozen?" The boy turned over and looked up at the detective, a contented look spreading over his face. "Come on here," said Stevenson, the child's gaze touching his heart, "let's get where it's warm." Stevenson took the boy, identified only as Johnny in police records, to the second precinct house where Second Sergeant William Ruddick (shown here, right) took the child in and began asking him why he was sleeping nights on the tracks. Johnny explained that he was an orphan, and while he had been placed with relatives nearby and had a bed in which to sleep, he preferred to stay out all night. The kindly sergeant, satisfied by Johnny's answers, sent him upstairs to police matron Hattie L. Seeley, who provided the nine year old with a warm bed for the remainder of the night. As for Second Sergeant William Ruddick, he was born on December 24, 1869, and became a patrolman on October 1, 1890. Ruddick lived at 710 West Highland Avenue.

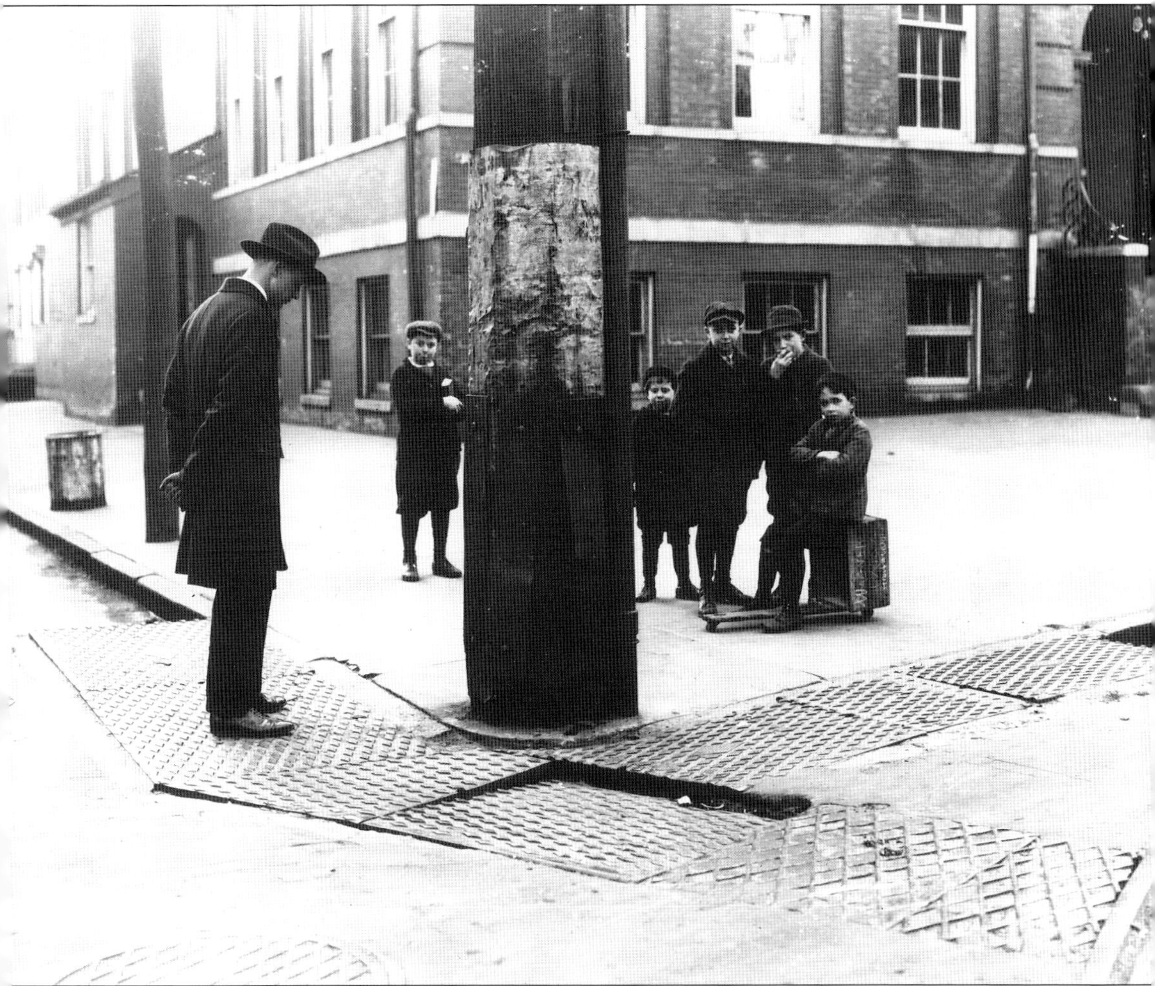

Harry C. Mann photographed the gentleman on the left and this group of schoolboys on December 16, 1920, outside the James Barron Hope School, a public elementary school, located at the corner of Holt and Fenchurch Streets. Note the homemade scooter made with a Wagner catsup crate. The school was formerly called the Holt Street School until November 1912, when names of Norfolk public schools were renamed for notable persons. James Barron Hope was born on March 23, 1829, in Portsmouth, Virginia, at Gosport Navy Yard, of which his grandfather, Commodore James Barron, was commandant. Hope graduated in 1847 from the College of William & Mary, and returned to his family home in Hampton, Virginia, to live. Like his famous grandfather, Hope had a temper not easily quelled. Two years after graduation, a running enmity between Hope and the Jones brothers, George and John Pembroke (an 1847 graduate of the United States Naval Academy), ended in a challenge to a duel from John Pembroke Jones. In April 1849, both young men met at Fortress Monroe, resulting in the serious wounding of Hope and Jones. Hope shot Jones with the same pistol used by his grandfather to kill Stephen Decatur in a duel 29 years earlier. After all this early notoriety, Hope began to write and publish. During the Civil War, he served as an Confederate army captain until war's end. Returning to Norfolk in 1865, he began writing for the *Virginian* newspaper, but is perhaps most famous as having been a founder of the *Landmark* in 1873. Hope was superintendent of Norfolk schools from 1886 to 1887. (Courtesy of the Library of Virginia.)

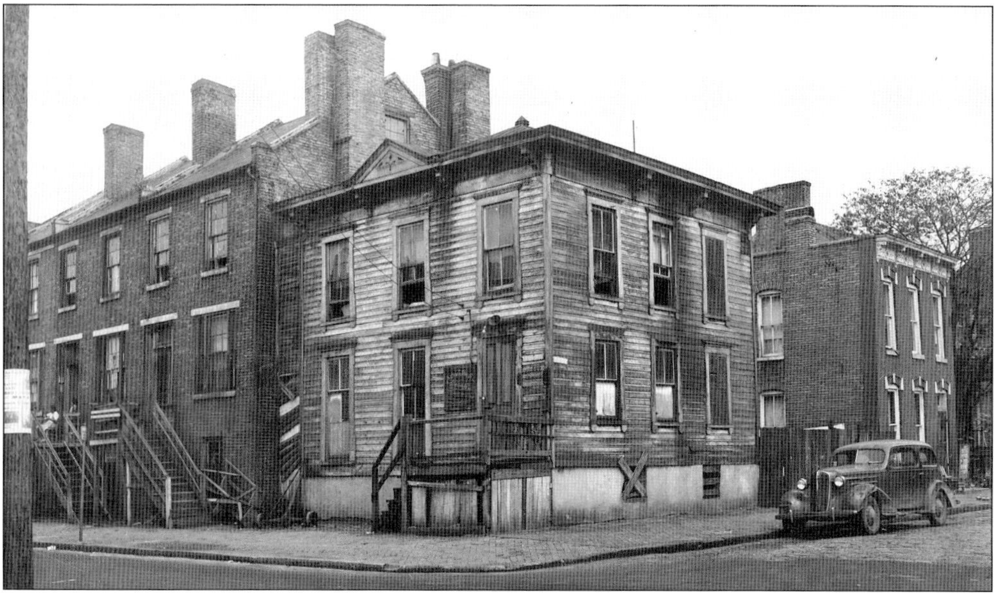

Antioch Baptist Church, located at the corner of Fenchurch and Mariner Streets, was the subject of this picture, taken May 7, 1946. Dilapidated and abandoned, the old-house-turned-church was hardly the house of worship it had been in years past. (Charles S. Borjes, photographer. Courtesy of Kirn Library.)

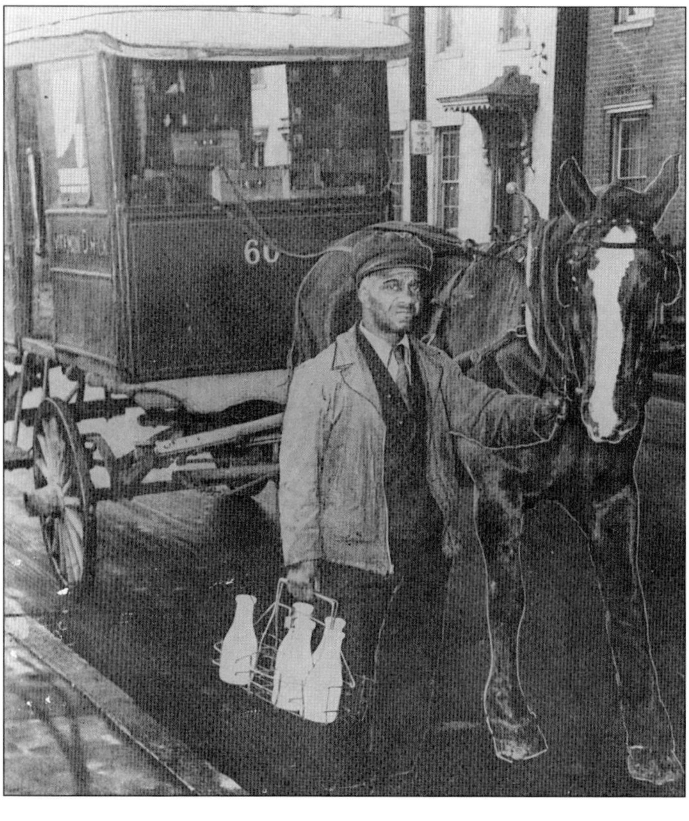

Oliver Hunter Jones had been a milk delivery man and salesman for 50 years when this picture was taken in 1949. Jones, a driver for Rosedale Dairy, lived at 715 Chapel Street. Rosedale Dairy, his employer, was owned and operated by Harry F. Wall, president; Thomas S. Lawrence, vice president; and H.M. Woodward, secretary. The dairy was located at Monticello Avenue and the corner of Ninth Street. (Courtesy of Kirn Library.)

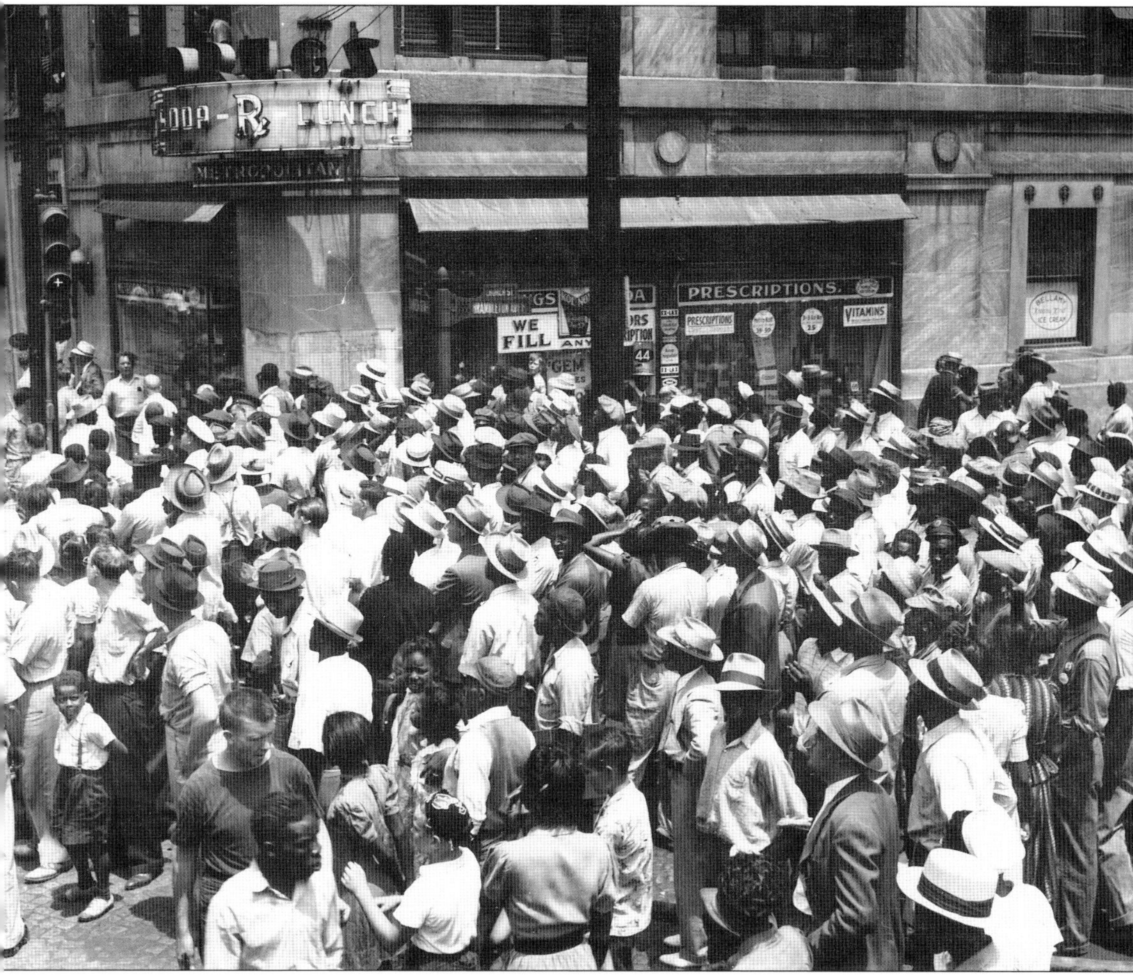

Spectators by the hundreds filled Church Street watching a fire on June 19, 1942. A three-alarm fire broke out in the F.W. Woolworth & Company's retail establishment at 709-711 Church Street the afternoon of June 19, claiming the life of two people, Ann Ruth Snead, an 18-year-old woman who was working her first day as a store clerk, and Thomas Edward Evans, a 14-year-old boy who lived at 117 Fenchurch Street. Snead was trapped helplessly on the second floor and later found dead from suffocation after she made frantic efforts to escape through heavily barred windows. People in the crowd could see Snead motioning for help, but efforts by firemen to rescue her proved futile as the iron bars that held her inside also kept them from coming to her aid. Details of the death of Evans, an African-American stock boy, were not expounded in the newspaper. His body was found in the debris the morning after the fire. Damage to the five-and-ten-cent store was confined largely to the second floor, which was used primarily as a stock room and was where the bodies were recovered. (Charles S. Borjes, photographer. Courtesy of Kirn Library.)

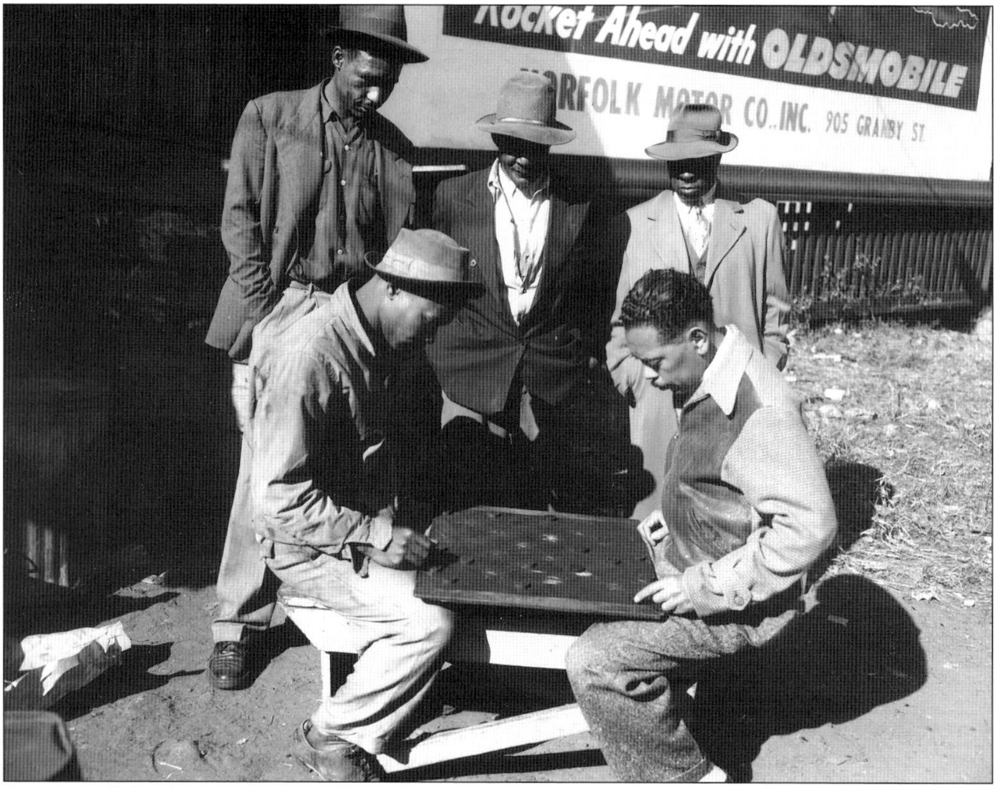

A game of checkers went on undisturbed at the busy intersection of Brambleton Avenue and Cumberland Street, November 6, 1950. Basking in the sun of an unseasonably warm 68-degree day, these gentlemen were oblivious to the screeching brakes and honking horns of traffic going by them. (Charles S. Borjes, photographer. Courtesy of Kirn Library.)

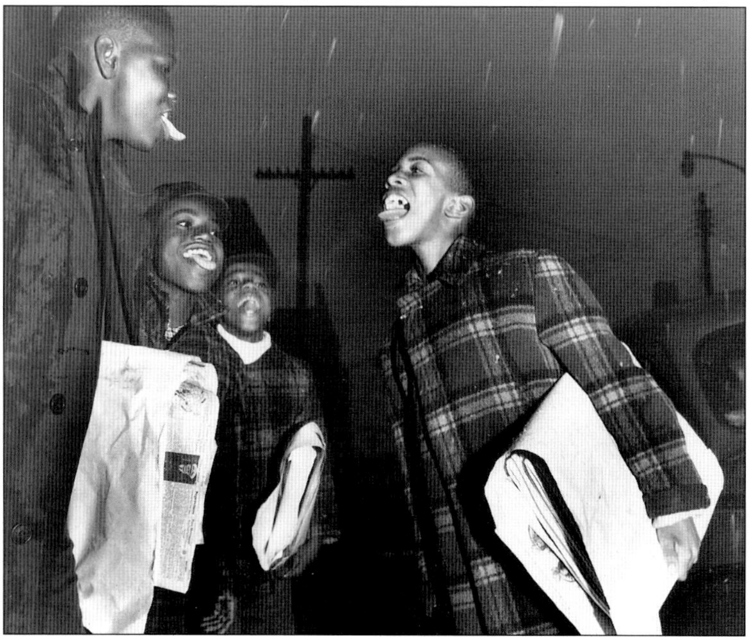

The paperboys in this playful image catch snow on their tongues, February 26, 1952. Norfolk youngsters rejoiced at the first real snow of the winter, described as a "damp fluffy affair," blown in on the wings of a developing nor'easter. Nearly an inch of snow fell before it turned to sleet and rain. (Charles S. Borjes, photographer. Courtesy of Kirn Library.)

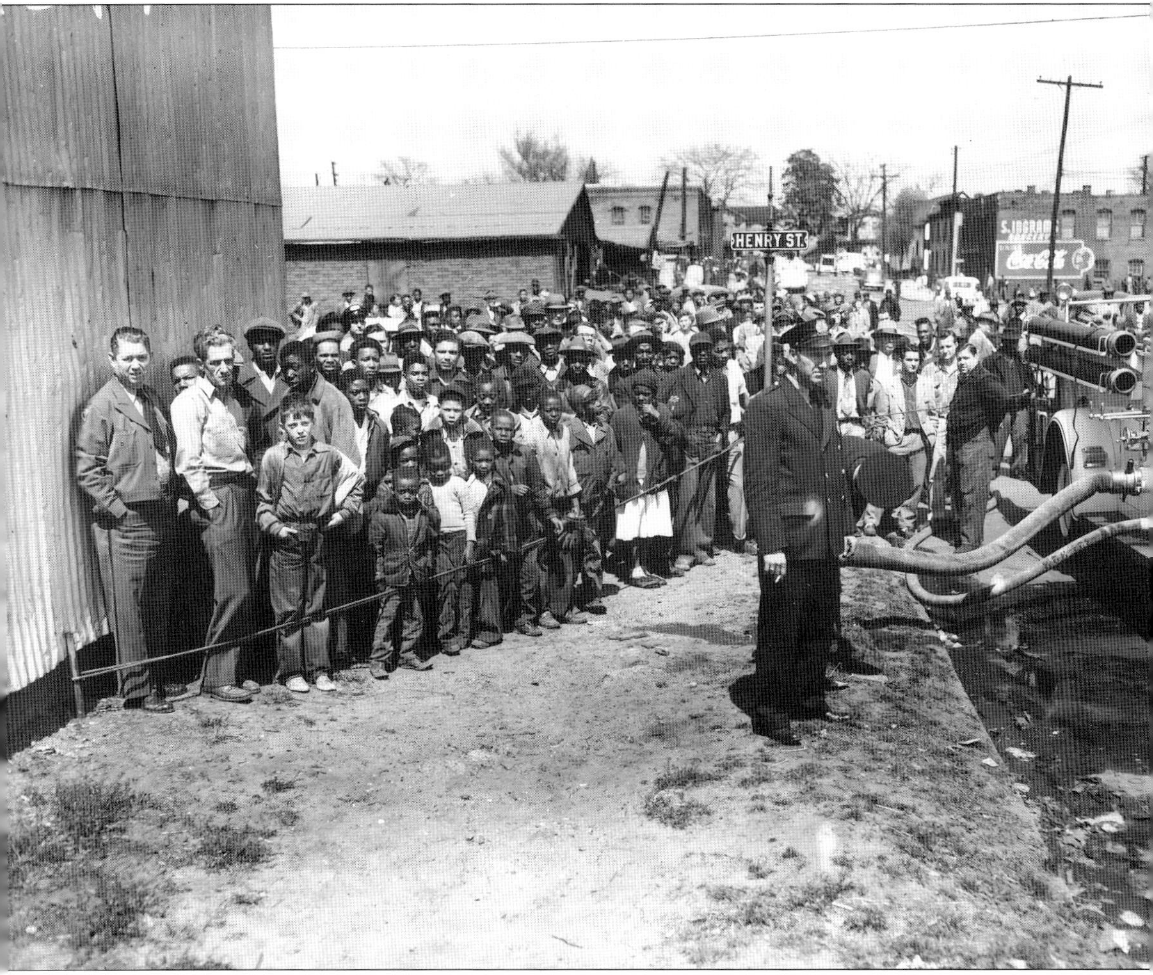

A noonday lunch crowd watched the fire at a storage warehouse at Calvert and Landing Streets from Henry Street, on April 9, 1952. The three-alarm fire broke out around midday and totally destroyed the warehouse and its contents: store fixtures belonging to Colonial Stores on the first floor and furniture owned by the Haynes Furniture Company on the second. The fire started in a pile of rubbish in the northwest corner of the corrugated metal warehouse and quickly spread. The building was owned by Israel Kanter. Leonard R. Strelitz, then vice president of Haynes Furniture, noted that Haynes had rented space in the warehouse after the loss of much of the company's stock in another warehouse fire two months before. A four-story Haynes warehouse on Commerce Street was destroyed on January 29. The April 9 blaze was visible throughout Norfolk. (Charles S. Borjes, photographer. Courtesy of Kirn Library.)

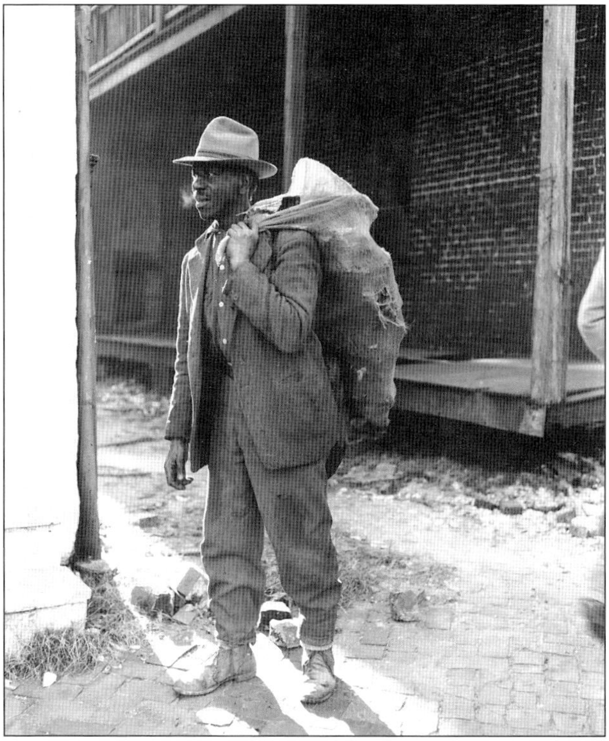

Gathering wood for his fire, December 19, 1953, this man prepares for the stinging climax of 48-hours-plus of sub-freezing temperatures. Temperatures were expected to be between 16 and 20 degrees. The all-time low for the date up to that time was 12 degrees, set in 1884. (Jim Mays, photographer. Courtesy of Kirn Library.)

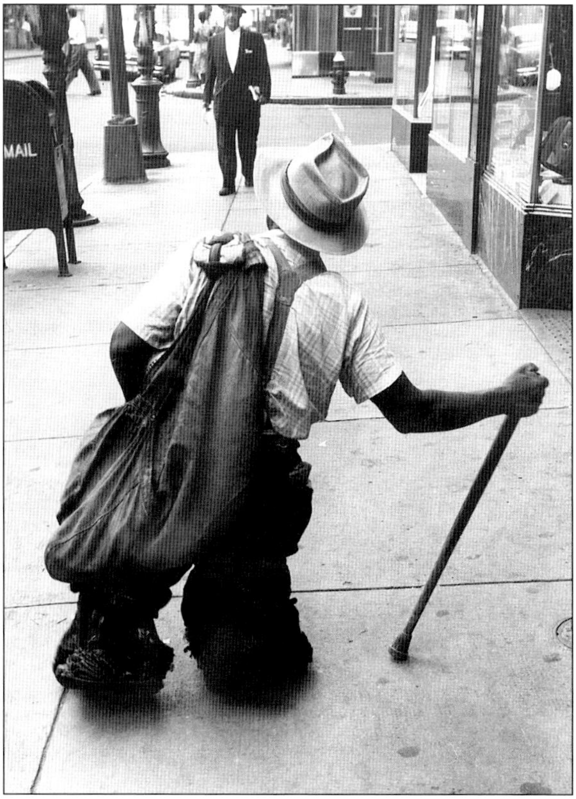

Legless newspaperman Joe McMillan was faithfully delivering his papers in the black community around Church Street *c.* 1956 when an unidentified photographer snapped his picture. (Courtesy of Kirn Library.)

John W. McCoy had been coming to the Norfolk City Market for a good 50 years when this picture was taken c. 1954. (Photographer unknown. Courtesy of Kirn Library.)

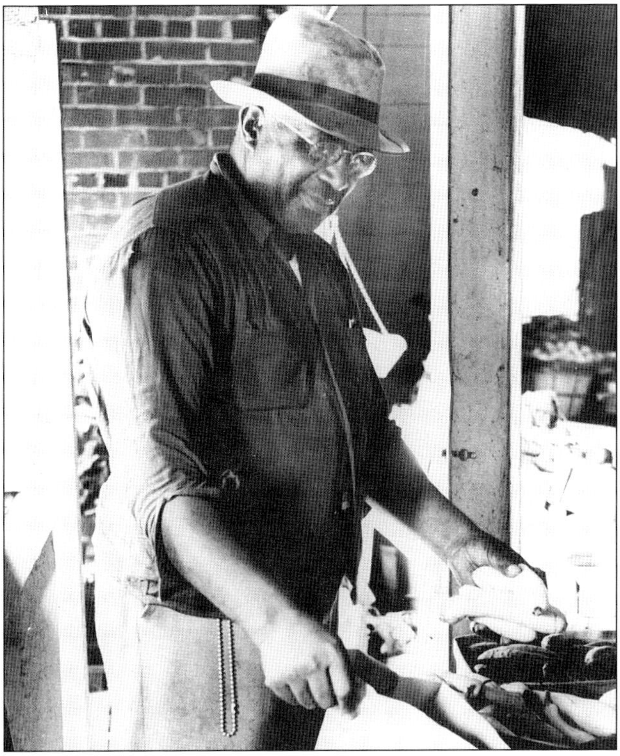

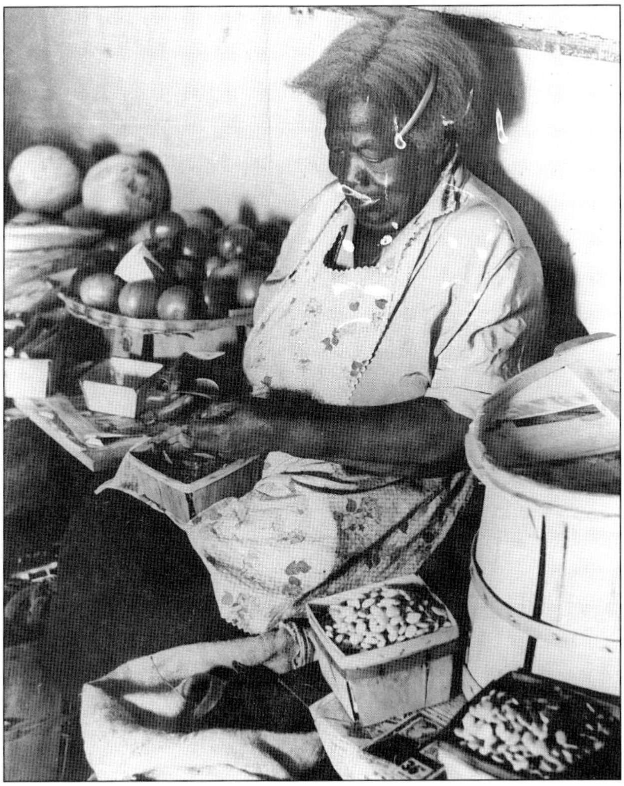

Rosa Butt, 80 years old when an unknown photographer took this picture of her, came to the Norfolk City Market to market her goods for 58 years each Friday and Saturday. The photograph was taken c. 1954. (Courtesy of Kirn Library.)

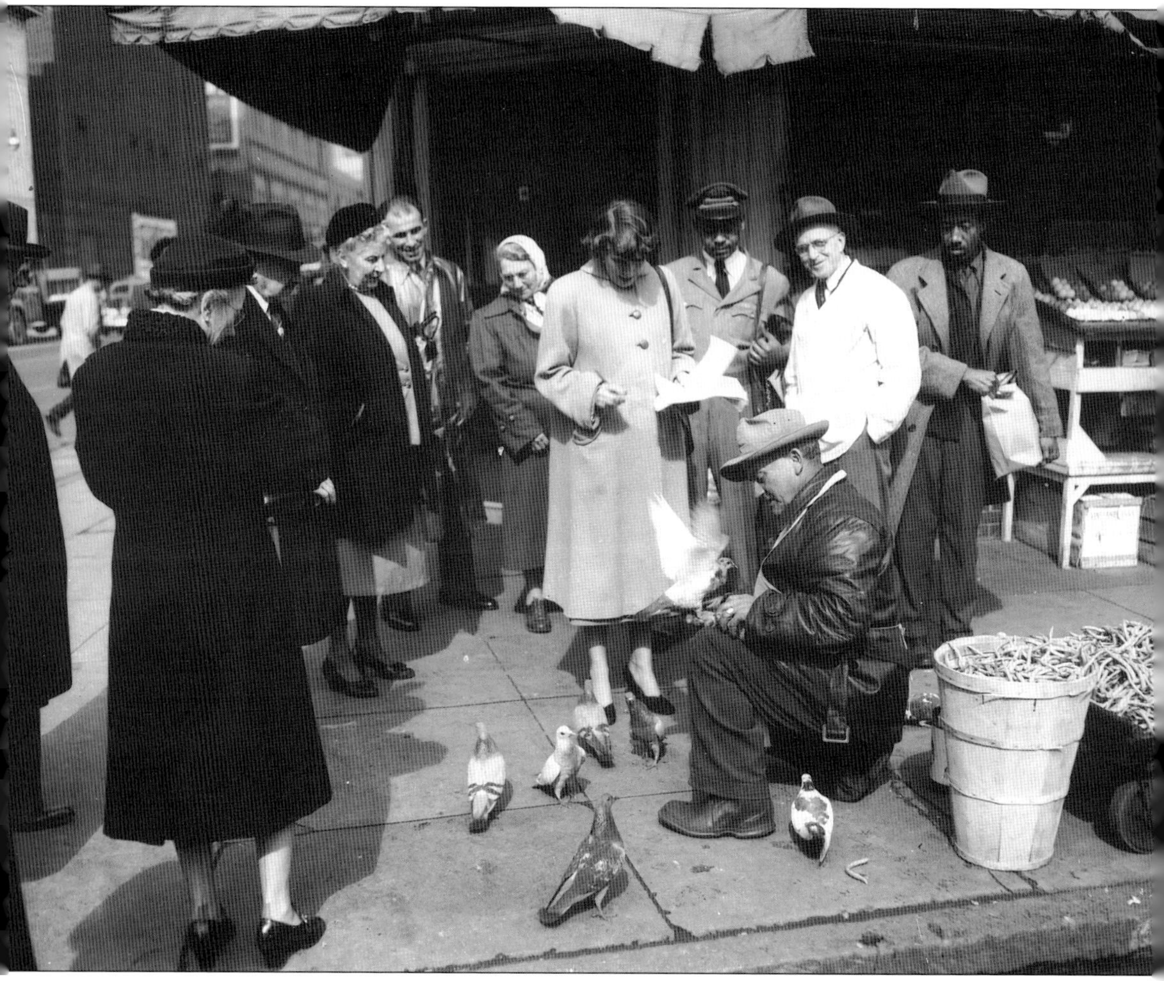

Making sure his almost 40 pigeons are fed their lunch before Norfolk's anti-pigeon ordinance became effective, Julian E. Fitchett, who operated an egg and produce business at the northeast corner of Monticello Avenue and Market Street, drew a friendly crowd of onlookers. Fitchett's stand was located within the bounds of the City Market complex, but his home was at 828 Holt Street. The city's pigeon ordinance forbade feeding the pigeons in the streets or public spaces. The new ordinance understandably upset Fitchett, who remarked: "I just can't understand why they want to stop me from feeding them. They (the pigeons) all know me, and I only have 40. My uncle has 200." At the age of 60, when Charles S. Borjes took this photograph on March 1, 1950, Fitchett had been feeding pigeons ever since he knew what birds were. He came to Norfolk from Virginia's Eastern Shore, operating a popcorn machine on Market Street before going into the egg and produce business in 1948. The Market Street pigeons were tame. Two months after moving into his stall at the City Market, Fitchett cemented his relationship with the birds. They responded to his whistle every morning at 11:30 a.m., eating his unpopped popcorn, or, to vary the menu, scratch feed. Fitchett had them eating out of his hand. Most of them had names, too, answering to names like "Whitey," "Speck," and "Spotty." On occasion, "Whitey" was loaned out to a Norfolk lodge for use in funerals of members. When unable to obtain a dove for a lodge funeral ritual, the lodge took "Whitey" to Forest Lawn, where he flew over the grave. It took the bird 30 minutes to fly back to Fitchett's stall on Market Street. (Courtesy of Kirn Library.)

Eight

Where the People Lived

"The morning comes in consciousness
Of faint stale smells of beer
From the sawdust-trampled street
With all its muddy feet that press
To early coffee-stands.
With the other masquerades
That time resumes,
One thinks of all the hands
That are raising dingy shades
In a thousand furnished rooms."

—From *Preludes*, 1936
T.S. (Thomas Stearns) Eliot, American-born English poet (1888–1965)

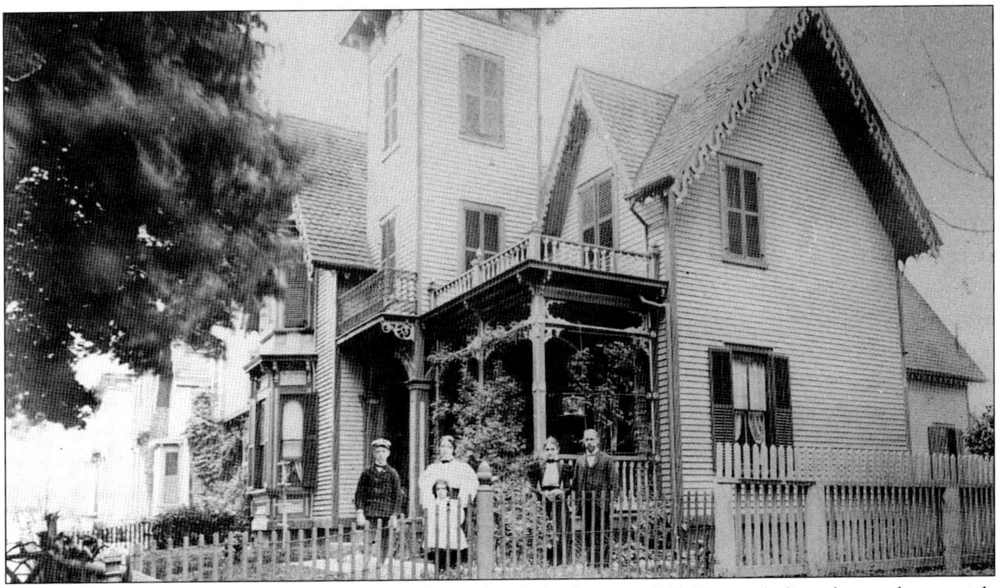

The James G. Gill residence was located at 257 Holt Street. Gill (far right) is shown here with his family. At the time this photograph was taken, 1897, Gill was in the wholesale grocery business, but in 1902, he added a two-bag roaster to his grocery operation at 282 Water Street, and thereby became the founder and president of the James G. Gill Company, coffee roasters, jobbers of tea, coffee, spice, and rice, of Norfolk. This is one of the few known photographs of Holt Street and its surrounding residential area. When Gill died in March of 1912, his son Frank continued to manage the business. Frank, though quite young when he took over the company, had a good reputation in Norfolk. The leading brands of coffee produced by Gill's at that time were "King of All" and "Queen's Blend" pure coffees.

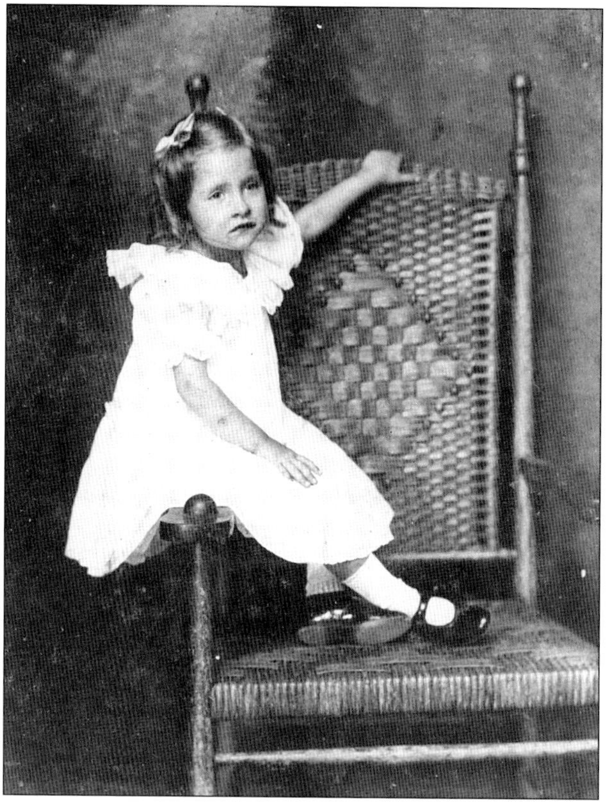

This lovely portrait of Frances Adams was taken *c.* 1905. Frances lived on Lincoln Street, located one block west of Church Street between Virginia Beach Boulevard and Brambleton Avenue.

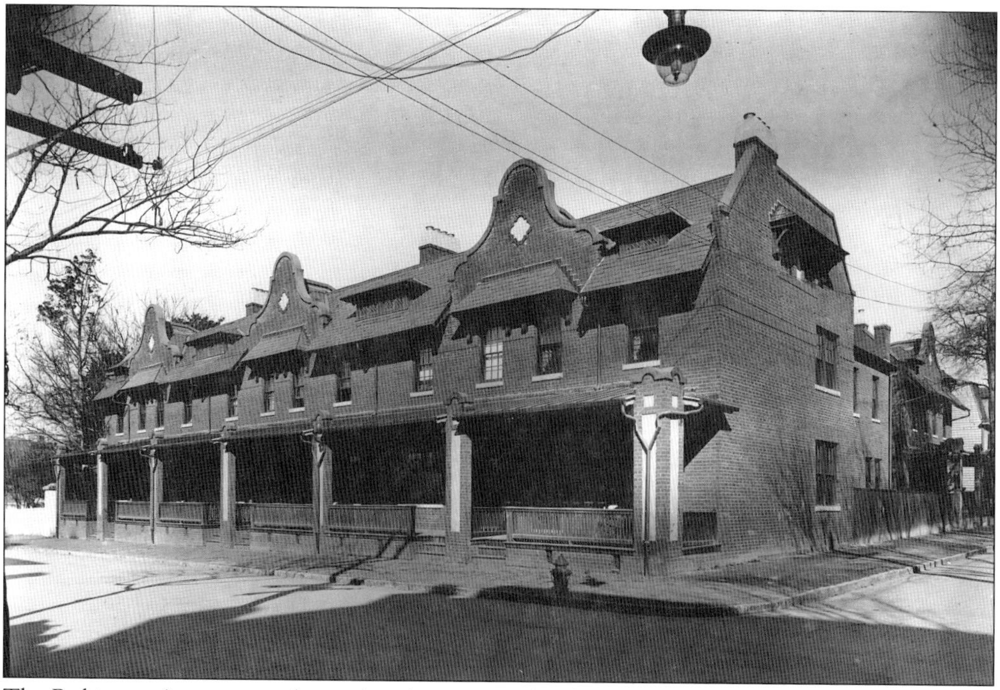

The Robinson Apartments, located at the corner of Holt and Walke Streets (1101 Holt Street), were photographed by Harry C. Mann about 1909. (Courtesy of the Library of Virginia.)

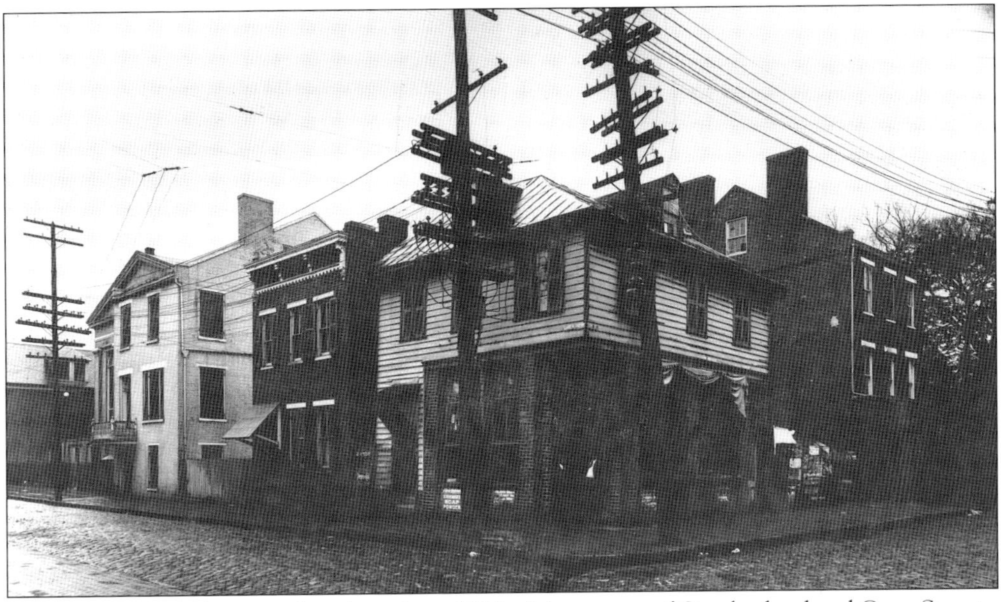

The scene in this photograph, taken about 1910 of the corner of Cumberland and Cove Streets, was one block off Church Street. The trees of Saint Paul's Episcopal Church churchyard are visible to the right. The owners of the small corner grocery store are barely visible standing in the doorway. There are visible advertisements for Star Soap, Kirkman's Soap Powder, and an ice-cold Pepsi Cola. (Harry C. Mann, photographer. Courtesy of the Library of Virginia.)

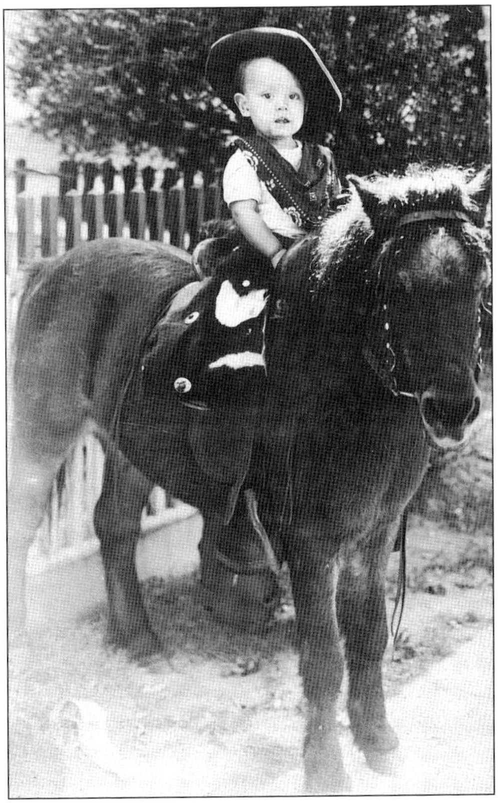

"Cowboys ride again!" This little boy lived on Park Avenue in the Brambleton section of Norfolk. The picture was taken by an unknown photographer in 1928.

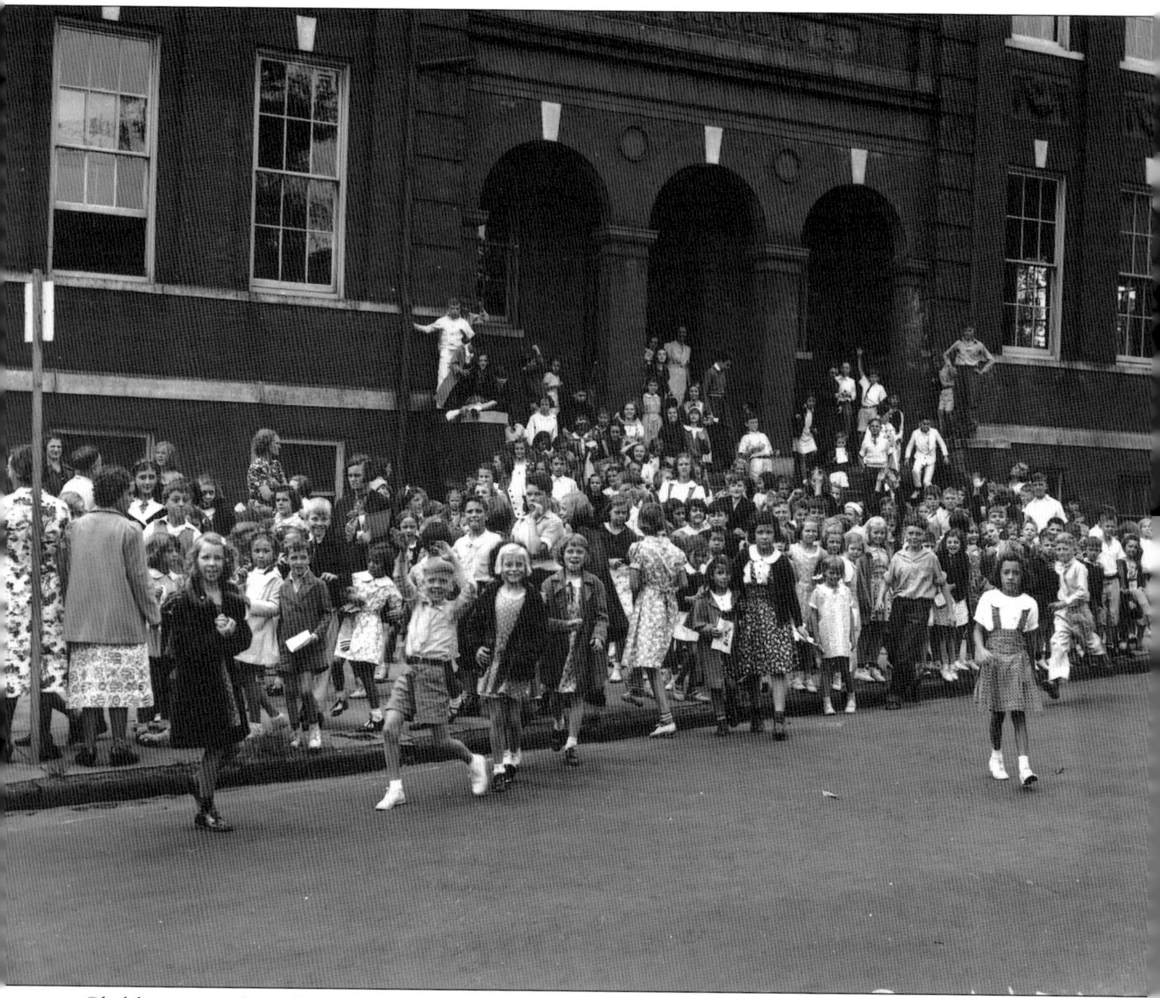

Children attending the James Barron Hope School, situated at the corner of Fenchurch and Holt Streets, put on smiles for photographer Charles S. Borjes on September 9, 1938, the first day of school. It is interesting to note that a significant number of school-aged children in the United States, even in 1938, used unconventional modes of transportation to get to school, employing the use of everything from motorboats, snowmobiles, and dogsleds to baskets swinging across steep canyons, to get to school. Children residing in particularly remote reaches of the nation had portable schoolhouses brought to them while others, for example, in the southeastern area of Oregon, had to move into a small town and live in a dormitory of the Crane School for the duration of the school year. Riding the school bus or simply walking to school was certainly a luxury for the children in this photograph, one they probably did not fully appreciate at the time. Somehow, these conventional modes of transporting oneself to school seem much safer than dangling twice a day in a basket hanging by a pulley from a heavy cable stretched over the Salmon River in Lemhi County, Idaho. Several children living in Lemhi County made that trip every day just to get their education. (Courtesy of Kirn Library.)

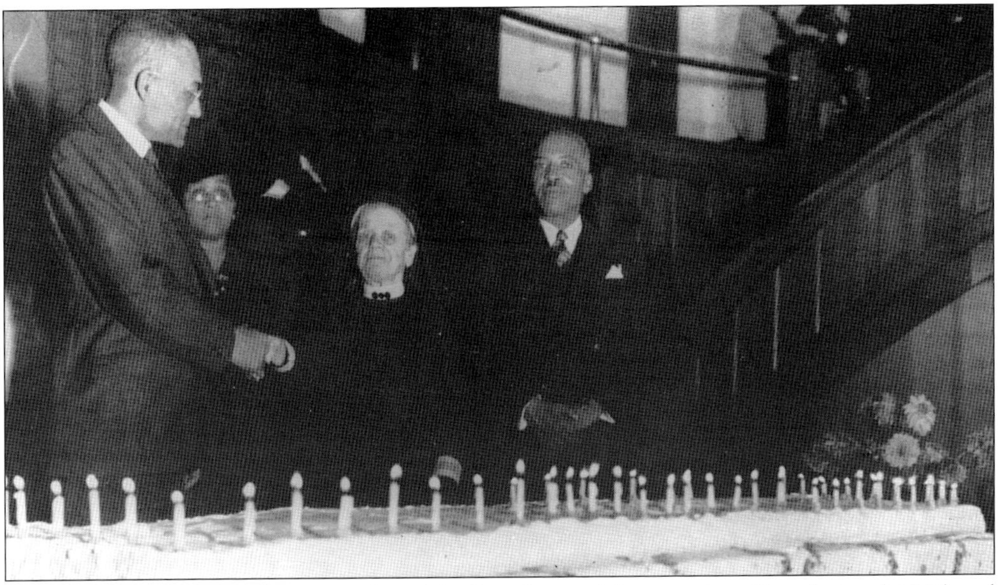

Mrs. Frank Anthony Walke, a member of the Daughters of the American Revolution (DAR) and United Daughters of the Confederacy (UDC), attended a 50th birthday party for the Reverend Richard B. Bowling (left, shaking Mrs. Walke's hand), pastor of First Baptist Church (414 Bute Street), in October 1941. The Reverend Dr. Russell C. Barbour, of Nashville, Tennessee (far right), was the guest minister for Reverend Bowling's celebration service. Mrs. Walke was the widow of Dr. Frank A. Walke, a surgeon in the Confederate army during the American Civil War. (Courtesy of Kirn Library.)

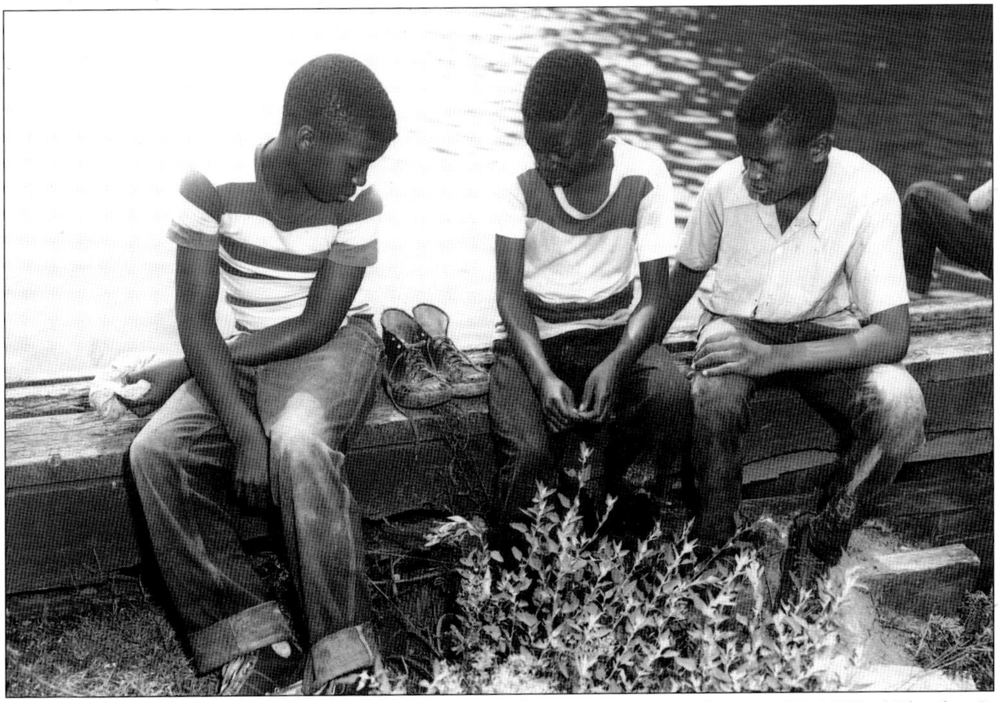

Friends gaze with sadness at the shoes of a young drowning victim, August 17, 1950. (Charles S. Borjes, photographer. Courtesy of Kirn Library.)

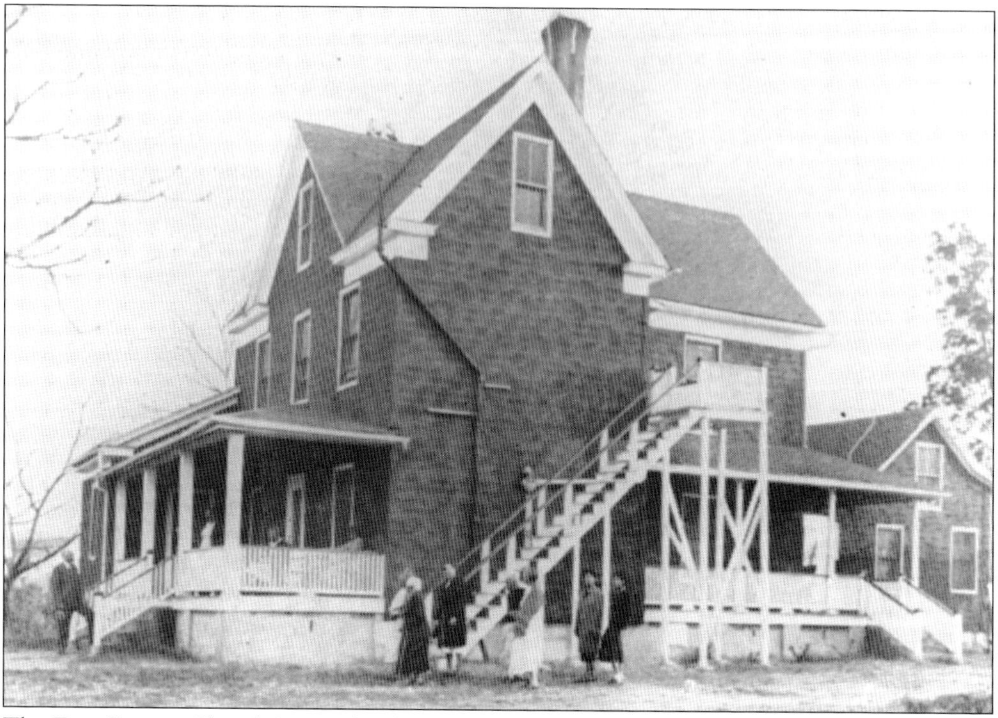

The First Baptist Church Home for the Aged, pictured here in 1949, was located off Church Street at 2730 Ludlow Street. (Courtesy of Kirn Library.)

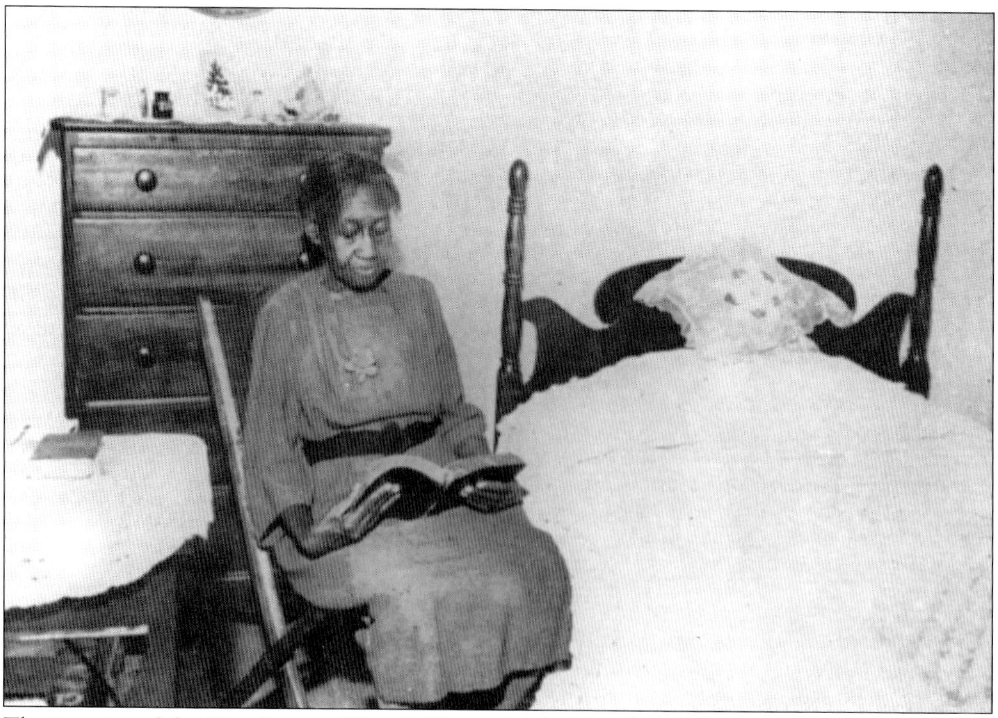

The interior of the First Baptist Church Home for the Aged included as many of the comforts of home for its residents as possible. (Courtesy of Kirn Library.)

An aged, but proud and elegant, African-American woman sat for this formal portrait by Charles S. Borjes c. 1950. In the words of Phillis Wheatley: "'Twas mercy brought me from my Pagan land,/ Taught my benighted soul to understand/That there's a God, that there's a Saviour too:/Once I redemption neither sought nor knew./Some view our sable race with scornful eye,/'Their colour is a diabolic dye.'/Remember, Christians, Negroes, black as Cain,/ May be refined, and join th' angelic train." [From *On Being Brought From Africa to America,* 1773; Phillis Wheatley, American poet (1754?–1784)]. (Courtesy of Kirn Library.)

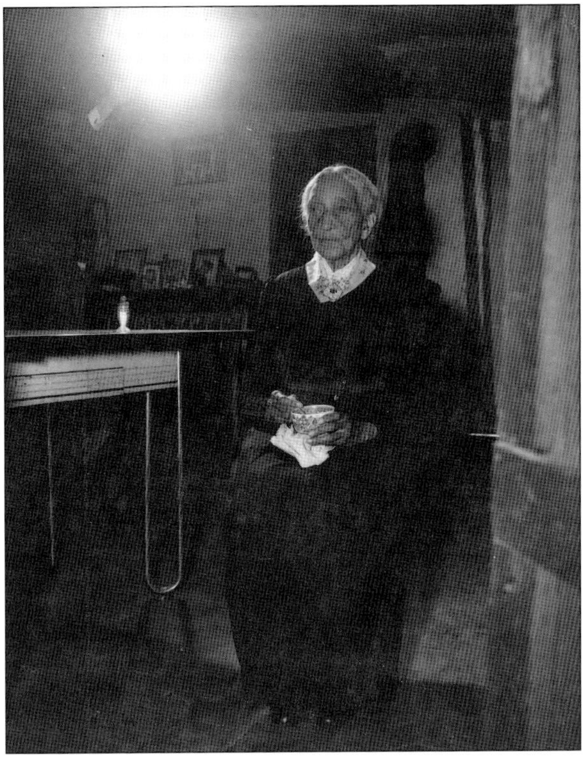

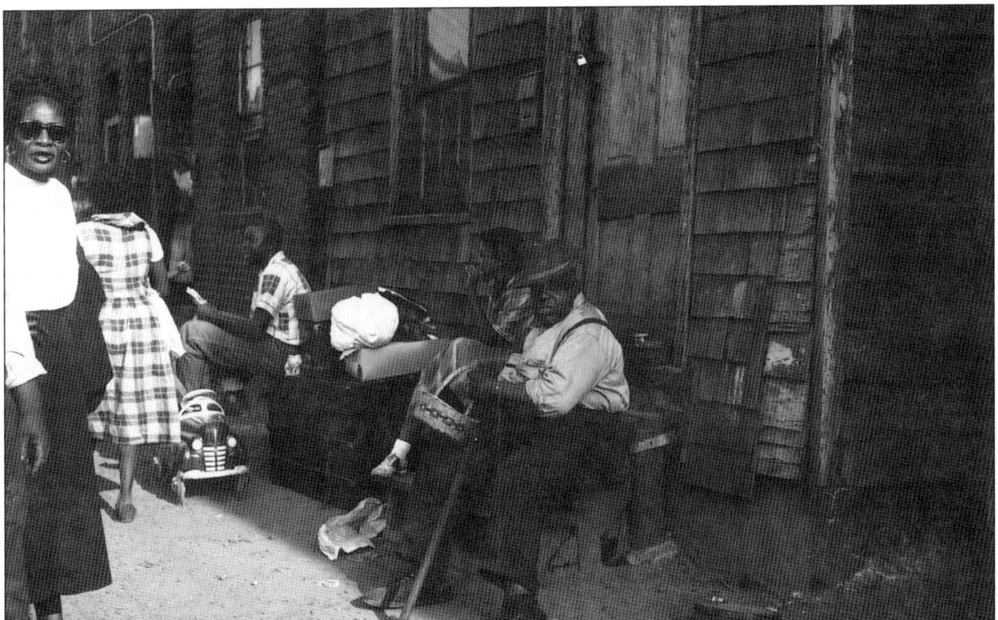

This image of Reilly Street, located in the neighborhood around St. Mary's of the Immaculate Conception Roman Catholic Church (now St. Mary's Basilica), was taken on May 26, 1953. This is one of Norfolk's oldest streets, having been called Second Cross in 1782. (Charles S. Borjes, photographer. Courtesy of Kirn Library.)

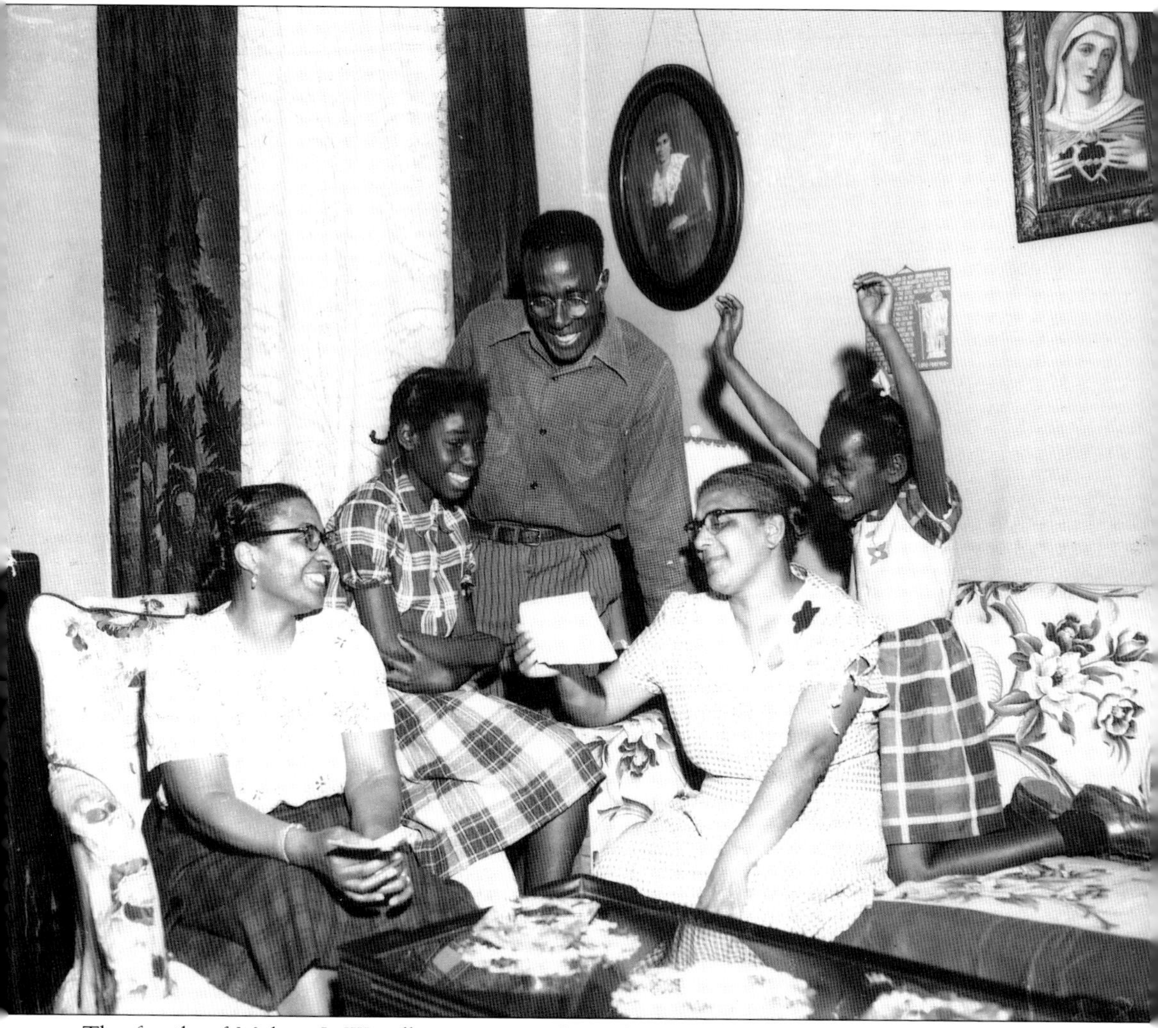

The family of Melvin J. Woodhouse received notification that their prisoner of war son was to be released the evening of April 24, 1953. Shown in their home at 406 Reilly Street were (left to right) Helen Bond, Melvin's aunt, holding the last letters received from her nephew; Gwendolyn Jones, Bond's granddaughter; George Woodhouse, the soldier's uncle; Ollie Mills, another aunt, looking at the Associated Press dispatch announcing her nephew's release; and Betty Jones, another granddaughter of Helen Bond. Ollie Mills, her sister Helen Bond, and brother George Woodhouse had raised Melvin since he was nine months old. The 32-year-old Woodhouse, a graduate of Booker T. Washington High School, served in WW II and re-entered the United States Army in June 1950. He was sent to Korea a few months later. The Department of Defense notified Ollie Mills on January 24, 1951, that Melvin had been missing in action since November 17, 1950. In December 1951, she received a letter from Melvin saying "he was getting along fine," only a few days before his name appeared on a list made public of Americans being held in communist prisoner of war camps. Woodhouse was detained in Prisoner of War Camp No. 4, North Korea. He became the first Norfolk soldier repatriated by the communists from North Korean prisoner of war camps after the truce at Panmunjom. Woodhouse's repatriation was also part of the first sick and wounded prisoner exchange of the Korean Conflict, a group which included 17 American, four British, four Turkish, and 75 South Korean military members. (Charles S. Borjes, photographer. Courtesy of Kirn Library.)

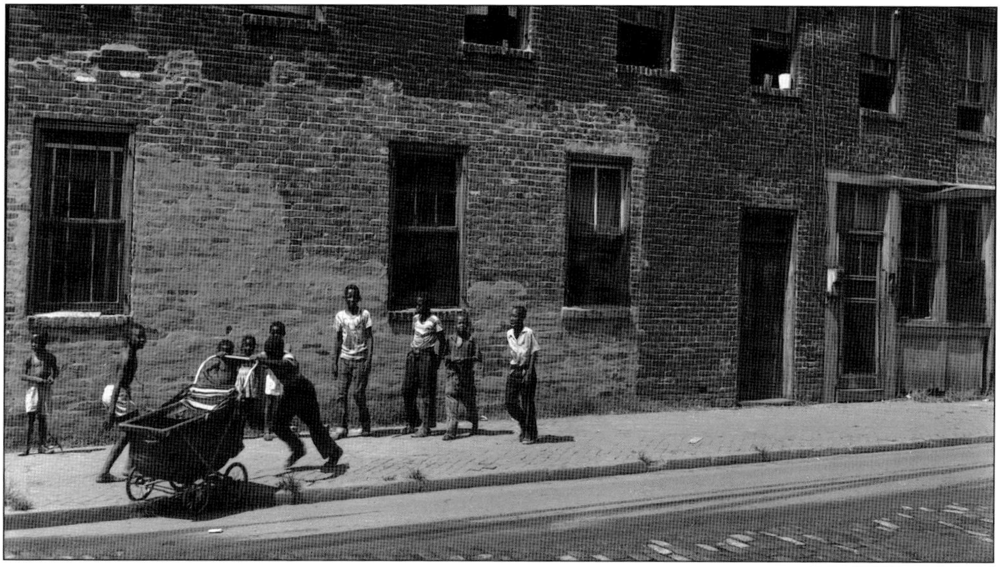

Pictured here are the slums, September 2, 1953. The scene is reminiscent of English poet Stephen Spender's lines from *An Elementary School Classroom in a Slum*, in which he wrote: "And yet, for these/Children, these windows, not this world, are world,/Where all their future's painted with a fog,/A narrow street sealed in with lead sky,/Far far from rivers, capes, and stars of words."(Jim Mays, photographer. Courtesy of Kirn Library.)

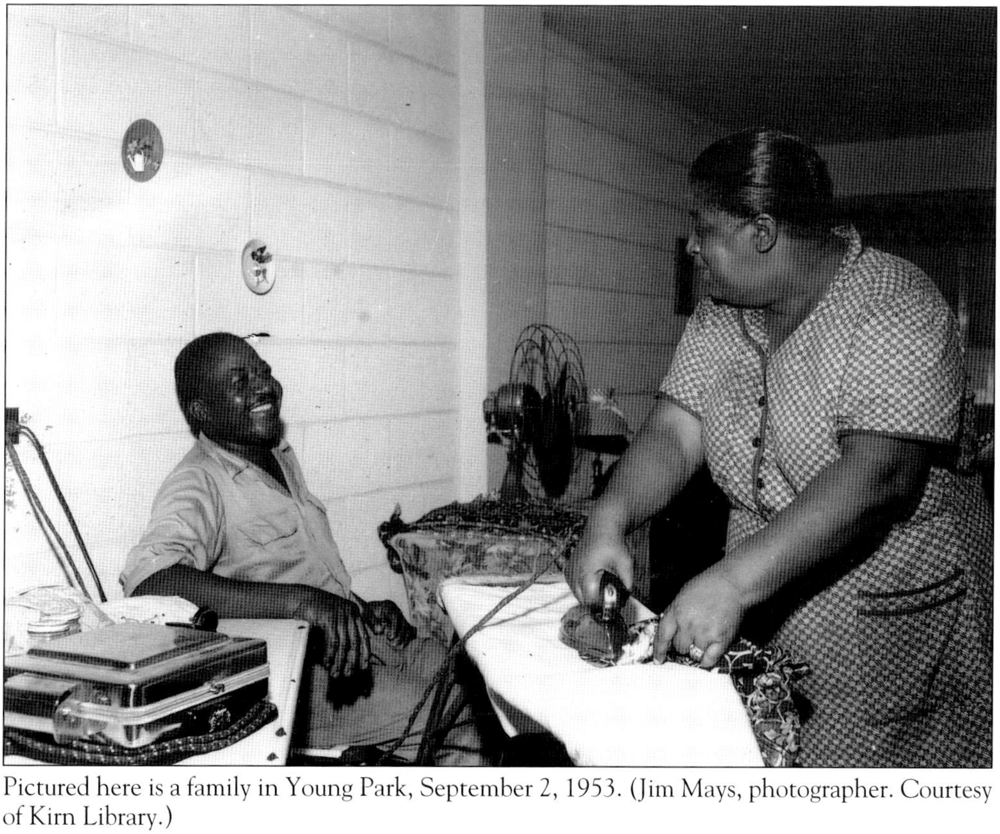

Pictured here is a family in Young Park, September 2, 1953. (Jim Mays, photographer. Courtesy of Kirn Library.)

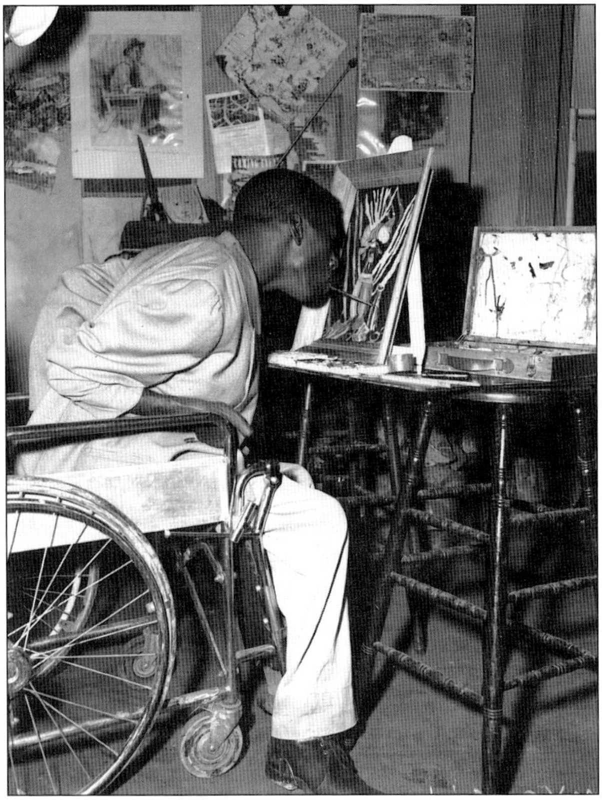

A handicapped artist, photographed by Jim Mays on May 29, 1954, works diligently on one of his paintings. (Courtesy of Kirn Library.)

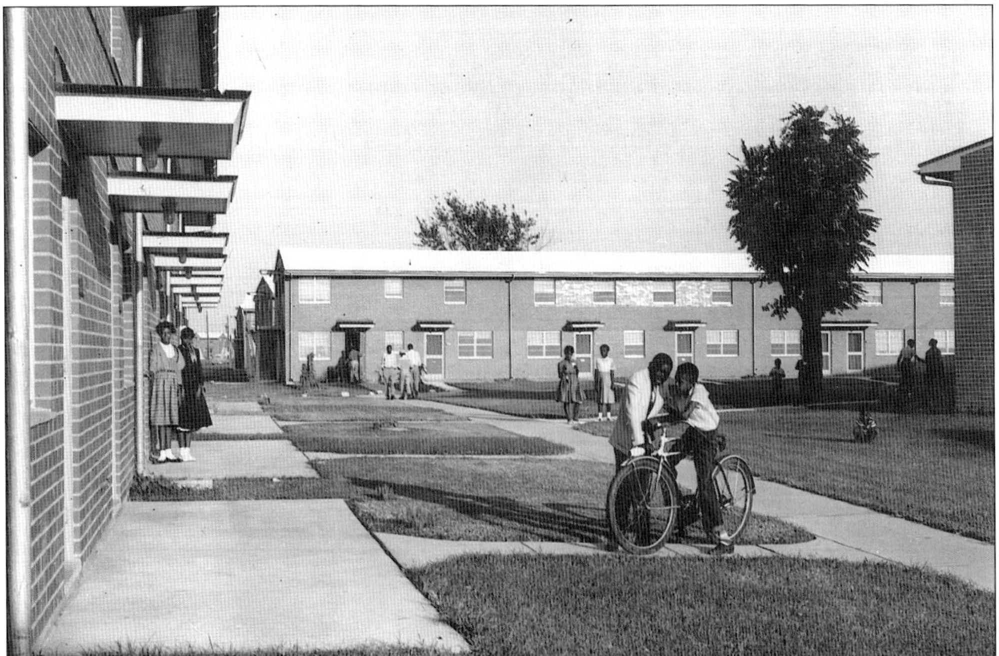

McIntosh Studio took this photograph at one of Norfolk Redevelopment and Housing Authority's housing projects on September 13, 1954. (Courtesy of Kirn Library.)

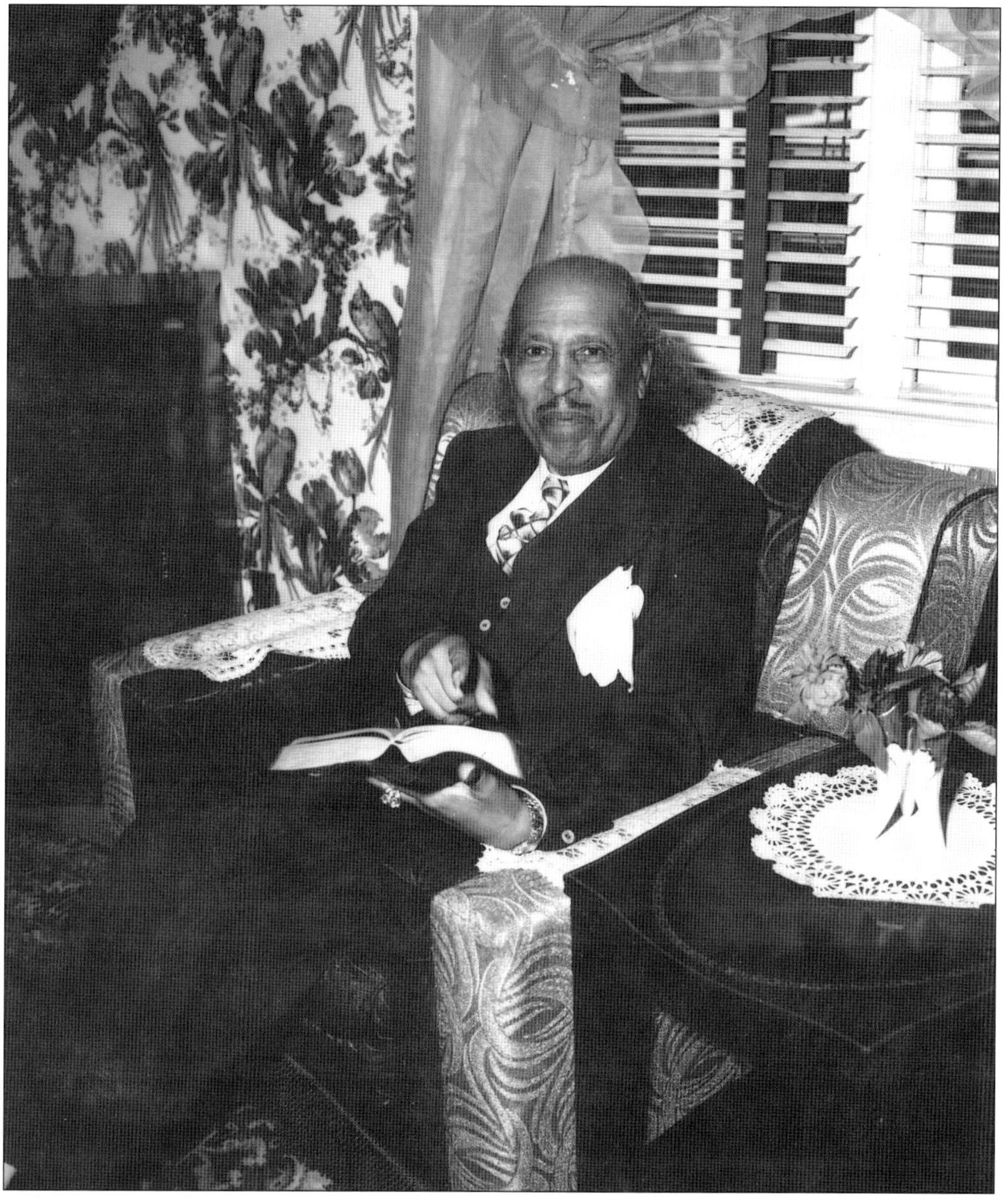

Bishop C.M. Madison, popularly known as "Daddy" Grace to his followers and founder of the national ecumenical United House of Prayer for All People, was photographed by Charles S. Borjes on July 1, 1952, in Norfolk. Once a year, usually in July, Madison, though headquartered in Philadelphia, made a trip to Norfolk to visit his church in the city. Treated like royalty, red carpets were rolled out for him as he stepped from a luxurious limousine and was ushered into the church. Over the years Madison became controversial for this luxurious lifestyle and flamboyant behavior. When residents in Augusta, Georgia, were recently asked to consider changing the name of Mill Street to Bishop C.M. Madison Boulevard, protests were loudest from non-United House churchgoers in the African-American community who noted that Madison did not represent all people, regardless of race or circumstance, nor did he seek a better America, noting in their comments the work of towering figures such as the Reverend Dr. Martin Luther King Jr. (Courtesy of Kirn Library.)

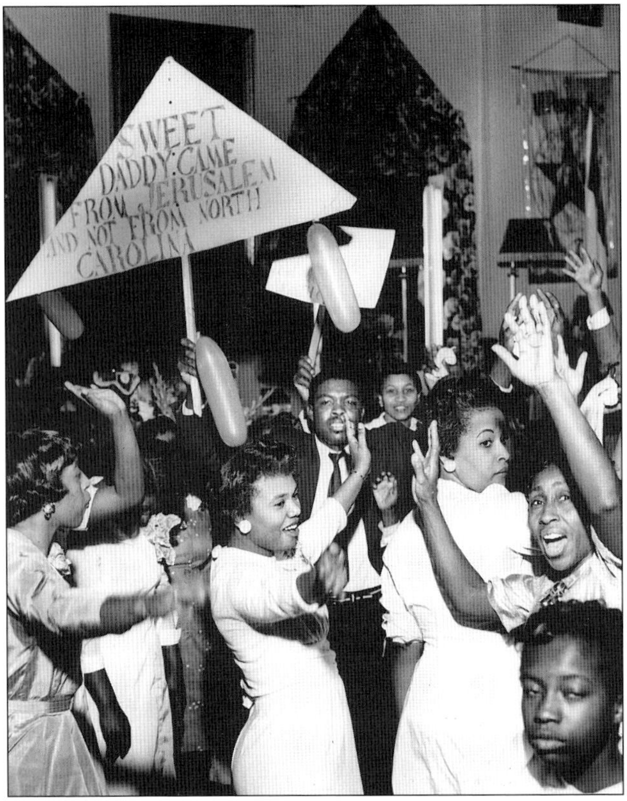

Bishop "Daddy" Grace's followers converged on the United House of Prayer for All People on Freemason Street on July 4, 1958, and later, took to the streets in a spirited parade.

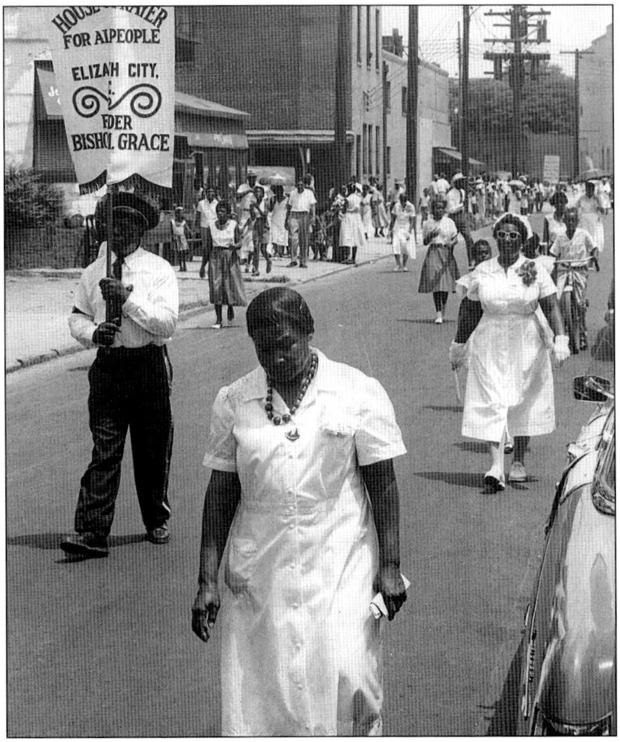

The hour-long parade of July 4, 1958, was in honor of "Daddy" Grace, though the bishop was not present for the festivities. Followers came from Elizabeth City, North Carolina, Newport News, and other localities to march in the Fourth of July parade. Women in the Norfolk congregation dressed in all white or yellow and carried umbrellas to protect them from the sun. Banners proclaiming, "My Rock Is Dad" and "House of Prayer Soul Hunters" filled the streets. Three bands, mostly playing jazz, marched down Freemason and Church Streets. The grand finale of the parade was a procession of girls dressed in light blue evening gowns. Behind them, in an open car sporting a sign on the trunk that read "Zorro Rides Again," rode the queen of the parade. (Courtesy of Kirn Library.)

Nine

Decades of Change

"Once I thought to write a history of the immigrants of America. Then I discovered that the immigrants were American history."

—Oscar Handlin, author of *The Uprooted*, 1951

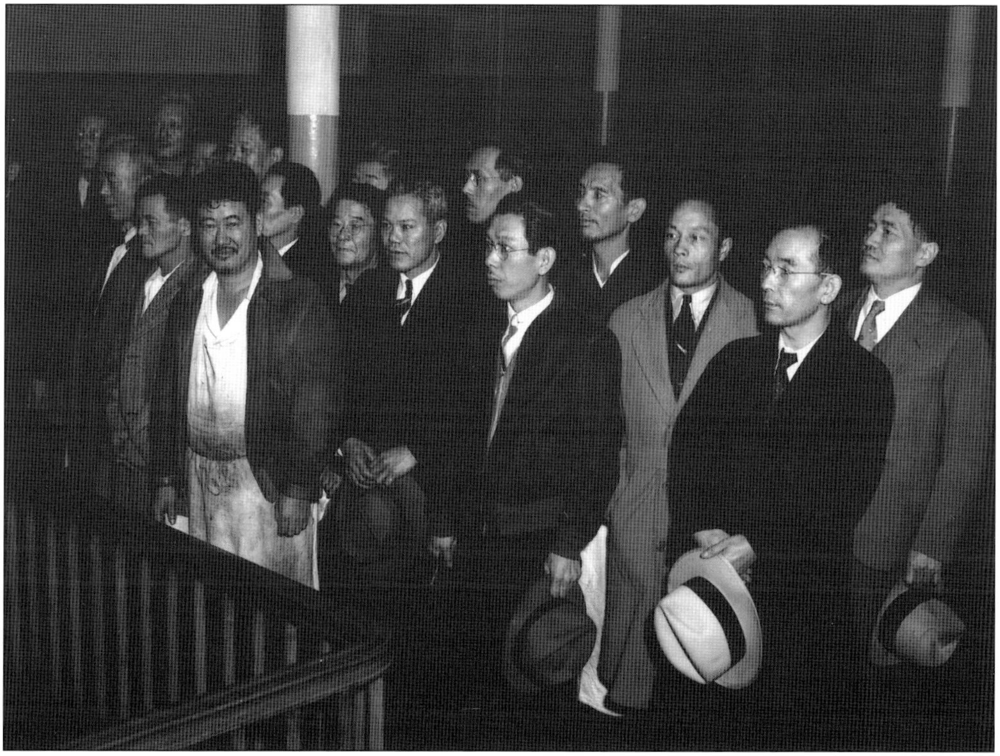

Japanese Americans and Japanese nationals were rounded up throughout Norfolk and surrounding cities and counties on December 7 and 8, 1941. Weeks before the Japanese attack on Pearl Harbor, Norfolk police aided by the Federal Bureau of Investigation and the United States Navy had compiled a list of residents of Japanese extraction. Those arrested were held for further investigation and fingerprinted. Men such as Wataru Tada, arrested in the second police precinct, operated a restaurant on Church Street and had raised his family in Norfolk since 1906. His daughter Alma was compelled to retain an attorney, Maurice B. Shapiro, to find out what was happening to her father, who was in custody, but unable to contact his family. When asked later about the Japanese attack on Pearl Harbor, Tada noted that "it was quite surprising to me. Perhaps it's because Japan has a lot of hot-heads in the government over there now." Tada did not, when interviewed, express anything but regret for the attack. After all, he had been an American citizen for 35 years. The Japanese community along Church Street was a strong one, many of them owning successful restaurants, laundries, and service enterprises. Examples of these included Thomas Tanaka and Hara Sumiji, who ran restaurants at 720 and 1103 Church Street, respectively. (Charles S. Borjes, photographer. Courtesy of Kirn Library.)

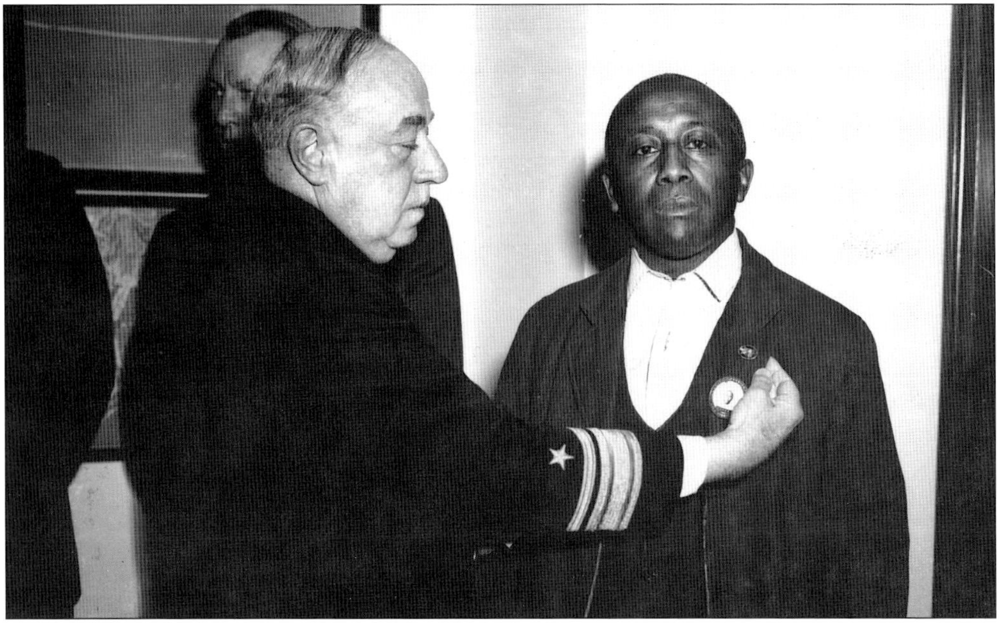

Rear Admiral Manley Simons presented Lushion Suzett of the Norfolk Naval Supply Depot with a service pin on February 11, 1942. Suzett lived at 1514 Outten Street in Huntersville. (H.D. Vollmer, photographer. Courtesy of Kirn Library.)

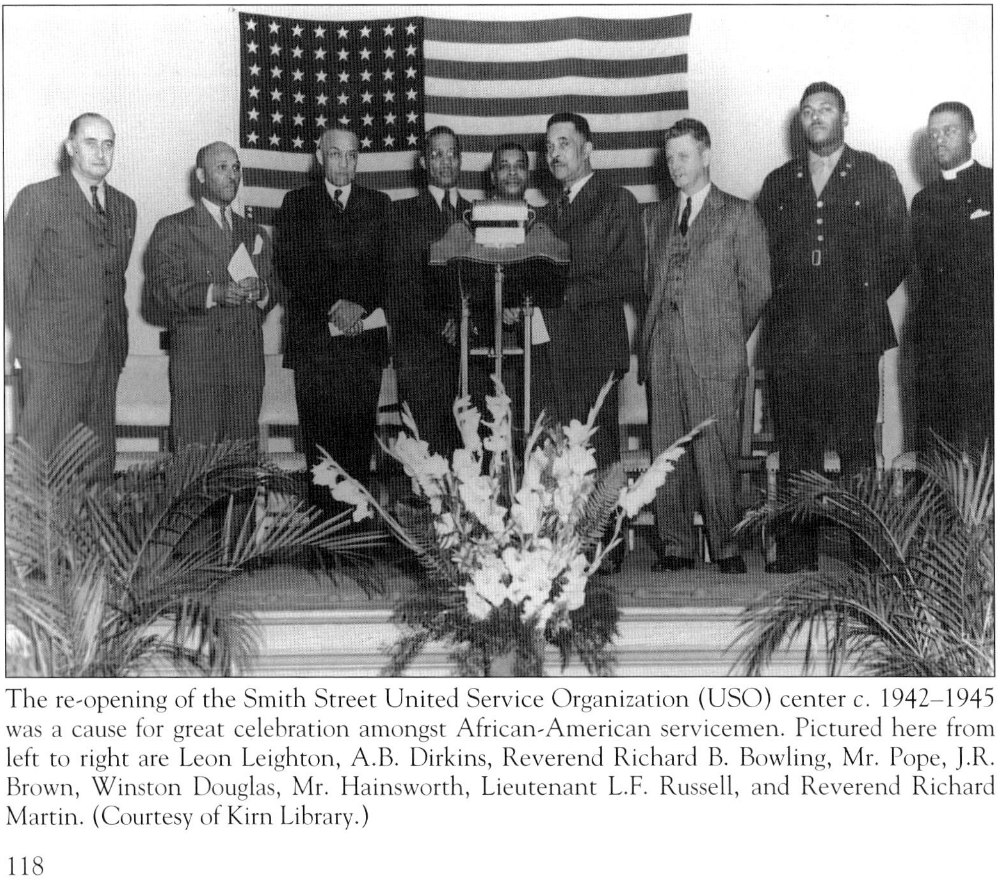

The re-opening of the Smith Street United Service Organization (USO) center *c*. 1942–1945 was a cause for great celebration amongst African-American servicemen. Pictured here from left to right are Leon Leighton, A.B. Dirkins, Reverend Richard B. Bowling, Mr. Pope, J.R. Brown, Winston Douglas, Mr. Hainsworth, Lieutenant L.F. Russell, and Reverend Richard Martin. (Courtesy of Kirn Library.)

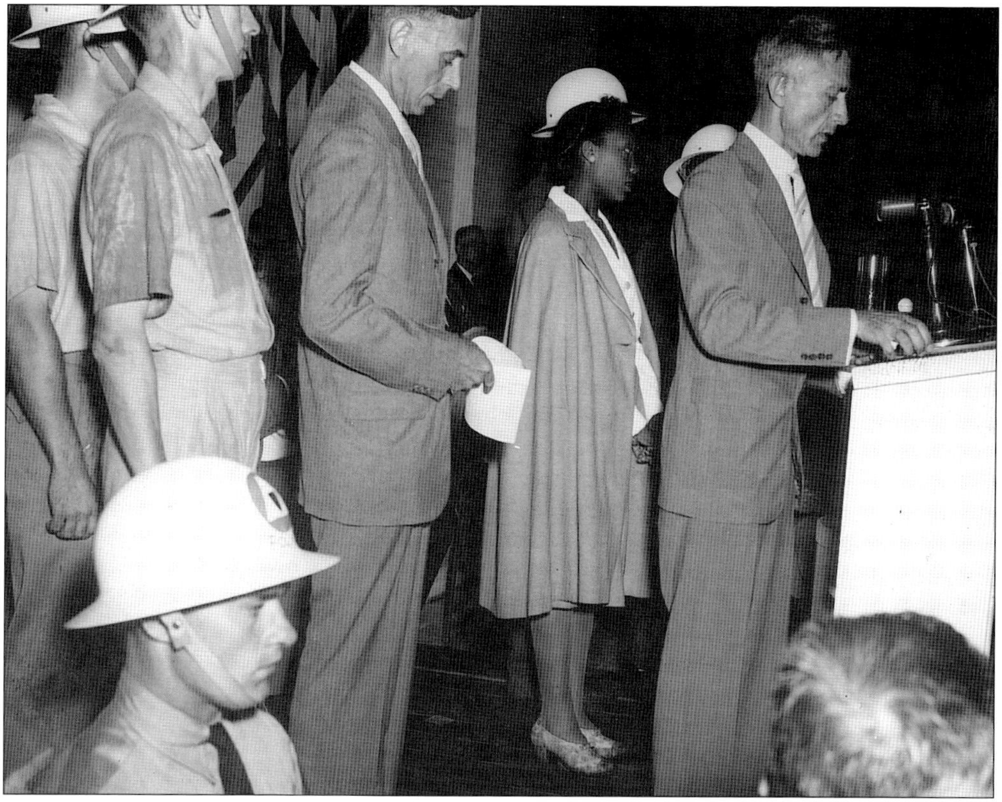

In numerous ways, WW II drew the entire Norfolk community together, black and white, in the war effort. A photographer from the United States Army Corps of Engineers, Norfolk District, took this picture on August 21, 1942, of a young African-American woman checking into a Civil Defense meeting. (Courtesy of the United States Army Corps of Engineers, Norfolk District.)

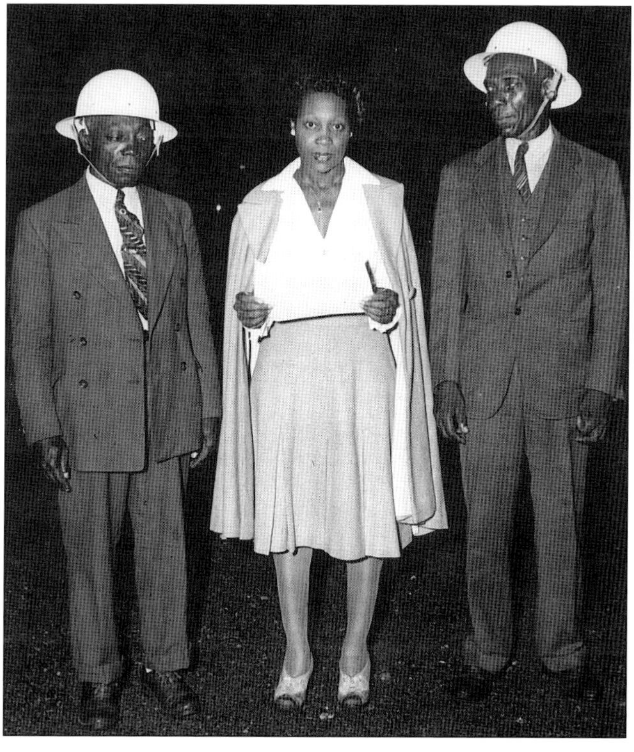

This image of air raid wardens, taken c. 1943, originally ran in the *Journal & Guide*, a publication for the African-American community. (Courtesy of Kirn Library.)

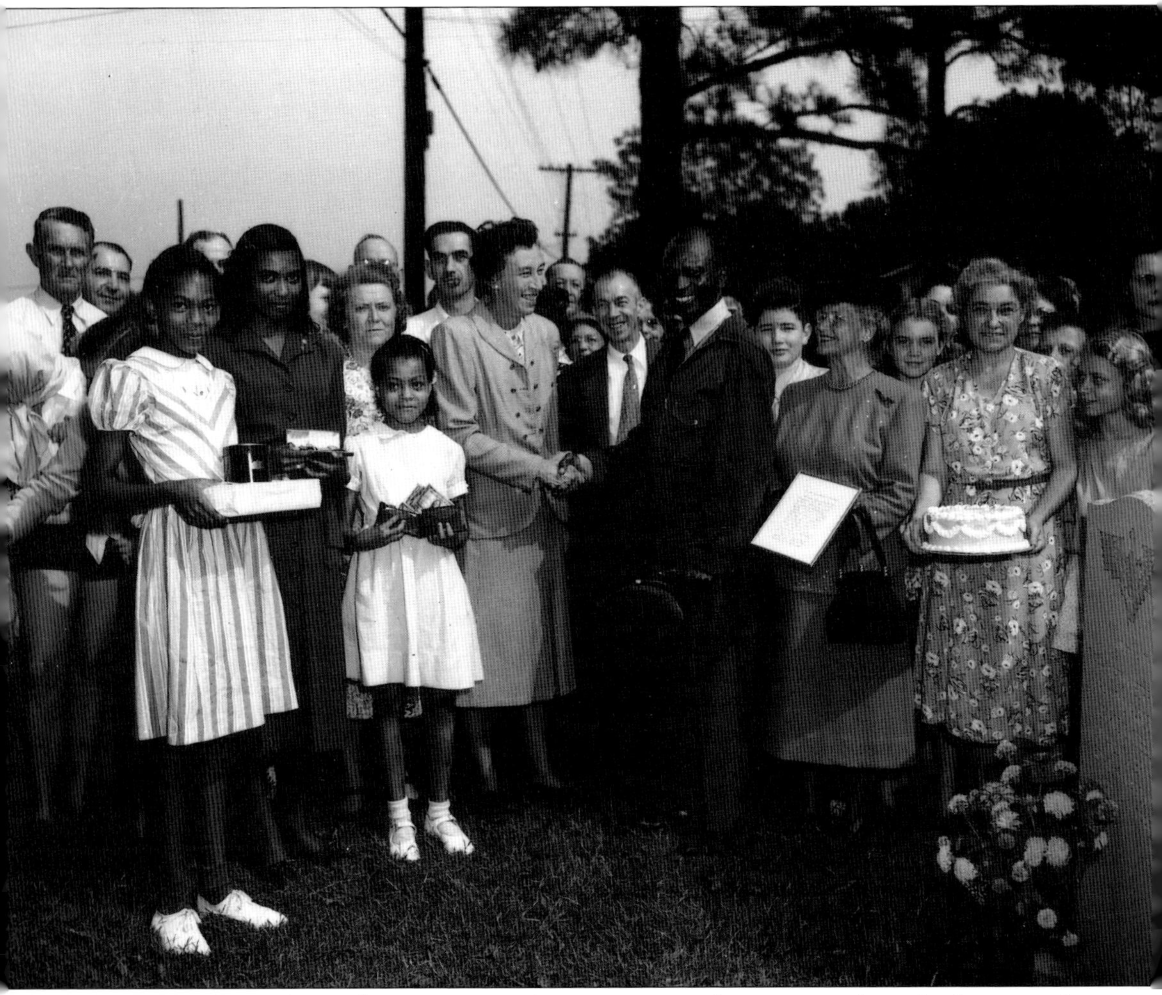

George H. Green (center), a veteran mail carrier, received presents and a cake from people along his route in honor of his 29 years of continuous service in Chesterfield Heights. This picture was taken on October 2, 1948. The woman shaking Green's hand is Mrs. C.A. Sousa. The woman holding the plaque to the right of Green is Mrs. Edward M. Albright. Nearly 100 Chesterfield Heights residents gathered at Earl's Court to wish their friend a warm goodbye. During his tenure as their mail carrier, Green, then 51 years old, had watched generations of families come and go. As newspaper reporter Cameron Gregory wrote of Green's departure from the neighborhood: "Green watched kids in rompers grow up and have children of their own. And, just as their fathers, this new generation has skipped down the streets behind him, tugging at his mail sack and getting an inevitable pat on the head. A modern Pied Piper, his popularity with the kids has surpassed the popsicle man's." Green went on to endear himself to families in West Ghent. He and his wife, Lillian, resided at 2708 Broad Creek Road. (Charles S. Borjes, photographer. Courtesy of Kirn Library.)

Booker T. Washington High School's graduation singers performed for commencement exercises on June 10, 1954. The singers, directed by I. Sherman Greene, and the presentation of a pageant entitled "A Day at Booker T. Washington High School" by a group of graduating seniors, were the highlights of the evening. Family members of the graduating class and other students packed the auditorium to see 88 boys and 115 girls file down the aisle to receive diplomas. Diplomas were presented by Winston Douglas, principal of the school, and Helen Laughon, a member of the Norfolk School Board. Elaine Overton, valedictorian, won a Bausch and Lomb Science Award, a scholarship from the Mu Sigma chapter of the Delta Sigma Theta sorority, and a scholarship to Hampton Institute. (Jim Mays, photographer. Courtesy of Kirn Library.)

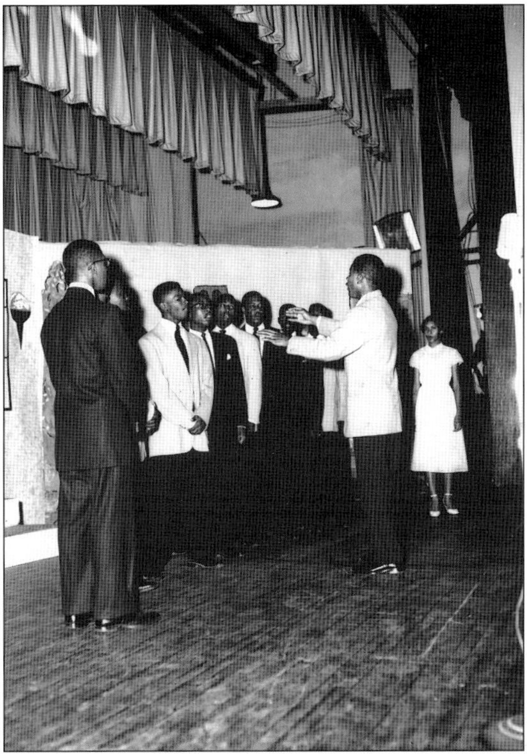

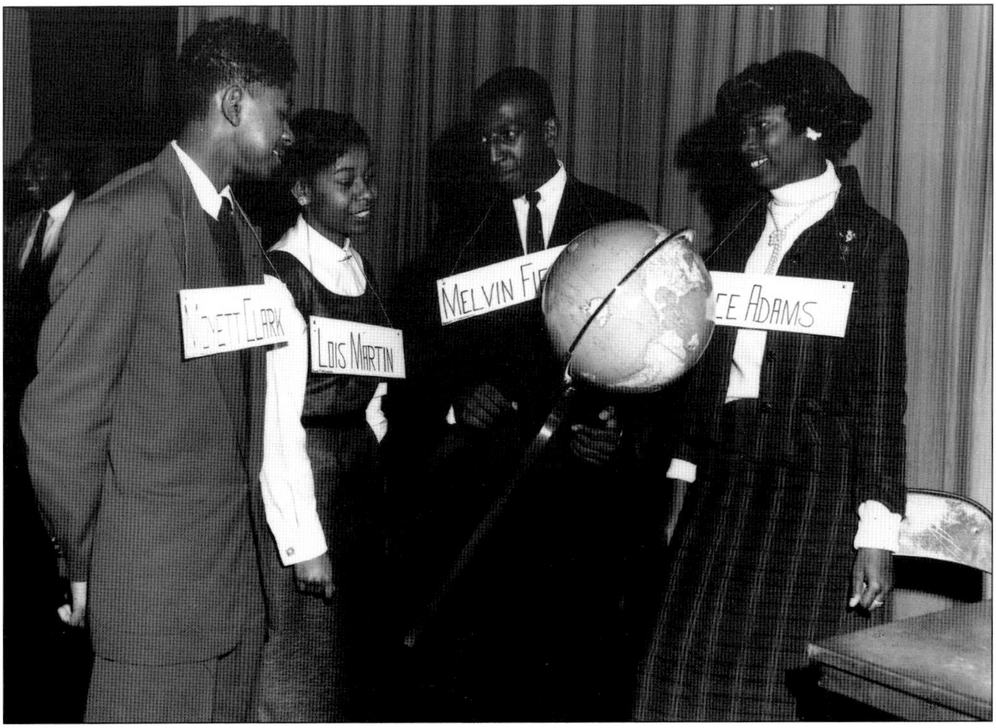

Pictured here are Booker T. Washington High School students, February 23, 1956. (Jim Mays, photographer. Courtesy of Kirn Library.)

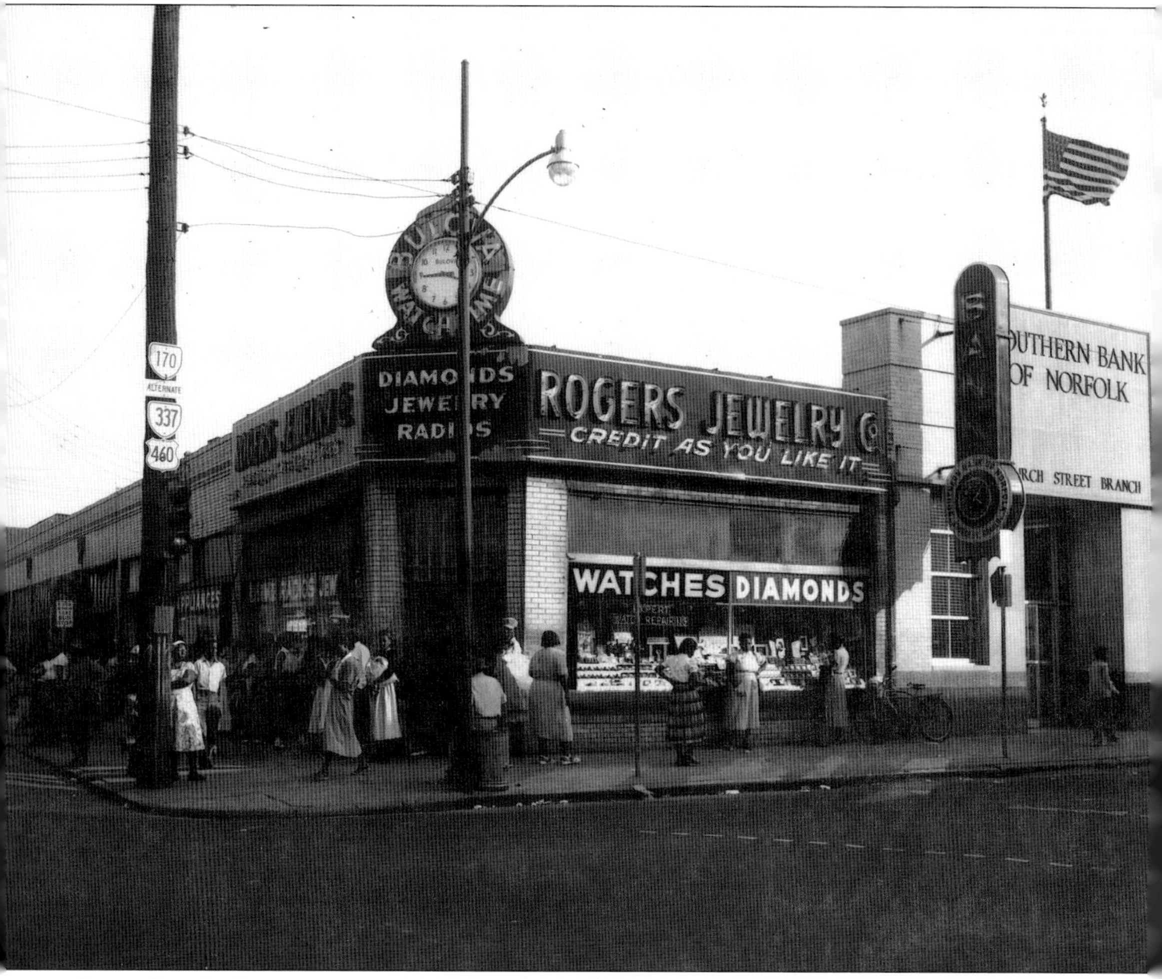

Rogers Jewelry Company was a mainstay at the southeast corner of Church Street and Brambleton Avenue at the time this picture was taken on September 18, 1953. The projected demolition of this structure, plus the Church Street branch of the Southern Bank of Norfolk, were at the heart of Norfolk Redevelopment and Housing Authority's completion of a million dollar right-of-way acquisition program in connection with the agency's expansion of Brambleton Avenue into a 2-mile, six-lane divided boulevard from Monticello Avenue to the Campostella Bridge. The most expensive acquisitions for the road expansion were the commercial properties on the southeast and southwest corners of Brambleton Avenue and Church Street, for which the authority paid $250,000. Landmarks vanished from the Norfolk landscape as the authority demolished the one-time celebrated Palais Royal dance hall, later converted to a bowling alley, on the southwest corner of Brambleton Avenue and Church Street, and the 60-year-old Hotel Mount Vernon, next-door. Farther west on Brambleton was the Carvel Theatre, another encroaching structure cleared to make way for the road widening. Two score or more business establishments along Brambleton Avenue were razed as part of the authority's Redevelopment Project No. 1, a major portion of which involved the demolishing of slum buildings which once stood on the site of the original 752-unit Young Park public housing development. (Jim Mays, photographer. Courtesy of Kirn Library.)

Ten

Between Memory and Reality

"The winter evening settles down
With smells of steaks in passageways.
Six o'clock.
The burnt-out ends of smoky days.
And now a gusty shower wraps
The grimy scraps
Of withered leaves about your feet
And newspapers from vacant lots;
The showers beat
On broken blinds and chimney-pots,
And at the corner of the street
A lonely cab-horse steams and stamps.
And then the lighting of the lamps."

—From *Preludes*, 1936
T.S. (Thomas Stearns) Eliot,
American-born English poet (1888–1965)

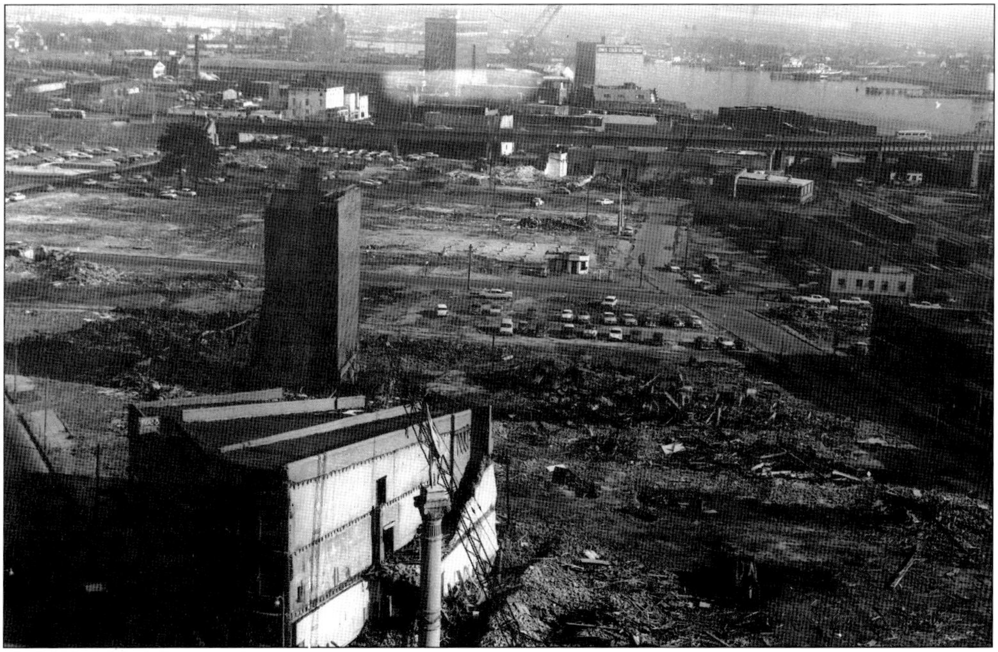

All that remained of the once vibrant areas of East Main, Union, and Church Streets were piles of rubble and a few buildings scheduled for demolition. As the redevelopment of downtown continued there would be scant resemblance to the days when the streets were full of people shoulder to shoulder, and the buildings exuded a character that only time and craftsmenship of two centuries or more could fashion. Carroll H. Walker took this picture on February 1, 1962. The tall building in the center is all that is left of the Gaiety Theatre. Walker snapped the picture from the top floor of the National Bank of Commerce building looking east atop what had been a busy Commercial Place; the Confederate Monument looms in the foreground. East Main Street is to the left, and Church Street runs left to right. Union Street is to the right.

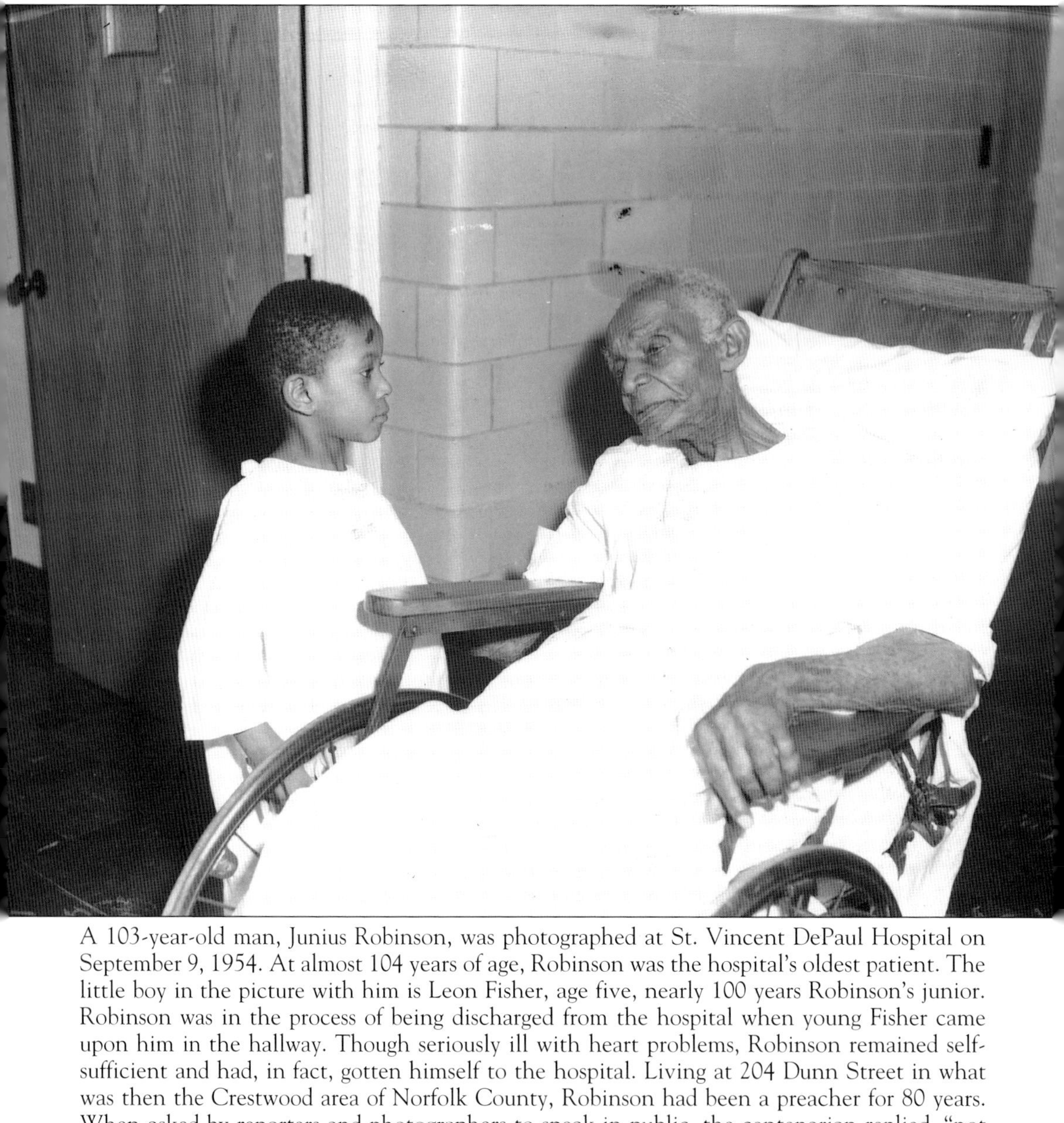

A 103-year-old man, Junius Robinson, was photographed at St. Vincent DePaul Hospital on September 9, 1954. At almost 104 years of age, Robinson was the hospital's oldest patient. The little boy in the picture with him is Leon Fisher, age five, nearly 100 years Robinson's junior. Robinson was in the process of being discharged from the hospital when young Fisher came upon him in the hallway. Though seriously ill with heart problems, Robinson remained self-sufficient and had, in fact, gotten himself to the hospital. Living at 204 Dunn Street in what was then the Crestwood area of Norfolk County, Robinson had been a preacher for 80 years. When asked by reporters and photographers to speak in public, the centenarian replied, "not enough people around." DePaul Hospital has served generations of families who grew up on Church Street and who now reside in all parts of Hampton Roads. (Jim Mays, photographer. Courtesy of Kirn Library.)

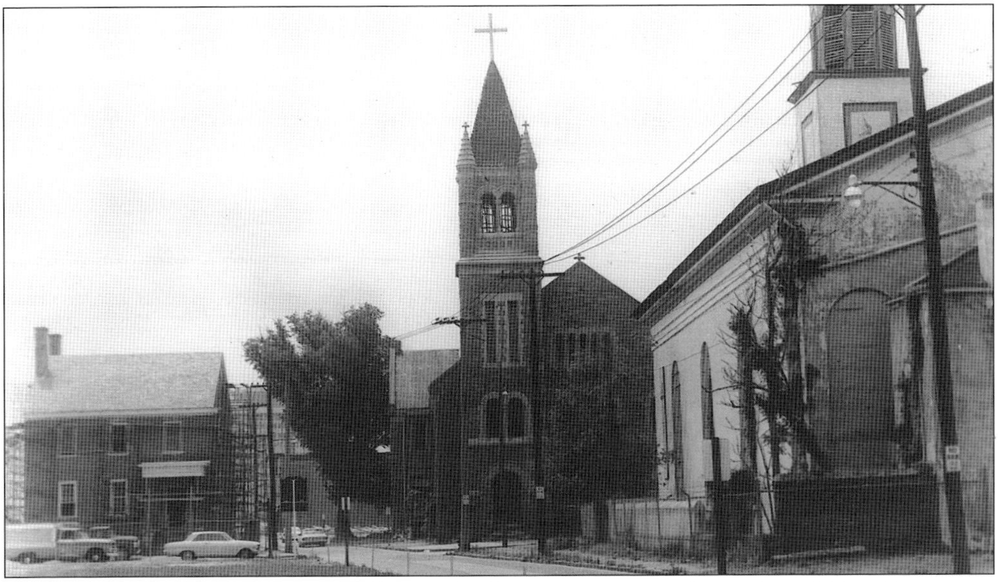

Times do change. Carroll H. Walker took this image of Cumberland and East Freemason Streets in 1960. The Willoughby-Baylor House is on the left, surrounded by scaffolding, and St. Joseph's Catholic Church (Colored) sits in the center, old Christ Church on the right. Lots in the foreground had already been cleared for redevelopment. St. Joseph's occupied the former Cumberland Street Methodist Church, located at the 400 block of East Freemason Street. In May 1924, the Cumberland Street Methodist congregation opted to sell its property and move to the "suburbs" north of downtown. The land and building were later purchased by Josephite priests. (Courtesy of Kirn Library.)

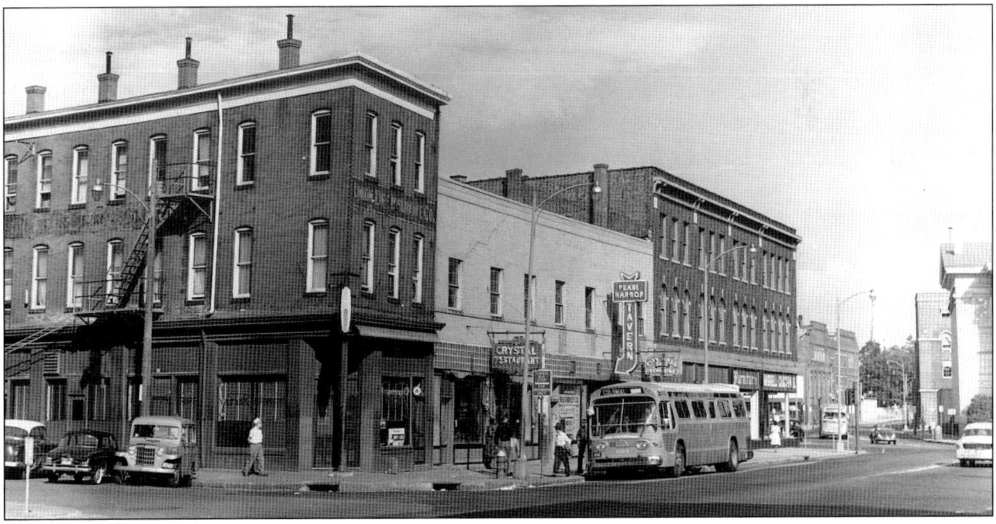

Looking east down City Hall Avenue, the view toward old St. Paul's Episcopal Church and the spire of St. Mary's of the Immaculate Conception Catholic Church is in stark contrast with earlier images of downtown Norfolk. Taken in August of 1960 by Carroll H. Walker, this portrait of an urban city center in decay has remained afixed in the minds of those who have spent nearly the last four decades planning and reshaping the future of downtown Norfolk. Church Street was truncated north of St. Paul's, and the buildings on the north side of City Hall Avenue (shown here) were razed to make way for progress.

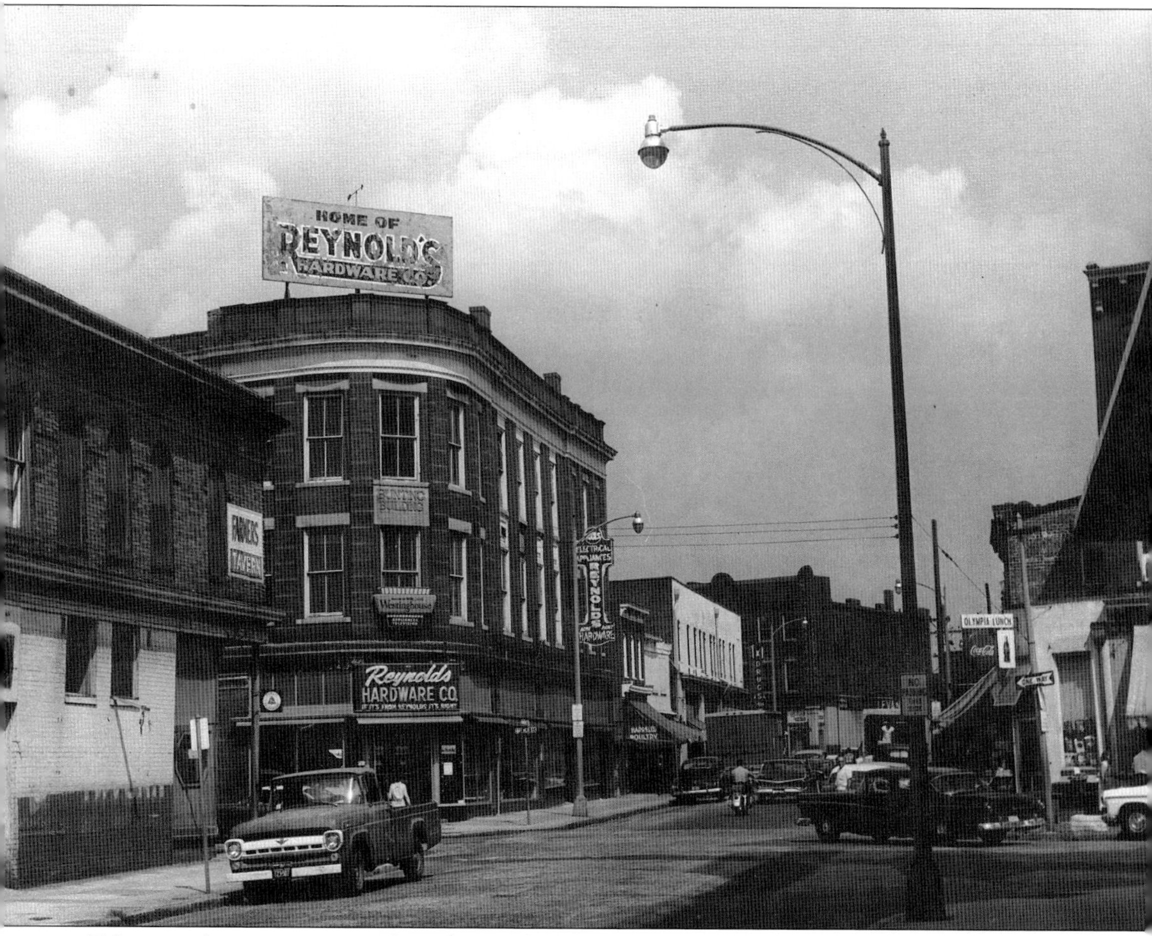

Taken at the intersection of Market and Brewer Streets, this image, also photographed by Carroll H. Walker in 1960, demonstrates the last vestiges of cobblestone streets and people actually making use of the intimate narrow thoroughfare that once defined the Church Street area. Small businesses still thrived and customers moved up and down the streets walking to their destinations, but notice the congestion created by vehicles of all description in the photograph. Within a couple of years, Church Street and its surrounding street grid would be expanded to accommodate the car, so many of the quaint establishments and family-owned enterprises obvious in Walker's picture would be out of business.

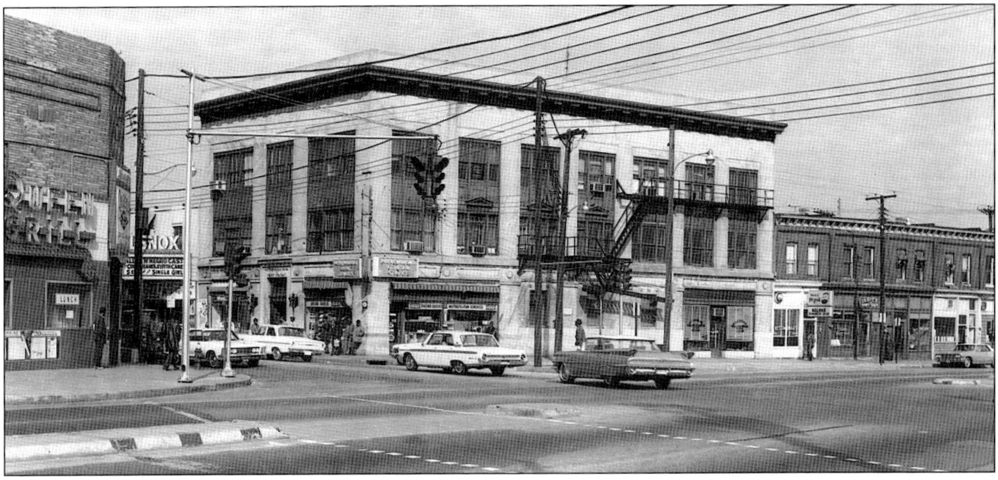

This is the way Church Street appeared on April 1, 1965, at its intersection with Brambleton Avenue. The gradual widening of Church Street to accommodate vehicular traffic changed the complexion of the street from pedestrian-friendly to an automobile-hungry thoroughfare. Many of the businesses that had flourished along the street for decades, dependent on foot traffic, faded quickly into yesteryear, unable to provide curb appeal to motorists. (Courtesy of Kirn Library.)

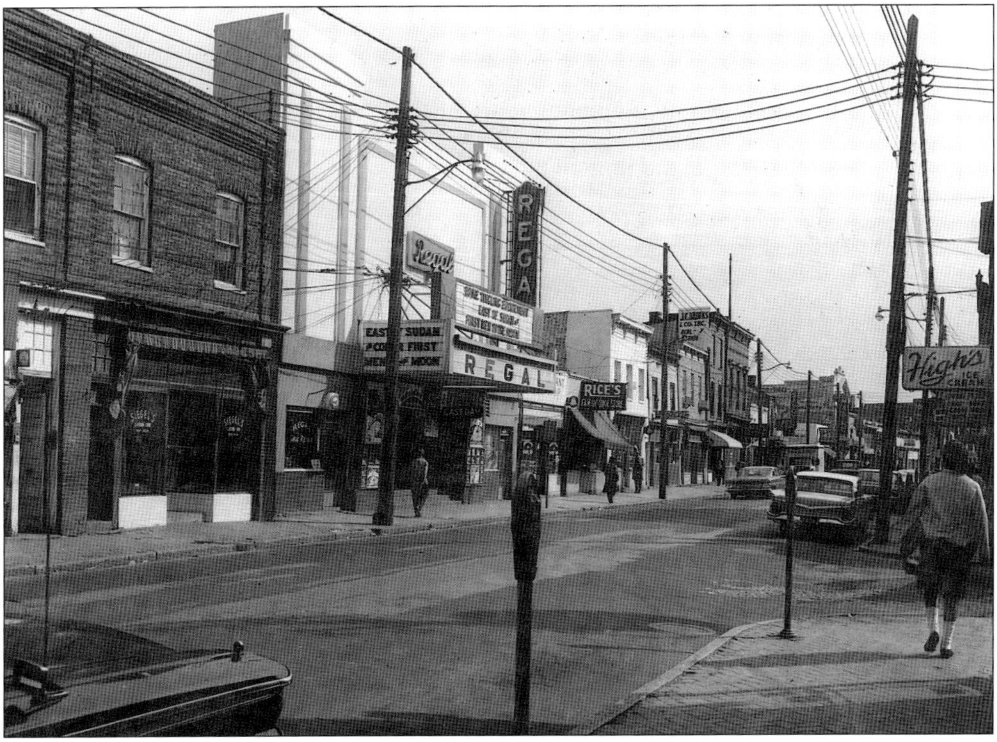

Looking south at the 800 block of Church Street, a photographer with Fariss Pictures stood at the corner of Church and Nichol Streets on April 1, 1965, to take this picture of the last remnant of the street's once-viable commercial corridor. Within a short span of time, redevelopment would lead to the razing of all the buildings in this image. (Courtesy of Kirn Library.)

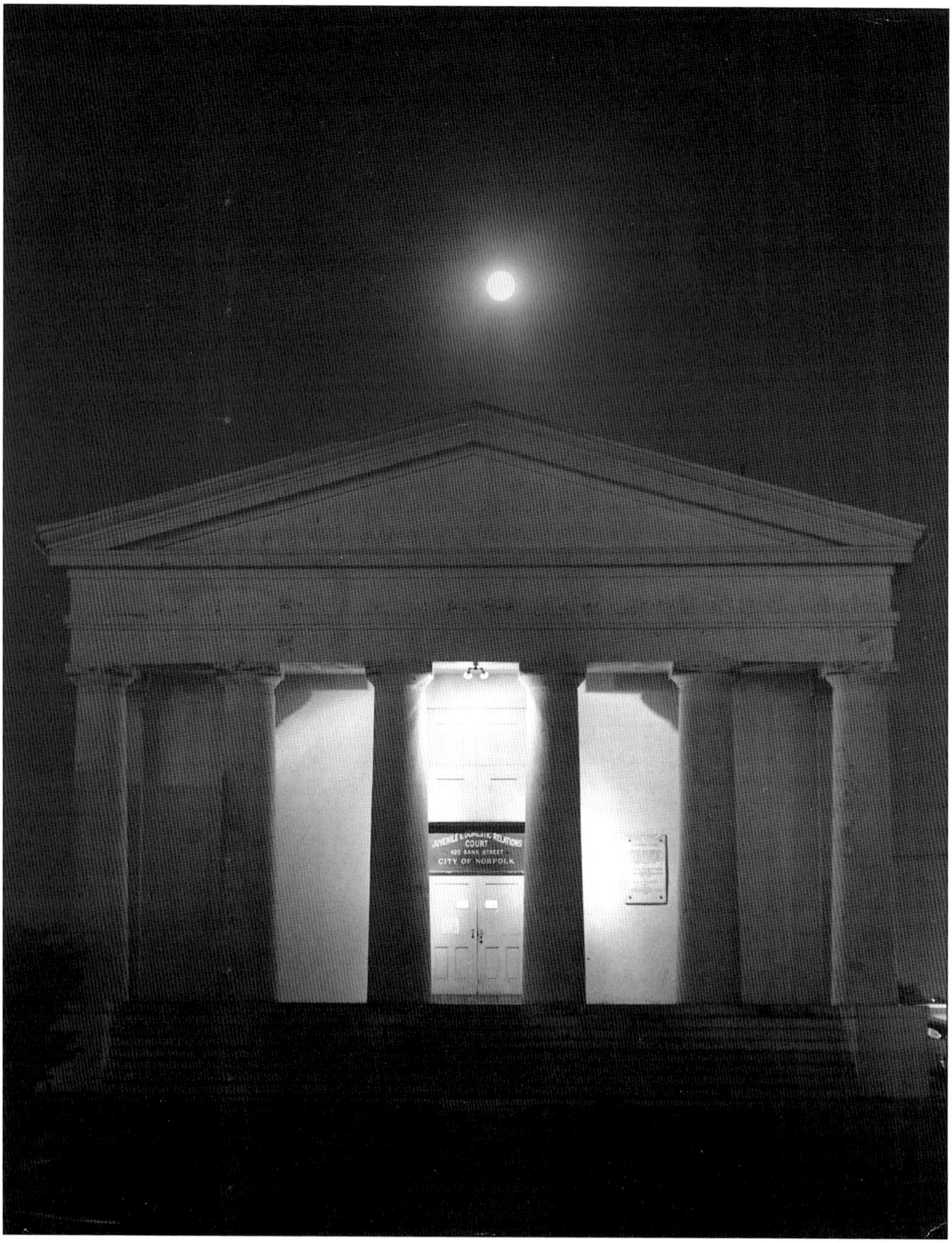

By the time Carroll H. Walker took this photograph of the old Norfolk Academy in 1970, it had become the home of the city of Norfolk's Juvenile and Domestic Relations Court, and the neighborhoods and businesses that once surrounded the building were long gone, leaving this once impressive historic building diminutive against a backdrop of civic arenas and strip shopping centers.